About This Book

Why is this topic important?

Games and gamification experiences are not going away. The engagement achieved through games means that gamification is a concept that needs to be part of every learning professional's tool box. Games provide meaning and context to learners, they provide a set of boundaries within a "safe" environment to explore, think, and "try things out."

Gamification is the ideal process for creating engaging learning environments. Game elements such as providing learners with permission to fail, encouragement of out-of-box thinking, and fostering a sense of control create rich learning experiences. The addition of game elements on top of traditional learning environments is a way of creating learning that aids in retention and is impactful. Learning professionals, managers, and others need to own the term "gamification" and use it to improve learning and performance within organizations.

What can you achieve with this book?

This book has a heavy emphasis on creating games for learning and not artificially incentivizing people through external rewards. The real value of game-based thinking and mechanics is to create meaningful learning experiences. This book is based on solid academic research conducted over dozens of years by many different researchers. Conclusions are based on peer-reviewed studies, and key takeaways are the direct result of empirical research. My goal was to bring together what is known about learning, games, and instruction and place all that knowledge in one place and to create design guidance for professionals who want to create impactful experiences for learners. With this information you can create engaging, exciting learning that impacts behavior and achieves desired outcomes.

As gaming concepts become more mainstream, organizations have begun to leverage games for instruction, but often the games are ill-conceived, linear in their approach, and not well designed. In other organizations, gamification of instruction is resisted because management is not aware of the growing body of research studies indicating the effectiveness of using game elements for enhancing learning.

How is this book organized?

This book is organized around four central themes. The first describes and defines the concept of gamification and dissects games to determine the elements that provide the most impact for the players and why these elements are critical to the success of games. The next theme is the research and theoretical basis for the use of games and game-based thinking. This theme provides results from dozens and dozens of studies providing insights into when game-based thinking and mechanics make for powerful learning tools. The third theme is that of matching game content with game design. Not all games are the same; the gamification of learning and instruction requires matching instructional content with game mechanics. This concept is explored in several chapters in the book. The fourth theme of the book is the actual design and development of the gamification of learning and instruction. The creation of a game design document is discussed, and a model for managing the entire process is described.

About the American Society for Training & Development

The American Society for Training & Development (ASTD) is the world's largest professional association dedicated to the training and development field. In more than 100 countries, ASTD's members work in organizations of all sizes, in the private and public sectors, as independent consultants, and as suppliers. Members connect locally in 130 U.S. chapters and with 30 international partners.

ASTD started in 1943 and in recent years has widened the profession's focus to align learning and performance to organizational results and is a sought-after voice on critical public policy issues. For more information, visit www.astd.org.

The Gamification of Learning and Instruction

Game-Based Methods and Strategies for Training and Education

Karl M. Kapp

Pfeiffer

A Wiley Imprint
www.pfeiffer.com

Published by Pfeiffer
An Imprint of Wiley
One Montgomery Street, Suite 1200, San Francisco, CA 94104-4594
www.pfeiffer.com

For additional copies/bulk purchases of this book in the U.S. please contact 800-274-4434.

Pfeiffer books and products are available through most bookstores. To contact Pfeiffer directly call our Customer Care Department within the U.S. at 800-274-4434, outside the U.S. at 317-572-3985, fax 317-572-4002, or visit www.pfeiffer.com.

Pfeiffer also publishes its books in a variety of electronic formats and by print-on-demand. Some material included with standard print versions of this book may not be included in e-books or in print-on-demand. If the version of this book that you purchased references media such as CD or DVD that was not included in your purchase, you may download this material at http://booksupport.wiley.com. For more information about Wiley products, visit www.wiley.com.

Library of Congress Cataloging-in-Publication Data

Kapp, Karl M.
    The gamification of learning and instruction : game-based methods and strategies for training and education / Karl M. Kapp.
        pages   cm
    ISBN 978-1-118-09634-5 (hardback)
        1. Educational games.   2. Simulation games in education.   3. Computer-assisted instruction.
    I. Title.
LB1029.G3K364   2012
371.33'4—dc23

                                                                                                        2011047543

Acquiring Editor:	Matthew Davis
Editorial Assistant:	Michael Zelenko
Director of Development:	Kathleen Dolan Davies
Production Editor:	Dawn Kilgore
Editor:	Rebecca Taff
Manufacturing Supervisor:	Becky Morgan

Printed in the United States of America

HB Printing 10   9   8   7   6   5   4   3
PB Printing 10   9   8   7   6   5   4   3   2   1

Contents

Chapter 11 Perspective of a Gamer, by Nathan Kapp 239

Chapter 12 Casual Game Site: DAU Case Study, by Alicia Sanchez 247

List of Figures and Tables

Figures

Tables

Contents on the Web

The following materials are available to download from:
www.pfeiffer.com/go/kapp.

password: professional

Articles

Basic Games for Teaching Different Types of Content

Five Elements that Make Games Engaging

Obstacles to Adoption of Games in Corporate Environments

Worksheet

Simulation/Game Development Worksheet

Foreword

AS I SIT DOWN to write this foreword, I reflect on how many games I encountered in the previous week.

I saw my youngest daughter playing Club Penguin on the Internet, my son playing Mario Super Slugger on the Wii, my oldest daughter playing Zoo Tycoon on a laptop, my sister-in-law tending her Farmville crops on Facebook, a friend playing Angry Birds on her iPhone, a Cancun cab driver explaining how he plays Call of Duty with others from around the globe, and the U.S. Naval War College describing to me their war game to assess their ability to deal with new conflicts that might arise from the climate crisis.

All of this just in the last *seven days*!

And I hesitated to actually list all those games by name, knowing that it will instantly date this book, just as the games I grew up with—Pong, Space Invaders, Zork—instantly date me.

Yes, from casual games to serious games, from smart phones to consoles, from toddlers to retirees, games and gamification are everywhere.

Although games themselves are not new—they've been played in the earliest civilizations—we have reached a confluence of technology and design where games have become ubiquitous and seem to have a unique ability to *engage* when we most need it.

In my book, *We* (Wiley, 2011), I explore the roots of the current employee engagement crisis, showing that job satisfaction around the world is at a record low, with stark consequences on business profits and individual health alike. Informed by survey research of over ten million employees in 150 countries, I also reveal what people need to feel engaged at work: growth and advancement, recognition and rewards, a higher goal to pursue, and a sense of teamwork. These are among the things that well-designed games and gamification efforts excel at.

It is this power of modern, digital games to engage that has caused "gamification" to become somewhat in vogue. Just as many industries benefited from the principles of industrial design, and interface design, and experience design . . . smart industries and businesses will quickly learn and adapt the principles of game design (or game "mechanics"). Game design indeed has broad utility for learning and development, for changing health behaviors, and for motivating at-work behaviors, among other things.

But we should also be cautious, as consultants and gurus treat "gamification" as a personal gold rush and try to add points, rewards, and badges to everything we do. Those things are elements of most games, and among the easier to implement, but those things alone do not a game make. The more challenging and beneficial aspects to gamification include the story, the challenge, the sense of control, decision making, and a sense of mastery—these are the elements of games that are of the most value.

When it comes specifically to learning events, we need to understand that, while we can benefit from the thoughtful application of gamification techniques, not every learning activity has to be a fully fledged game. Learning professionals can add game elements like curiosity, challenge, avatars, distributed practice, or storytelling to the learning we develop. Designers should strive to take the best of games—not the worst like points and badges—and leverage that to create successful engaging programs.

Karl Kapp has written a book that is empirically solid. He shares peer-reviewed research to back up claims, assertions, and ideas. Several meta-analysis studies conclusively show what is successful for game-based learning and what is not. His years of experience as a graduate school professor, consultant to government and industry, and National Science Foundation investigator enables him to share the most relevant, applicable conclusions.

Yet, this is no dry academic tome; Karl has written the definitive guide to gamification, which itself is accessible and engaging. He brings trends to life and illustrates the principles of gamification through numerous examples from real-world games. Whether he's describing the Cisco "Binary Game," the U.S. Navy's multi-player anti-piracy game, or even the importance of aesthetics in a simple chess piece, Karl captivates the reader and ensures comprehension page after page.

There is no doubt that "gamification" is an important and powerful weapon in the arsenal for learning, marketing, and behavior change of any kind. This book is a valuable guide for all who are trying to understand or adopt these important design principles.

Kevin Kruse
New York Times best-selling author of *We:*
How to Increase Performance and Profits Through Full Engagement

Preface

GAMIFICATION IS A BIZARRE word. What does it mean? Why does it matter? How can it be related to serious learning? Questions I find myself discussing with my students and clients all the time. The only people I don't have to explain it to are my kids. They get it. They got it. They are part of it. When my one son gives my other son 10 points for getting him a soda, that's gamification (where those 10 points go and what they are used for, I have no idea). When my son times himself to see how quickly he can rattle off the definitions of economic terms as a study technique, that's gamification. When my son sits down to learn algebra in a first-person game, that's gamification.

On its surface, gamification is simply the use of game mechanics to make learning and instruction more fun. It seems "fake" artificial or like a shortcut. It's not. Underneath the surface is the idea of engagement, story, autonomy, and meaning. Games give experiences meaning, they provide a set of boundaries within a "safe" environment to explore, think and "try things out." Games provide motivation to succeed and reduce the sting of failure.

You can always hit the reset button or strive to be in the championship game again next year—only this time you'll win.

Games are the ideal learning environment with their built-in permission to fail, encouragement of out-of-box thinking, and sense of control. The addition of game elements on top of traditional learning environments is a way of leveraging the power of engagement and imagination. In e-learning we need to use games instead of presenting text and multiple-choice questions on an endless parade of screens with little feedback or assessment of knowledge gained. In the classroom, we need gamification to avoid the endless stream of bullets we hurl at trainees in an uninspiring lecture format.

Don't think of gamification as only the use of badges, rewards and points; instead, think of the engaging elements of why people play games—it's not just for the points—its for the sense of engagement, immediate feedback, feeling of accomplishment, and success of striving against a challenge and overcoming it.

This is what learning is about. We learning professionals (academics, teachers, corporate trainers, instructional designers) know gamification; we've done it, we've turned boring content into engaging classroom activities, we've immersed learners in case studies, we've set the bar. Now is not the time to walk away from the concept of gamification; now is the time to take it back to add richer meaning and depth to the term. Let's make gamification mean something to learning and instruction. Let's situate learners in authentic environments in which they can practice their skills and gain immediate feedback on progress and accomplishments, earn recognition for doing well, and feel good for overcoming a challenge. All that sure beats the heck out of answering a multiple-choice question.

This book has a heavy emphasis on creating games for learning and not artificially incentivizing people through external rewards. The real value of the game-based mechanics is to create meaningful learning experiences. This book is based on solid academic research conducted over dozens of years by many different researchers. Conclusions are based on peer-reviewed studies, and key takeaways are direct results of empirical research. My goal was to bring together what is known about learning, games, and instruction and place all that knowledge in one place and to create design guidance for learning professions who want to create impactful experiences for learners.

What's Coming in This Book

This books looks at several aspects of gamification from its definition to examples to determining how to match instructional content to specific game design features. Gamification is a multifaceted concept, and each chapter in the book examines one of the facets.

The first chapter introduces terminology. What is a game? What is gamification? What does that mean to faculty members, college instructors, instructional designers, and other learning and development practitioners? The chapter provides examples of gamification and parses the term into its component elements.

Chapter Two examines the individual elements that make up a game from the rules to the aesthetics and describes how they all contribute to game play. It is important to note that it takes more than just one game element to make a game; the combination of many of these elements makes playing a game engaging.

In Chapter Three, the theories behind the elements of gamification are presented. The chapter covers operant conditioning and the reinforcement schedules, but only as one of many elements that make games engaging. Self-Determination Theory is described and related to games. Also explored are the concepts of distributed practice, social learning theory, achieving the flow state, scaffolding, and the power of episodic memory.

Chapter Four reviews research studies describing the effectiveness of games as well as the effectiveness of specific game elements such as the use of avatars and third-person versus first-person perspective. The goal of the chapter is to provide support to the argument that game-based learning and gamification are effective for changing behavior and creating positive learning outcomes.

The fifth chapter looks at how gamification can be used for learning and problem solving. The chapter explores how games help with hand-eye coordination, how they are good for young and old learners, and how they have been used to encourage and promote pro-social behavior. The chapter explores how game interfaces and mechanics are being used to solve difficult scientific and geo-political problems.

Chapter Six is a discussion of both the different types of game players and the different types of games that exist. Cooperation, competitive, and the self-expression aspects of games are addressed, as are the different needs of novice, expert, and master-level players.

Chapter Seven presents a framework for developing games that teach higher order thinking skills from predicting outcomes, to synthesizing content to ultimately problem solving. The chapter also presents suggestions to help with the process of developing a game to solve a specific problem.

In Chapter Eight methods are presented for creating game-based learning in the cognitive domains of declarative, conceptual, and procedural knowledge as well as rules-based learning. Also covered are the affective or emotional domain, the psychomotor domain, and the teaching of soft skills like negotiating and leadership.

How does one manage the process of designing and building a game? Chapter Nine addresses those issues by contrasting two project management methods, the ADDIE method and the Scrum method. The chapter also provides an outline that can be used for the creation of a gamification-design document.

The first guest contributor appears in Chapter Ten. Lucas Blair, a game designer at MAYA Design and Ph.D. candidate in modeling and simulation at the University of Central Florida. Lucas carefully outlines a taxonomy for building game reward structures.

The next guest contributor is Nathan Kapp, who wrote Chapter Eleven. Nathan has been playing video games his entire life. He provides an insider's perspective on what games mean to the upcoming generation, the games he has played, and what he has learned from games and how he has applied that knowledge to other areas of his life. The chapter nicely "validates" the theory and research presented earlier. Nathan provides living proof of the impact of games.

The third guest contributor, providing Chapter Twelve, is Alicia Sanchez, the "Games Czar" of Defense Acquisition University, where she oversees the use of games and simulations in their curriculum. She describes how they have established a games common designed to reinforce concepts that should be known throughout the organization and not aimed at one particular task.

Koreen Olbrish is the final guest. She wrote Chapter Thirteen. In the chapter she outlines how alternative reality games are moving game concepts into the field and out of classrooms. She provides basic definitions and describes how they can augment traditional instruction and learning.

Chapter Fourteen provides two final examples of gamification in action and provides a couple of next step action items to further your research and study on gamification. The best way to experience gamification is first-hand.

The Best Way to Read This Book

This book provides the research-backed recommendations to change how organizations look at games and to provide a method of creating effective learning through gamification. It can be used as a primer or introductory text to introduce the topic of gamification, but it is also designed as a practical field-book to help teams in the midst of gamification projects.

If you are reading this book as a primer, it makes most sense to read the chapters in chronological order. Pause after each part to ensure you understand the key arguments, research findings, and positions in each chapter, and then move on to the next part.

Another approach is to cover the contents of the book as a team. Divide your team, department, or faculty into reading clubs and read a chapter each week. Then, once a week, the group should get together and discuss the salient and thought-provoking points. Can you implement the takeaways? How can you help the organization design meaningful games for learning? What guidelines should you establish for the gamification of learning in your organization? How can you get this data about the effectiveness of these game elements in the hands of upper management? How can you implement these ideas?

This group approach will spark discussion, provide insightful solutions, and guide you to develop your own methods of applying the ideas and concepts in this book to your own organization or classroom. It will also begin discussions about the future of learning within your organization that may not have occurred otherwise. These conversations, even when slightly off-topic, will be valuable in strengthening your organization in terms of maximizing the use of game-based methods for learning.

If you are in the midst of designing a gamification project, I encourage you to become intimately familiar with the key takeaways at the end of every chapter. Work with your peers on the design team to ensure that everyone understands each of these takeaways and what they mean to the creation of gamified learning and instruction.

Graduate and undergraduate students will particularly find this book of interest as a foundation to building dissertations, pursing lines of research, and as a generation that have grown up playing video games.

Continuing the Discussion

A topic like gamification does not remain static, it is continually evolving as technology and our understanding of how gamificaiton can foster learning and collaboration continue to grow. In an effort to continue the dialogue in real time and to make real progress in helping others I've created a Facebook page for easy collaboration, posting of games and interactions among readers. The page is http://tinyurl.com/gamificationLI.

Enjoy the book. I hope you have as much fun reading it as I did writing it. I wish you all the best in your quest to bring a gamification to learning and instruction. And have fun doing it!

Karl Kapp
Danville, Pennsylvania

Acknowledgments

WRITING A BOOK IS A JOURNEY and a process with many people contributing bits and pieces along the way. Thanks to Nathan and Nicholas—the gamers who inspired this work and who inspire me on a daily basis. Also to my wife Nancy, who had to put up with my incessant recanting of the "fascinating" research I kept discovering. Special thanks to Dorothy Kapp, thanks, mom! Thanks to the "runner chicks" and Mike.

Thanks to Carrie McKeague, the chief learning officer of Kaplan-EduNeering, who helped with permissions and with images, and to Danny Collins of Kaplan-EduNeering, who assisted with screen captures and describing some of the projects he's involved with in terms of games and 3D. In fact, a big thanks to the entire Kaplan-EduNeering team for their support, encouragement, and the opportunity to do great work with them.

Thanks to everyone at Bloomsburg University: the wonderful students who contribute so much in their ideas, enthusiasm, and energy. The faculty, Helmut Doll, Mary Nicholson, and Tim Phillips; a more talented, dedicated, and caring group of faculty cannot be found. Thanks to Tina Barnes,

Karen Swartz, Tammy Matthews, and Brian Seely, who make the department and institute function.

Thanks to John Greco at UnitedHealthcare, who secured some great case studies and screen captures for me. Thanks also to John Rice, whose innovative work helped make Chapter Seven possible. And to Jim Helein at Windwalker who helped secure screen shots.

Thanks also to all the readers of my blog who challenge, inspire, and motivate me to do the best work I can. This includes great conversations about gamification I had on my blog with Kathy Sierra and Sebastian Deterding. Those were fascinating, providing interesting insights and sparking new ideas which made their way into the book. Thanks also to Andrew Hughes, president of Designing Digitally, who has done some great work with gamification with all kinds of content. Also, to Kristen Bittner, who created the interesting and delightful artwork that appears throughout the book. Thanks to Ron Burns and all his great work with the corporate 3D world ProtoSphere.

Also, a thank you to Eric Milks, who was invaluable in his assistance with the National Science Foundation game project. And thanks to the entire team: Michael Hacker, David Burghardt, , Deborah Hecht, Gordon Snyder, Bert Flugman, Jim Kiggens, Jessica Andrezze, Matthew Cohen, Kyle Bean, Cecilia Mason, Heather Gee, Tom Robertson, David Shaw, Gordon Snyder, Jr., Laura Saxman, Jim Lauckhard, Caterina La Fata, Maria Russo, Kevin Oswald, Nicholas Cimorelli, Seth Baker, and other team members I may have omitted accidently. The project and team are extraordinary.

Thanks to Brett Bixler, lead instructional designer and educational gaming commons evangelist at Penn State University, who took the time to review the book and make insightful comments prior to publication.

Thanks to my wonderful contributors, Nathan Kapp, Koreen Olbrish, Lucas Blair, Kris Rockwell, Eric Milks, Alicia Sanchez, and Judy Unrien. A wink and a nod to Bonnie Scepkowski, Heath Miller, and Ellen Leinfuss And thanks to Matthew Davis, Michael Zelenko, Dawn Kilgore, Rebecca Taff, and the entire team at Pfeiffer.

Karl M. Kapp
Bloomsburg, Pennsylvania
February 2012

About the Author

KARL M. KAPP is a professor of instructional technology in Bloomsburg University's Department of Instructional Technology in Bloomsburg, Pennsylvania. In Bloomsburg's graduate program, he teaches a capstone course using problem-based learning in which students are formed into "companies," write a business plan, receive an e-learning request for proposal (RFP), write a forty-page proposal, develop a working prototype, and present their solution to representatives from various learning and e-learning corporations throughout the United States. He teaches a course titled "Learning in 3D," which teaches graduate students how to design learning in virtual immersive environments. Kapp teaches an instructional game design course and is the co-principle investigator for a National Science Foundation grant to create a video game to teach middle school children engineering, math and science concepts. The game is called Survival Master (go to http://gaming2learn.org/ to learn more).

Additionally, as the assistant director of Bloomsburg University's acclaimed Institute for Interactive Technologies (IIT), Kapp helps government, corporate, and non-profit organizations leverage learning technologies to positively impact employee productivity and organizational profitability through the effective use of learning. He provides advice on e-learning design, learning infrastructures, and e-learning technologies to such companies and organizations as AstraZeneca, Pennsylvania Department of Public Welfare, Toys R Us, Kaplan-Eduneering, Kellogg's, Sovereign Bank, and various federal government agencies.

Kapp consults with learning technology companies and government organizations. Additionally, he advises Fortune 500 companies on the use of technology for transferring knowledge to their employees. He has been interviewed by such magazines as *Training, T &D, Software Strategies, Knowledge Management, Distance Learning,* and *PharmaVoice* and by general television, and radio programs concerning his work with learning and technology.

Kapp is a frequent keynote speaker, workshop leader, moderator, and panelist at national and international conferences as well as events for private corporations and universities. He has authored or co-authored four books on the convergence of learning and technology: *Integrated Learning for ERP Success; Winning e-Learning Proposals; Gadgets, Games and Gizmos for Learning;* and *Learning in 3D.*

Kapp consults with organizations in a variety of areas, including helping them devise strategies around virtual immersive environments, game-based learning, gamification of learning and instruction, mobile learning solutions, learning through social networking, gamification of knowledge, instructional design, and learning strategy development. He earned an Ed.D. in instructional design and technology from the University of Pittsburgh.

You can keep up with Kapp's musings and occasional rants on his widely read "Kapp Notes" blog at www.kaplaneduneering.com/kappnotes/

Contributors

Lucas Blair is a game designer at MAYA Design and Ph.D. candidate in modeling and simulation at the University of Central Florida. His dissertation topic, "The Use of Video Game Achievements to Enhance Player Performance, Self-Efficacy and Motivation," was investigated at RETRO Laboratory. He earned an M.S. in instructional technology from Bloomsburg University.

Nathan Kapp is a rising high school senior headed to college. His goal is to study business and economics. He placed first in the Future Business Leaders of America (FBLA) regional competition in the event of "Entrepreneurship." He plays a variety of video games such as Call of Duty, NBA Live, the Madden Franchise, and Little Big Planet and is a frequent visitor to www.addictinggames.com.

Eric D. Milks is the plant training manager for Kellogg Company in Muncy, Pennsylvania. He is advocate for new training initiatives and is continually pursuing options to better connect with the next generation of manufacturing employees. Prior to Kellogg's, he served many years as the project manager at the Institute for Interactive Technologies and continues to serve in an adjunct faculty role for the Department of Instructional Technology at Bloomsburg University. He also gives presentations and workshops on instructional design and authoring applications. For the last couple of years, he has been heavily involved in the conception and design of a middle school–based educational video game funded by the National Science Foundation. In his spare time, when he is not "gaming," he has focused his attention to the growth and the possibilities of the m-learning market.

Koreen Olbrish, CEO, founded Tandem Learning to address an unmet need in the learning space. Applying her background in experiential learning and technology for education, Olbrish advocates new ways of leveraging technology for enterprise learning with emphasis on performance improvement and behavioral change. She has strong ties to education, having received her master's in science in curriculum and instruction from Penn State University and helping start Freire Charter School in Philadelphia in 1999. The majority of her experience has been in the development of enterprise learning solutions, with particular expertise in simulations, serious games, and the application of virtual worlds for learning.

Kris Rockwell is CEO and founder of Hybrid Learning Systems. Prior to starting Hybrid, Rockwell worked for US Airways developing and implementing computer-based training (CBT) and desktop simulation systems for the flight training department. For the past eight years, Rockwell has focused on mobile learning content development and delivery and serious games. He also serves as the head of the Aviation Industry CBT Committee (AICC) Emerging Technology Subcommittee. His work with Smart Graphics has appeared in the Adobe Systems website and he has been featured in *Civil Aviation Training* magazine as well as *Military Training and Simulation* magazine, and the *Defense Management Journal* in the UK. In addition to his work in the e-learning world, Rockwell has served as an adjunct teacher in the multimedia program at Duquesne University in Pittsburgh, Pennsylvania.

He has presented at the International Air Transport Association, NASA/ FAA Operating Documents Workshop IV, mLearn 2009, DevLearn 2009, DevLearn 2010, WritersUA 2010, and ForumOxford 2010 at Oxford University.

Alicia Sanchez, Ph.D., is the "Games Czar" for Defense Acquisition University (DAU), where she specializes in the implementation of games and simulations in a variety of learning environments. Sanchez completed her Ph.D. at the University of Central Florida in the modeling and simulation program. She has served as a research psychologist at the Naval Air Warfare Center, as research faculty for the Institute of Simulation and Training, as adjunct faculty for UCF's digital media program, and as a research scientist for the Virginia Modeling Analysis and Simulation Center. Her work with simulation and games has focused on K-12 literacy and STEM, Intact Team Training and, most recently, acquisition. Within those areas Sanchez has served as executive producer and/or designer on over twenty games and earned recognition from CLO, Brandon Hall, PBS, and the SGS&C. Recently she launched the first ever DoD Casual Games site; since its launch in December 2010 the site has been visited over 250,000 times. She has presented internationally at conferences, including GDC, NATO, Harvard, GLS, and IITSEC.

Judy Unrein, MBA, has worked in the training and development industry since 1997 as a trainer, project manager, and instructional designer. She currently designs learning solutions for Artisan E-Learning, and she speaks and writes frequently about e-learning design and technology for a variety of organizations and publications, including her blog at onehundredfortywords.com. She has an MBA and an M.Ed. in instructional design.

What Is Gamification?

CHAPTER QUESTIONS

At the end of this chapter, you should be able to answer these questions:

- What is a game?
- What is gamification?
- What are three examples of adding game-based elements to traditional learning environments to improve learning and retention?
- What are the advantages of using game-based techniques for the creation and implementation of performance improvement initiatives?

Introduction

You have ten seconds.

Name three countries that begin with the letter "U." Go.

Ten, nine, eight, seven, six, five, four, three, two, one. Hint, check Endnote 1 for answers.[1]

How did you do? Did you get the obvious one? Did you get all three? Did you get more than three? Did you turn to the back of the book? Did answers pop into your head? If you tried to answer the question or looked in the back of the book, you experienced *gamification.*

People like playing games; they are fun and engaging. In fact, a recent survey showed that 55 percent of people would be interested in working for a company that offered games as a way to increase productivity.[2] So maybe your vision of gamification is rewards, badges, and points for doing everyday stuff at work or even for brushing your teeth. But that's a narrow way of looking at gamification; a broader, more encompassing and more helpful way of looking at gamification exists.

Following are several examples of concepts that fit with my definition of gamification. See whether you can develop a definition of the term before one is provided in the text. Or see whether your concept of gamification is the same concept discussed in this book . . . but be prepared, it may not be. Ready, set . . . go.

Gamification in Action

Lack of physical activity is a growing challenge putting millions of people at risk, but it's not due to a lack of information or knowledge. Plenty of people know they should exercise and can recite all the benefits of physical activity when asked. But sadly, this knowledge is not reflected in their behavior. Few people exercise or even elect extra physical activity when given the opportunity. For instance, many people exiting a subway take the escalator to get to street level rather than the stairs, even when the escalator is busy and the stairs empty. But all that changed in one town when they transformed a subway exiting staircase into a set of black and white piano keys,

Figure 1.1. Taking the Stairs and Making Music!

Image reprinted with permission of the artist, Kristin Bittner.

each step producing a different musical note when stepped on, as depicted in Figure 1.1. After the piano-type steps were installed, behavior changed. People started to engage with the keys and elected to take the stairs making music as they entered and exited the subway station. The use of the staircase increased 66 percent.[3]

Running was never a favorite activity of Rachel's; she didn't like to run in the rain or cold, or even if when it was hot or muggy. She couldn't bring herself to jump out of bed in the morning, put on a pair of running shoes, and pound the pavement; she just wasn't that into it. Until she downloaded *Zombies, Run!* The mobile application changed everything.

It wasn't an ordinary application to track running time, number of miles completed, and pacing, Sure, it tracked all that, but it also involved her in an interactive game. As she runs, she plays the role of a character known as Runner 5. Her job is to go out into a zombie-infested post-apocalyptic environment and collect supplies to bring back to her home base.

She puts on her headphones, starts the application and, as she is running, the application periodically indicates when she has collected key items required to support her virtual base. It also warns her when zombie hordes are closing in and she needs to increase her speed. Several times a run, she finds herself chased by zombies and unknowingly doing interval training. All the while, the application records her pace and number of miles; when she returns home, she uploads the information to a website to track her progress. She also tracks the rebuilding of her base using items collects during her run.

Now she can't wait to run. She is actively engaged in the story, and her running miles have increased over the past few months as she finds herself running more so she can rebuild her base faster and find out her next mission as Runner 5.[4]

Sam knows first-hand just how dangerous it can be working on a loading dock. One day, he was unloading product from a delivery truck with his 9,000 pound forklift when he forgot to check behind him as he backed up. What he didn't see was that a co-worker had placed a stack of pallets immediately behind him blocking his right-of-way. As Sam's forklift moved backward, it caught the edge of the pallet and began to tip. Instinctively, Sam tried to jump out of the forklift. Unfortunately, his foot caught, the forklift tipped all the way over on landed on him. He saw himself being killed instantly.

Sam wasn't hurt—not even a scratch. Of course, he did lose one life and 100 life points for his mistake, which made him mad because it dropped his standings in the virtual safety leaderboard. Sam was driving a virtual forklift in a virtual networked simulated environment with an instructor and four other trainees. The entire incident took place online as part of a training activity. After the incident, the instructor used the opportunity to explain to the group several points of forklift and loading dock safety. To this day, Sam has never had a safety incident on an actual loading dock. He contributes that record partly to the training he has received in the loading dock simulator.[5]

Professor Jones, a new faculty member at a large university, teaches large classes. She has over three hundred students per class but, on average, her students have almost 100 percent attendance. Other faculty members marvel at how she is able to accomplish this task because many students use large classes are an excuse to cut class. But to Professor Jones, the process is simple. Each class period she tracks attendance, demands student interactivity, and evaluates the quality of each and every student's answer to questions she poses during her lectures. Students log onto a website and see their progress against themselves and others on a class leader board. Professor Jones uses an audience response system to make the process for three hundred students manageable.

Every student is assigned a response pad at the beginning of the semester containing his or her student identification number. In every class, Professor Jones poses dozens of questions from the reading interspersed into her lecture. Students respond by clicking a button that corresponds to an answer. The results are instantly loaded to the class website, and students track how they are doing in real time.

Elizabeth's organization is the envy of many. Its members never have to actively recruit; people come to them, drawn by their reputation, and the ones who fit well and make a positive contribution end up being welcomed into the group. Elizabeth has learned from other start-ups the importance of good communication and giving everyone a common vision he or she can believe in. She is a good day-to-day manager but is also careful to step aside and allow others the opportunity to lead. She is charismatic by nature, but uses this strength to make everyone on the team feel like part of something special, rather than hogging the spotlight. When there's a disagreement, everyone on the team knows that she can be counted on to be fair and practical.

She credits her abilities with learning from other leaders. Remembering the first person to promote her into a management position, she says, "This guy was amazing. . . . Everyone loved him. No one could argue with him. And I learned it wasn't just because he was a leader. It was his attitude. He was always open to other ideas, but he also knew how to stick firmly to something he knew would work. It's not about being able to force people to do what you want to them to do; it's about getting people to try what you want and seeing how things work, and staying open to new ideas."

By the time Elizabeth was promoted to her first management position at work, she had years of management and leadership experience from leading one of the most successful guilds on her World of Warcraft server.[6]

Emanuel's factory wasn't doing well. The team members were working as quickly as they could, but they never got ahead of their problems. The plastic inventory components were stacked up around the work centers, customer satisfaction rates were low, and product wasn't flowing through the factory in a timely manner. The only consolation was that none of the competitors' factories looked much better. Emanuel's frustration level was beginning to grow and he could feel himself getting angry; he just didn't know how to improve production. It was at this time that the instructor stepped in and explained to the four teams sitting around the lean manufacturing game boards how they could improve.

The instructor from a lean manufacturing consulting firm demonstrated techniques for streamlining the factory floor layout on the game board and provided ideas for moving materials from work cell to work cell based on upstream demand and not simply meeting a quota. After the demonstration by the instructor, Emanuel and his fellow teammates reconfigured their mock factory and moved their plastic inventory pieces based on the new advice. During this process, something became glaringly obvious to Emanuel. Quickly moving inventory from work center to work center wasn't as productive as only moving inventory when the downstream work center need it. Emanuel had read that advice and heard it spoken by instructors, but he never really understood or trusted that idea until he witnessed the dramatic results during the playing of the game. Four weeks later, the product line Emanuel supervised benefited from his new insight by waiting for downstream demand before producing the needed inventory. Production on Emanuel's line increased by 20 percent, while scrap decreased by 15 percent.

Are these concepts you think of when you hear the term "gamification," or are you still thinking rewards, badges, and points?

What Is a Game?

Before we can go too much further in describing or defining the concept of gamification, we must first define the root of the word gamification. What is a game? There have been many different definitions and attempts at defining the term "game," but I think one of the closest definitions for application in an instructional setting was put forth by Katie Salen and Eric Zimmerman in their book *Rules of Play: Game Design Fundamentals.*

> "A game is a system in which players engage in an artificial conflict, defined by rules, that results in a quantifiable outcome."[7]

Even this excellent definition needs to be modified to fit a learning context, let's replace few words from their original definition and add the concept of emotional reaction based on idea of fun presented by Raph Koster is his seminal work, *A Theory of Fun.*[8]

> "A game is a system in which players engage in an abstract challenge, defined by rules, interactivity, and feedback, that results in a quantifiable outcome often eliciting an emotional reaction."

Let's look at each element of the definition:

- *System.* A set of interconnected elements occur within the "space" of the game. A score is related to behaviors and activities that, in turn, are related to a strategy or movement of pieces. The system aspect is the idea that each part of a game impacts and is integrated with other parts of the game. Scores are linked to actions, and actions are limited by rules.

- *Players.* Games involve a person interacting with game content or with other players. This happens in first-person shooters, board games, and games like Tetris. The person playing the game is the player. Later we'll refer to the players of games as "learners." The act of playing a game often results in learning, and learners are our target audience for gamification of instruction. But, for now, in this context—defining a game—we'll stick with the concept of player.

- *Abstract.* Games typically involve an abstraction of reality and typically take place in a narrowly defined "game space." This means that a game contains elements of a realistic situation or the essence of the situation but is not an exact replica. This is true of the game Monopoly, which mimics some of the essence of real estate transactions and business dealings, but is not an accurate portrayal of those transactions.

- *Challenge*. Games challenge players to achieve goals and outcomes that are not simple or straightforward. For example, even a simple game like Tic-Tac-Toe is a challenge when you play against another person who has equal knowledge of the game. A game becomes boring when the challenge no longer exists. But even the challenge involved with the card game of Solitaire provides enough challenge that the player continues to try to achieve the winning state within the game.

- *Rules*. The rules of the game define the game. They are the structure that allows the artificial construct to occur. They define the sequence of play, the winning state, and what is "fair" and what is "not fair" within the confines of the game environment.

- *Interactivity*. Games involve interactions. Players interact with one another, with the game system, and with the content presented during the game. Interactivity is a large part of games.

- *Feedback*. A hallmark of games is the feedback they provide to players. Feedback within a game is typically instant, direct, and clear. Players are able to take in the feedback and attempt corrections or changes based on both the positive feedback they receive as well as negative feedback.

- *Quantifiable Outcome*. Games are designed so that the winning state is concrete. The result of a well-designed game is that the player clearly knows when he or she has won or lost. There is no ambiguity. There is a score, level, or winning state (checkmate) that defines a clear outcome. This is one element that distinguishes games from a state of "play," which has no defined end state or quantifiable outcome. This is also one of the traits that make games ideal for instructional settings.

- *Emotional Reaction*. Games typically involve emotion. From the "thrill of victory" to "the agony of defeat," a wide range of emotions enter into games. The feeling of completing a game in many cases is as exhilarating as is the actual playing of the game. But at times frustration, anger, and sadness can be part of a game as well. Games, more than most human interactions, evoke strong emotions on many levels.

Together these disparate elements combine to make an event that is larger than the individual elements. A **player** gets caught up in playing a game because the instant **feedback** and constant **interaction** are related to the **challenge** of the game, which is defined by the **rules,** which all work within the **system** to provoke an **emotional reaction** and, finally, result in a **quantifiable outcome** within an **abstract** version of a larger system.

What Is Gamification?

All of the examples in the opening of this chapter have one thing in common: they use elements traditionally thought of as game-like or "fun" to promote learning and engagement. The positive outcomes and behavior changes described are the result of the process of "gamification."

Deciding whether to take the stairs or escalator is typically not a decision based on fun, but add keys that make music when you step on them and fun plays a major role. Graphing your runs and challenging yourself and others to reach the next level provides feedback and interactivity not typically available. Learning to be safe is serious business, but placing the person in a safe environment and letting him or her gain experience through trial and error brings an allowable element of failure into the process. Leadership training programs are typically boring, dry, and highly politicized, whereas leading a guild and gaining experience rallying the troops to succeed on a raid is engaging. Playing a board game is usually reserved for family fun night, but when properly configured and used in a corporate setting, insights can be gained that could not otherwise be possible. Motivating over three hundred students in a large lecture class to attend on a regular basis can be a daunting task without the motivation of a leader board.

Game-based techniques or gamification, when employed properly, have the power to engage, inform, and educate. Gabe Zichermann who wrote the book *Game-Based Marketing,* defines the term gamification as the "process of using game thinking and mechanics to engage audiences and solve problems."[9] Amy Jo Kim, author of *Community Building on the Web* and a well-known designer of social games, defined the term gamification as "using game techniques to make activities more engaging and fun."[10] The consultancy firm The Gartner Group defines gamification as "the broad trend of employing game mechanics to non-game environments such as innovation, marketing, training, employee performance, health and social change."[11] Wikipedia defines the concept thus:

> "Gamification is the use of game play mechanics for non-game applications (also known as 'funware'), particularly consumer-oriented web and mobile sites, in order to encourage people to adopt the applications. It also strives to encourage users to engage in desired behaviors in connection with the applications. Gamification works by making technology more engaging, and by encouraging desired behaviors, taking advantage of humans' psychological predisposition to engage in gaming. The technique can encourage people to perform chores that they ordinarily consider boring, such as completing surveys, shopping, or reading websites."[12]

Combining elements from these definitions and getting rid of the emphasis of getting people to do things they ordinarily consider boring, results in defining the term gamification as:

> "Gamification is using game-based mechanics, aesthetics and game thinking to engage people, motivate action, promote learning, and solve problems."

Let's look at each element of the definition:

- *Game-Based.* The concepts outlined in the definition of "game" described above apply to gamification. The goal is to create a system in which learners, players, consumers, and employees engage in an abstract challenge, defined by rules, interactivity, and feedback that results in a quantifiable outcome ideally eliciting an emotional reaction. The goal is to create a game in which people want to invest brain share, time, and energy.

- *Mechanics.* The mechanics of playing a game include levels, earning badges, point systems, scores, and time constraints. These are the elements that are used in many games. Mechanics alone are insufficient to turn a boring experience into a game-like engaging experience, but they are crucial building blocks used during the gamification process.

- *Aesthetics.* Without engaging graphics or a well-designed experienced, gamification cannot be successful. The user interface or the look and feel of an experience is an essential element in the process of gamification. How an experience is aesthetically perceived by a person greatly influences his or her willingness to accept gamification.

- *Game Thinking.* This is perhaps the most important element of gamification. It is the idea of thinking about an everyday experience like jogging or running and converting it into an activity that has elements of competition, cooperation, exploration and storytelling.[13] It is how running becomes a social process. Friends compete against each other while simultaneously offering encouragement in a cooperative environment and the runner tells the story of running one thousand miles or of escaping zombies. It is how the management of a virtual factory provides the insights into the operations of a real factory. It's how leadership skills are learned guiding others on quests.

- *Engage.* An explicit goal of the gamification process is to gain a person's attention and to involve him or her in the process you have created. Engagement of an individual is a primary focus of gamification.

- *People.* These can be learners, consumers, or players. These are the individuals who will be engaged in the created process and who will be motivated to take action.

- *Motivate Action.* Motivation is a process that energizes and gives direction, purpose or meaning to behavior and actions. For individuals to be motivated, the challenge must not be too hard or too simple. Driving participation in an action or activity is a core element in gamification.

- *Promote Learning.* Gamification can be used to promote learning because many of the elements of gamification are based on educational psychology and are techniques that designers of instruction, teachers, and professors have been using for years. Items such as assigning points to activities, presenting corrective feedback, and encouraging collaboration on projects have been the staples of many educational practitioners. The difference is that gamification provides another layer of interest and a new way weaving together those elements into an engaging game space that both motivates and educates learners.

- *Solve Problems.* Gamification has a high potential to help solve problems. The cooperative nature of games can focus more than one individual on solving a problem. The competitive nature of games encourages many to do their best to accomplish the goal of winning.

What Gamification Is Not

Now that we have defined the term gamification, let's define what gamification is not. There are a number of commonly held misconceptions about gamification that must be addressed so that the true potential of gamification can be realized. Gamification is not . . .

- *Badges, Points, and Rewards.* Unfortunately, the least exciting and least useful elements of games have been labeled "gamification." This is unfortunate because the real power of game-based thinking is in the other elements of games: engagement, storytelling, visualization of characters, and problem solving. Those are the foundations upon which gamification needs to be built. Unfortunately, a few people are devaluing the term "gamification" when it could have real use in describing how to take engagement and learning to the next level. Learning professionals, who have been adding "real" game elements to learning, such as interactivity, storytelling, and problem solving, need to take back the word "gamification" and use it for themselves.

- *Trivialization of Learning.* Gamification is not a cheapening or dilution of "real learning." Serious learning scenarios are undertaken within game spaces all the time from military games, to sales incentives, to practicing medical procedures or preparing for standardized tests. Gamified learning can, and is, difficult, challenging, and stressful. Well-designed games help learners acquire skills, knowledge, and abilities in short, concentrated periods of time with high retention rates and effective recall. Do not think of games for learning in the same way as you think of games for children. Gamification is a serious approach to accelerating the experience curve of the learning, teaching complex subjects, and systems thinking.

- *New.* In spite of the rapid growth of the concept of gamification, the elements of gamification are not new. The military has been using "war games," simulations, and goal-driven experiences to train personnel for centuries. In fact, many historians believe that a 7th century game called Chaturanga may be the first game that used pieces to serve as military figures on a fictional battlefield. The pieces represented foot soldiers, elephants, and chariots, which moved about on a playing board much like the modern chessboard.[14]

Teachers, faculty members, and corporate trainers have been using game-like techniques for a long time as well. Instructors, trainers, and professors embed stories in the form of case studies to wrap experiences for learners, create challenges to engage learners, and set goals and provide feedback on progress while providing a safe environment for learners to practice skills. All of these are elements of gamification.

What is new is the emphasis of bringing all of these elements together in an engaging manner under the single concept of gamification. The focus on the relationships and dependencies of these elements is new. The rapidly growing acceptance of game thinking and game mechanics applied to performance, learning, and instruction is forcing a re-examination of how games impact learning and performance.

- *Foreign to Learning Professionals.* It is critical to remember that learning and development professionals are uniquely qualified to lead the gamification effort within organizations. The elements of interactive design that are buried in good instructional design strategies need to be surfaced and applied to the creation of online and face-to-face learning events to create compelling interactive experiences while leveraging the best from game-based experiences.

- *Perfect for Every Learning Situation.* There are many situations for which gamification will not work. Too often the learning profession embraces a new concept as the answer to all learning problems and overhypes the concept to the point of backlash. It is important to approach the gamification of content and learning carefully and methodically. If gamification is seen as a panacea and applied to every single learning event, it will quickly become trivialized and non-impactful. Stay focused on using gamification for the right learning outcomes.

- *Easy to Create.* Creating an effective game or properly gamifying content is not an insignificant task. It takes a great deal of design and up-front work to determine which game elements should map to which types of content and what incentives and rewards work with what type of environment. It also takes time to develop the right theme, the correct method of scoring, and the best way to determine the winning states. In short, it is not easy to create a game that is both fun to play and instructional.

- *Only Game Mechanics.* Bolting one or two game elements onto boring content is not an effective use of gamification. A huge mistake made by novice designers or others who attempt to embrace gamification is that they only look at the mechanics of the game such as scores, points, rewards, badges, and so forth, and neglect other, more critical, elements of effective gamification. The best approach is to consider the entire experience of the learner and not just one or two elements. Storytelling comes into play, as do the motivational aspects of the learning. The entire experience must work together. If a piece or part is missing and the environment is not congruent with the learning, the results can be disastrous. It is the interplay of different elements all adding up to more than the sum of the parts that makes an experience worthwhile.

Gamification Versus Serious Games

To some the difference between the terms "serious games" and "gamification" is simple. A serious game is an experience designed using game mechanics and game thinking to educate individuals in a specific content domain. There are serious games for leadership, sale techniques, and other business topics as well as many serious games in the realm of healthcare. These folks approach the serious game as a noble use of game mechanics and a way to engage and interact with learners.

On the other hand, they view the concept of "gamification" as a trivial use of game mechanics to artificially engage learners and others in activities in which they would otherwise not engage. They see the addition of points, rewards, and badges to activities as trivial and not a serious use of the "essence" of games or game-based learning. To them, gamification is leaderboards and high scores artificially tacked onto real-life situations.

As indicated above, these are not the traits of gamification as defined in this book. In fact, the definition of "gamification" as merely adding game mechanics to non-game situations to encourage engagement is a narrow approach; an approach that does not lead to learning, engagement, or productivity improvements.

Gamification as defined here is *a careful and considered application of game thinking to solving problems and encouraging learning using all the elements of games that are appropriate.* When you get right down to it, the goals of both are relatively the same. Serious games and gamification are both trying to solve a problem, motivate people, and promote learning using game-based thinking and techniques.

Serious games tend to take the approach of using a game within a well-defined game space like a game board or within a computer browser, while gamification tends to take the use of a game outside of a defined space and apply the concept to items like walking up steps, tracking the number of miles run, or making a sales call. But even these are artificial distinctions.

When an instructional designer develops a game to teach the sales process within an organization, is that the gamification of sales techniques or is it a serious game? Is asking students to answer questions about physics using an audience response system to obtain a certain grade a serious game with serious consequences (like passing or failing) or simply gamification of a serious subject? Is the process of tracking all the food you eat and the steps you take with sensors prior to having heart surgery a serious game or the gamification of pre-surgical preparation? Is a game designed to teach you how to exercise and run after the surgery a serious game or the gamification of a recovery plan? An argument might be that the musical stairs example in the beginning of the chapter was an example of play but not an example of gamification because there was no goal to accomplish and, therefore, the example is of play and not gamification.

Looking at it another way, the musical stairs example cited earlier doesn't have an artificial goal or objective from the players' perspective like a serious game. The people using the stairs want to get to the top (intrinsic motivation) and the music adds a little extrinsic motivation and engagement or interactivity (game mechanics) to the process. However, the designers of the musical steps did have a very specific goal . . . get people to use the stairs. And is getting to the top of the stairs a goal?

People using reward points (an oft-noted gamification technique) have an intrinsic goal (fly to a beach for vacation). The slight extrinsic motivation is that they might be able to fly for free or reduced price if they acquire enough points. The goal of the designers of the reward system is to persuade the people to fly more on their airline. The completion criteria is taking the flight for free.

Employees playing a game teaching better sales negotiation skills have an intrinsic goal to become better salespeople, and the "game environment" is extrinsic motivation with an artificial goal (defeat the anti-sales aliens, for example). The sales folks could learn sales skills without the "serious game." But management really wants them to sell more by taking to heart the "gamified" learning content.

So each activity has an intrinsic goal (reach top of steps, fly for free, learn to sell better), each has extrinsic elements (music, points,) each has a clear end point (top of stairs, a free flight, sales game ends), and each is designed specifically to illicit a serious outcome (taking stairs for health, sell more airline tickets, sell more product.) Is only the airline rewards example "gamification"? I don't think so. I think all are examples of gamification.

Is something only a "game" if the people engaged in the activity have a goal? If a designer involves people in a game without their awareness—like the step example–is that a game? Stated another way, if a designer has a clear goal for the desired outcome and the players aren't aware of it, is it still a game? Is adding game elements (points, time constraints, leaderboards) to traditional instructional content (learning how to be a better salesperson) the "gamification" of content?

For the purpose of this book, the delivery of content—for a purpose other than pure entertainment—using game-based thinking and mechanics is gamification. Placing artificial goals on items like taking the stairs is a game—the goal is to get to the top of the steps but to be engaged in the process. In this book, the creation of a serious game falls under the process of gamification. So, yes, climbing the musical stairs, earning frequent flyer miles, and teaching sales skills with a game are all gamification because all of these processes fit under the definition of using game-based mechanics, aesthetics, and game thinking to engage people, motivate action, promote learning, and solve problems. Building a game based on content to be learned is really the gamification of the content; the same thought processes, techniques, and approach needs to be applied as when one is gamifying a website or a set of stairs.

In this book, the use of serious games will be considered a form of gamification because serious games are a specific sub-set of the meta-concept of gamification. Gamification encompasses the idea of adding game elements, game thinking, and game mechanics to learning content. The goal of gamification is to take content that is typically presented as a lecture or an e-learning course and add game-based elements (story, challenge, feedback, rewards, etc.) and create a gamified learning opportunity either in the form of a full-fledged educational game, in the form of game-elements on top of normal tasks like running for exercise, or in the form of an engaging classroom experience wherein the learners participate in a story-based challenge to master the content presented.

The core underlying element of gamification is game play and that is why the chapters in this book study games and game elements. Understanding how games work and influence learners will help professionals understand how to create future learning experiences that are engaging, motivational, and lead to increased retention and application of knowledge.

Growth of Gamification

The gamification trend is growing, with no signs of slowing down. Elements from games are making their way into corporate training departments through avatars, increased problem-based learning, and interactive learning experiences. Colleges and universities through audience response systems, online simulations and interactive storytelling are quickly integrating game-thinking into the curriculum. The influence of games and game elements is growing at a rapid pace.

One of the reasons for this growth is that the average video game player has been playing games for over twelve years and more and more people at all ages are playing games. In fact, 26 percent of people playing games are over fifty, which is an increase from a mere 9 percent in 1999.[15] Video games are main stream and becoming more popular yearly.

In the United States, computer and video game software sales generate over $10.5 billion a year and 67 percent of American households play computer or video games. Additionally, nearly sixty-two million U.S. Internet users, or 27 percent of the online audience, will play at least one game on a social network monthly making social gaming a billion dollar a year business.[16] With online and social games growing at a rapid pace. The massively multiplayer online role play game (MMORPG) industry, with well-known games like World of Warcraft, RuneScape, Disney Toontown, Club Penguin, and Eve Online, itself is valued at over $4 billion. [17]

But these numbers are dwarfed by the world wide video and computer game industry, which is valued at over $105 billion.[18] With the United Kingdom spending $270 million and France spending $220 million just on MMORPGs games. In Japan, spending on game consoles and handheld devices is approximately $2.2 billion per year.

As the proliferation of video and computer games increases, the gamification industry itself is growing at a staggering rate. More than 50 percent of organizations that manage innovation process will gamify those processes within the next decade.[19] Also within the decade, the overall market for gamification is predicted grow to $1.6 billion, up from a reported $100 million in 2011.[20] Within the next five years, a gamified service for consumer goods marketing and customer retention will become as important as Facebook, Twitter, or Amazon, and more than 70 percent of Global 2000 organizations will have at least one gamified application.[21]

Who Is Using Gamificaiton?

A number of organizations are using gamification to train workers, educate students, solve problems, and generate new ideas and concepts. These organizations range from business schools to software companies to pharmaceutical companies to government organizations, and beyond. In almost every industry it is possible to find an example of the gamification of learning, innovation, and problem solving.

Cisco developed a game it calls "The Binary Game," which is an arcade game that looks like Tetris. The idea is to teach people the basic idea of binary numbers. The player doesn't need to know binary numbers to play but actually learns the concept while playing. Within five minutes, the game exposes the players to the forty to fifty binary problems. Quickly, the players recognize patterns and develop strategies because they are trying to beat the game. Those patterns and strategies are actually giving them ability to think in binary.[22]

IBM created an interactive first-person thinker game called INNOV8, which teaches the complex idea of business process management by making players responsible for making decisions that impact the fictitious company named After, Inc. The game, is used in business and information technology programs in hundreds of schools around the world. The interactive, 3-D educational game was designed to bridge the gap in understanding between IT teams and business leaders in an organization.

In the game, students make business decisions based on materials within the game, collaboration with classmates, and in game discussions with characters that provide various amounts of information. Skills learned include business problem solving, prioritization, and consensus building. The game provides a type of virtual internship that allows students to examine the ramifications of their decisions in a safe environment where they won't really get fired or lose a bonus based on a bad decision.[23] It is a gamified approach to teaching decision making and business acumen.

Of course, the military has always been a huge advocate of games and has gamified military strategy, war preparedness, and tactical training. Military organizations worldwide have found that, when dealing with life and death, game-based training scenarios make an impact on the learners.

But a new wrinkle in military gamification is the use of games to solve military problems. In this case, the U.S. military is trying to generate new ideas on how to battle Somali pirates through the use of a massive multiplayer game. The initiative involves the military creating a game-based environment and crowdsourcing military problems to civilians. The goal is to find innovative solutions by observing what players do within the game environment.

The game platform is called a massive multiplayer online war game leveraging the Internet (MMOWGLI) and will have more than one thousand online players who will immerse themselves in the game environment focused on defeating the efforts of Somali pirates. This unique use of gamification is the first time the American military has integrated crowdsourcing and gamification into traditional military war games.

The game, created by the Office of Naval Research (ONR), is designed to test the feasibility of using massively multiplayer online games to solve difficult and non-conventional strategic problems. The first integration of the game focuses on combating Somalia piracy but the platform is designed so it can be adapted to a variety of military situations. The goal is to see whether the game will help the military gain insights into fighting off piracy in the Horn of Africa and Gulf of Aden. Players negotiate the logistics of arming ships, determine the likelihood of pirate attacks, and carefully consider the financial, jurisdictional, and temporal difficulties of military action needed to support commercial shipping and cruise ships. Then they set sail and face pirate attacks; they will then see whether they successfully prepared.

If unsuccessful, players make adjustments and try again. All the while, the military will track what happens, hoping that the scaled-up participant pool offers novel combinations of actions and ideas that, ultimately, assist with solving the real-life problem.[24]

The United Kingdom's Department for Work and Pensions created a game called Idea Street. The goal behind the game was to decentralize innovation and generate ideas from its 120,000 people across the organization. Idea Street is a social collaboration platform with the addition of game mechanics. The mechanics included points, leader boards, and a "buzz index." Within the first eighteen months, Idea Street had approximately 4,500 users and had generated 1,400 ideas, sixty-three of which had gone forward to implementation.[25]

In the area of innovation and idea generation, Hilton's Embassy Suites used game techniques in a customer loyalty campaign targeting 50,000 of Embassy Suites' most loyal guests. The company solicited participation with ten different approaches, including direct mail, e-mail, and asking customers to play a game. The game option proved most effective. The people targeted by the game (five thousand) were most likely to open e-mails and later spent the most money. That group accounted for about $200,000 of the additional $1 million in revenue generated by the campaign.[26]

Implications and Importance to the Future of Learning

Learning professionals must understand the growing trend of applying game-based sensibilities to the development of instruction through creating time-based activities, leveling up of learning experiences, storytelling, avatars, and other techniques. Yes, points and leaderboards will be a part of that, but they are not the main focus; all elements of games need to be brought to bear intelligently and carefully.

The growing use of avatars, the increasing popularity of massively multiplayer online role play games, and the addition of point systems, badges, and leaderboards in realms such as economics, retail sales, and finance are leading to a proliferation of gamified collaborative and learning techniques. This is not a waning trend; rather it is gaining momentum and acceptance in more and more fields. Learning and development professionals must follow that trend or be left behind. This is especially true when applied to areas not typically thought of as material appropriate for "games."

This is also crucial because traditional methods of learning are losing favor, most page-turning e-learning modules are boring people who have grown up playing video games for an average of twelve years. Time and attention of learners is limited, and learning professionals must focus on providing an engaging and goal-oriented solution to the training and teaching dilemma. A focus on gamification increases engagement, relevance, and immersion and assists with the transfer of learning to the actual situation.

Learning professionals will be called upon to match different game strategies with different types of learning content to create the right learning outcome. College faculty, learning professionals, and others in the field of learning and education must gain knowledge of how gamification techniques can be used in a variety of settings to improve learning, retention, and application of knowledge. Learning and development professionals and educators are in a unique position to seize the opportunity to create interactive experiences for internal employees, students, and customers using gamification.

In the next chapter, we'll examine the individual elements that contribute to making a game engaging. Knowledge of these elements will assist with the gamification of content to be learned.

■ ■ ■

Key Takeaways

The key takeaways from this chapter are

- A "game" is a system in which players engage in an abstract challenge, defined by rules, interactivity, and feedback, that results in a quantifiable outcome often eliciting an emotional reaction.

- "Gamification" is using game-based mechanics, aesthetics, and game thinking to engage people, motivate action, promote learning, and solve problems.

- Gamification is not the superficial addition of points, rewards, and badges to learning experiences.

- Gamification is growing; soon a gamified service for consumer goods marketing and customer retention will become as important as Facebook, Twitter, or Amazon.

- Global 2000 organizations are quickly putting gamification into place.

- Gamification techniques can be applied to learning applications within any type of industry, from the military to retail to computer services to manufacturing organizations.

- Serious games are created by using game-based mechanics, aesthetics, and game thinking to engage people, motivate action, promote learning, and solve problems. In other words, they are created through the gamification of traditional learning content.

- Learning professionals, educators, and faculty members have many of the skills, knowledge, and abilities to take a leadership position in the gamification of learning and instruction.

It's in the Game: Understanding Game Elements

CHAPTER QUESTIONS

At the end of this chapter, you should be able to answer the following questions:

- What are the various elements that are contained within games?
- How would you compare and contrast game element and mechanics and typical instructional design?
- How do game elements work individually and collectively to create the game playing experience?

Introduction

What makes a game motivational, exciting, or irresistible? Why can some games be played over and over again, while others are a one and done? The answers to these questions and others boil down to the game elements or game mechanics that contribute to interest in playing a game. This chapter explores the more common elements and describes how they contribute to game play. Although an import consideration is that a single element or even one or two elements alone cannot make an engaging, immersive learning environment. It is the interrelationship of the elements that makes a game engaging.

Abstractions of Concepts and Reality

Imagine trying to duplicate all the complexity of running a major city, creating an amusement park, or gearing up for a military assault. These are involved and complicated processes and the backdrops for a variety of engaging and fun games. Games based on this complex subject matter work, not because they include all the complexities, but precisely because they reduce the complexity and use broad generalizations to represent reality. The player is involved in an abstraction of events, ideas, and reality.

Games are based on models of the real world. A game may be regarded as a dynamic model of reality in which the model provides a representation of reality at a particular period of time. This is known in the academic literature as an *operating model*, as distinct from verbal, graphic, mathematical, or physical models. It is also important to note that the modeled reality may be hypothetical, imagined, or fictional as is often in the case in games like Dungeons and Dragons and video games like the Halo series.[1]

Abstracted reality has a number of advantages over reality. First, it helps the player manage the conceptual space being experienced. In other words, it helps the player understand what is going on within the game. It minimizes the complexity. The game Monopoly and the game Chess are abstractions to such a degree that financial monopolies and military strategy are literally reduced to the space of a game board. This makes it possible for players to engage with the concepts of strategy and financial acquisition without having to experience war or being in a monopoly themselves. It is possible to manage the concepts easily within the abstracted space.

The second advantage is that cause and effect can be more clearly identified. In a large, interconnected system like a city, raising taxes might eventually cause people to move away and the long-term impact might be an erosion of the tax base, but waiting years for that to happen doesn't provide a clear cause and effect relationship to those living in the city. Additionally, issues such as quality of life, availability of employers, quality of school systems, and other factors influence people's willingness to stay within a given location. Games highlight relationships and make those relationships more clearly linked so that once a city manager raises taxes, non-character players begin moving out of the city in one or two subsequent turns.

Third, abstracting reality removes extraneous factors. Reality is messy; there are a lot of events that happen in real life that would not make playing a game very interesting. Everyday occurrences in reality make for uninteresting game play. Few games force a player to stop all activity and get a haircut or go to the dentist. Important in real life, removed in games.

In games with guns, it takes many real-life fatal shots to bring down the game character. A hospital visit for that wound to the shoulder—out of the question. Reloading is required but happens infrequently, and for some reason cases of bullets are strewn all over the place.

If that weren't the case, every time a player was shot, he or she would be required to visit the hospital and be bedridden for weeks or would die instantly and end the game. Games remove elements of reality to keep the player focused on the essence of the game. Removing extraneous factors keeps the game moving and the player involved. Too many elements of reality and the game ceases to be engaging.

Fourth, it reduces the time required to grasp the concepts. In complex systems the ability to grasp all the concepts and ideas involved can be overwhelming. For example, without training, driving a race car can be a complicated and frightening ordeal, but in racing games the controls are abstractions of reality and easier to use than in real life. The abstraction of the interface and the game concepts makes it easier to grasp complex processes.

Goals

To many, the difference between a game and play is the introduction of a goal. Sure, you and your friends can casually run around the park and play on the jungle gym, but when someone says, "I bet I can beat you to the other end of the playground," suddenly play time is over and a game begins.

The simple introduction of a goal adds purpose, focus, and measurable outcomes. You now have a method to measure the quality of play or, at least, certain aspects of the play. Exploration of the park and the surroundings are over and a focus on a specific outcome now becomes the main activity. Introducing a goal or a series of goals to a casual play situation usually creates a game.

As stated in Salen and Zimmerman's work, *Rules of Play: Game Design Fundamentals:* "Goals are fundamental to games . . . at the outcome of a game, the goals are either reached or not reached and this quantifiable outcome is part of our definition of games."[2] Game goals, unlike instructional goals, which are sometimes broad sweeping statements (understand good customer service), are specific and unambiguous. Typically, there is no doubt whether or not a game goal was achieved. Either you defeat the dragon or you die trying, you solve the puzzle or you can't figure it out, you take over territory or you forfeit ground.

In many games, goals are clear and visible both figuratively and literary. In the causal game of Tetris, the goal is to prevent the blocks from reaching the top of the screen. As you are playing the game, you see your progress on the screen by observing how far away the blocks are from the top of the screen. You see, at every point in the game, exactly how you are doing.

Even a simple game like Tic-Tac-Toe provides visual cues as to how each player is performing. You can see where your opponent placed the X's and the open spots left for your O's. The race to the other side of the playground described before provides visual cues as to progress. You can see who finishes first. In fact, that visual cue determines who wins.

Visually understanding how far you are from a goal provides incentive, feedback, and an indication of progress as well as a measurement against others. "Hey, I scored 21,001 in that game; that's 1 better than you." The goal of the game is the primary device for determining level of effort at a certain point in the game, strategies, moves, and, ultimately, who wins. The goal sustains the game and keeps players moving forward.

A goal gives the player the freedom and autonomy to pursue it using different approaches and methods. Knowing the goal, one can apply different techniques to achieve the goal. It seems counter-intuitive, but clear goals like "rescue the princess" provide the player with choices. You can go directly to the princess and fight the dragon or you can go through the forest and collect the necessary weaponry to beat the dragon or you can build a flying machine and bypass the dragon altogether.

But goals have to be well structured and sequenced to have sustained meaning and to motivate players to achieve those goals. In instructional terms, you have to create a terminal goal and support that goal with a series of enabling objectives. These enabling objectives serve as small incremental steps that allow a player to move from one accomplishment to the next.

The reason for this is two-fold. First, once a player accomplishes the goal of the game, the game is over. Once you've solved the puzzle, rescued the princess, or taken over all the territory, you are done. "In this sense, a game's goal is the death of play."[3] Achieving the goal of the game means the game is over. So a number of smaller goals leading to a larger goal are important in providing sustained play. You don't want the game to end too early.

The second is that a goal can be difficult to achieve without building prerequisite skills necessary to achieve the goal. For example, one cannot rescue the princess unless he or she first learns to slay dragons. In games, defeating the final villain or enemy often requires learning a combination of skills, often at different levels in the game, and then using that combination of skills to defeat the game or, in other words, to achieve the ultimate goal.

Rules

At its simplest form, a game is just a set of defined rules. There are rules indicating the maximum number of players who can play a game, rules describing how to score points, rules indicating what is allowed in the game, and, in the case of digital games, rules that apply to writing the code that makes the video game character jump. Without rules, games would not exist. Rules are designed specifically to limit player actions and keep the game manageable.

But the multiple levels of rules within games is not always clear and, when designing a game or using game-based elements to enhance learning, understanding the different levels of rules is important. In the book *Rules of Play: Game Design Fundamentals*, the authors define different types of rules that apply to games.[4]

- *Operational Rules.* These are the rule that describe how the game is played. When you want to play a game and someone explains that you can't open the door until you collect the right key, he is describing an operational rule. Or he tells you that collecting two thousand tokens allows you to buy a cooler snowboard, which is also an operational rule. Once you gain a basic understanding of operational rules, you can play the game.

- *Constituative Rules or Foundational Rules.* These are the underlying formal structures dictating game functionality. An example is the mathematical formulas used to calculate how many times the number 6 will appear on a die. These tend to be abstract and need only be understood by the designer of the game. However, occasionally a player can determine these underlying rules and use them to his or her advantage. In the 1990s a group of math students from MIT used a method of counting cards in the card game Black Jack to win millions of dollars at casinos in Las Vegas. They achieved this feat by moving beyond the operational rules governing the game such as "the cards from 2 through 9 are valued at their face value" and "the 10 card, Jack, Queen, and King are all valued at 10" to the foundational rules such as "We are playing with three decks, which means there are 156 cards and that means there are a total of forty-eight high cards and four of them have been played already, so the probability that the next card is a high card is .28."[5]

- *Implicit Rules or Behavior Rules.* These are the rules that govern the social contract between two or more players, in other words, the rules related to being a good sport about the game—game etiquette. These are implied rules and are usually not written. Yet, they have a powerful influence over the game. If they are violated, it is usually a penalty and in a team game can constitute the player being kicked out.

- *Instructional Rules.* Another set of rules exist in an instructional game. These are the rules that you want the learner to know and internalize after the game is played. It is the reason the game is being created in the first place. These rules are the rules that govern the learning within the process of the game. For example, we were creating an online board game to teach inventory managers concepts and ideas to reduce inventory within the organization. One of the rules was that if the player selected a wrong answer, the inventory levels in the factory went up. So the player with the lowest score won the game, not the player with the highest score. This was a conscious choice to reinforce the instructional rule that lower inventory was desirable. The actual game play would not have changed if the score went down, but the instructional lesson may have been diminished if it had.

Conflict, Competition, or Cooperation

Games involve conflict, competition, or cooperation. A conflict is a challenge provided by a meaningful opponent. To win a challenge, the player must actively defeat an opponent. This occurs when one team works against another in a football game, or in an online first-person shooter where one player faces off against another to see who will be the last player "standing" at the end of the game. This can also be a scenario whereby a player is in conflict with the game system. Elements of the game attempt to thwart player progress, such as non-player characters shooting at the player while working toward their objective. The meaning of the play in the context of conflict is to become a winner while avoiding a loss at the hands of an opponent.[6] This is typically accomplished by inflicting damage on the opponent, by scoring more points against the opponent, or by hindering the progress of the opponent.

Competition is where opponents are "constrained from impeding each other and instead devote the entirety of their attentions to optimizing their own performance."[7] This occurs in racing games. Two players race to the finish line and each tries to go as quickly as possible but they don't interfere with one another. In this case the meaning of the play is to achieve the best possible accomplishment against the environment, obstacles, and the opponent. Winning is accomplished by being faster, cleverer, or more skilled than the opponents.

Cooperation is the act of working with others to achieve a mutually desirable and beneficial outcome. This is the social aspect of games that many players enjoy. In these types of games, the more individuals work together, the more they are able to achieve. FarmVille, the online social networking game that lets a person run his or her own virtual farm, uses the concept of cooperation with its co-op farming elements. Often in role-play games, two or more players of different player types must team together to overcome an obstacle or accomplish a goal. Working together and achieving a goal is the winning state of cooperative play.

While it is helpful to consider the elements of conflict, competition, and cooperation separately, often good game design includes elements of all three. In the online role-play game World of Warcraft, players can battle each other, they can form guilds to accomplish cooperative goals, and they compete with others to achieve certain quests as quickly as possible. The game intertwines the three elements to provide an engaging game play environment.

Time

Time is an element that has many dimensions as it relates to game design and game play. The most obvious is to use time as a motivator for player activity and action. As soon as that timer appears in the upper corner of an instructional video game screen and starts to count down (or in some cases up), it raises the stress level and motivates action. Players no longer loiter, leisurely explore an area, or wait to see what happens next. Instead, they focus, jump into action, and begin to undertake the tasks needed to accomplish the level or game's goal. In this way, time serves to spur player action and to force the player to work under pressure. This can be valuable in mimicking certain work conditions under which time is a key success factor, such as resolving a customer complaint as quickly as possible in a call center and then answering the next call or completing a task within a certain amount of time.

Time can also be a resource that needs to be allocated during a game. The allocation of time to one task and then another task can be critical to success. For example, in many games it is important to gather treasure, but if the player spends all his or her time looking for treasure, he or she may not complete a level in the allocated time or may lose out on gathering other rewards. In more corporate focused games, players can learn how much time they should spend on one activity while balancing their overall time allotment. Players may be put into situations in which they have to decide, "Should I spend my time answering all my e-mails or focus on voicemail or have fewer face-to-face meetings?" Prioritizing activities because of time constraints can be a challenge in terms of determining what time is spent on what activity, a challenge people deal with on a daily basis.

Video games allow the designer of the game to compress time to show consequences of actions more quickly than during the natural course of events. In an actual situation, a person may have to wait months for the results of an action, such as the decision to build an apartment building, hoping it can be filled with tenants. In a video game, those months can be compressed into minutes. In the game Civilization V, hundreds of years go by in a matter of a few hours as the players take turns moving warriors, ships, and settlers. Without the convention of compressed time, games would be onerous and boring.

Reward Structures

Badges, points, and rewards are not all bad; it's just that they are not the only component to gamification. Understanding how reward structures can work and how to integrate these structures into games is important. Reward structures have a role to play as an integral part of games and not the focus of a gamification effort.

While it's fun to obtain a high score on a video game, it is just as fun to let others know you are the one who received the high score and to imaging

being on the top of the leaderboard, as depicted in Figure 2.1. Game designers are aware of this and, early in arcade games, they created a leaderboard to
add a social component to what was then essentially a solitary endeavor. The
leaderboard is a list of the top scores in the game so whoever plays the game
could see all the players' names or initials and scores. It was a simple inven-
tion but created a powerful motivator to play the game again and again and
gave players a chance to socially interact in discussions around the game
and high scores. It also gave bragging rights and social capital to the individuals who achieved the high scores.

In addition to leaderboards, games also provide players with instant
reward in the form of points. Sometimes those points are directly related to

Figure 2.1. The Goal? Be at the Top of the Leaderboard.

Image reprinted with permission of the artist, Kristin Bittner.

#	NAME	SCORE
1		2798
2	N. Hawkins	2764
3	B. Marten	2750
4	H. Chin	2682
5	G. Brown	2657
6	R. Olen	2571
7	E. Williams	2546
8	A. Johnson	2530
9	P. Ramirez	2511
10	D. Duncan	2459

the activity. In football video game Madden NFL 12, when a player scores a touchdown, the team earns 6 points. In the social networking game Mafia Wars, points are earned by completing jobs or winning fights, which are both activities directly related to the narrative of the game, which is running a criminal empire. In other games like Super Mario Brothers, you can earn points by collecting coins, which is not essential to the goal of the game, which is make it to the castle and rescue Princess Toadstool from Bowser.

In addition to points, many games have extra abilities or prizes that can be earned for accomplishing certain tasks within the game. In the video game Call of Duty, rewards can be translated into an upgrade of weapons or the ability to have special tactics available. For example, a kill streak (killing eleven opponents without being killed yourself) enables you to "call in the dogs," which provides dogs who sniff out enemies.

There are two views on rewards and badges: one is to make them as easy to get as possible early in a game so that players are hooked and want to continue playing. The other school of thought is to avoid easy badges that are not related to activities that are rewarding in and of themselves. For example, in Call of Duty to have a kill streak of eleven is a good accomplishment in and of itself. The subsequent ability to "call in the dogs" is nice but not the main motivator for trying to have an eleven-kill streak. It is better to link activities within the game to reward than to have random rewards.

Unfortunately, e-learning courses and classroom instruction do not offer easily traceable progress reports like leaderboards, badges, or rewards. Wouldn't it be great to have a corporate leaderboard so employees could know how well they were doing? Or have badges employees wear to know how accomplished they are? The gamification of work provides added incentive to employees through carefully crafted rewards structures.

Feedback

One of the features video games, board games, and other types of games have over traditional learning environments is the frequency and intensity of feedback. Feedback in games is almost constant. In a video game the player has real-time feedback on progress toward goal, amount of life or energy left, location, time remaining, how much "stuff" they have in inventory, and even how other players are doing. In fact, often a screen or a player will flash to indicate the danger of being eliminated with the next wrong move. On a board game you can see where your piece is related to others, you know who is taking the next turn, and you can see how much progress is to be made with the roll of the dice and how close you and your opponents are to successfully finishing.

Games provide informational feedback. Feedback in learning or playing games is designed to evoke the correct behavior, thoughts, or actions. Games provide information upon which the player can act. The informational feedback is designed to indicate the degree of "rightness" or "wrongness" of a response, action, or activity. Feedback immediately informs the learner if he or she did the right thing, the wrong thing, or somewhere in the middle but doesn't tell the learner how to correct the action.

The second form of feedback is to provide information to the leaner to guide him or her toward the correct outcome. If you did the wrong thing, you should be prompted, guided, or pointed toward a more appropriate action or activity but not told exactly what to do, if nothing else, through the knowledge that the activity you chose was not correct. Often these two feedback mechanisms overlap. If you are playing a video game as a spy and you enter a door and an alarm goes off and bad guys instantly become alert, you know you went in the wrong door, but that action also informs you. Look for other options for entering the building such as that open window you passed on the way to the door. It is not didactic; it doesn't tell the player, "no" you should do X instead of Y. Instead, the player suffers or rejoices in the consequences of the actions taken.

In game designer parlance, the term often used for effective, exciting, and engaging feedback is "juicy." When creating feedback, designers strive for juiciness. So what is juicy feedback? Well-known game designer and researcher, Robin Hunicke describes juicy feedback as having the following characteristics:[8]

- *Tactile*—The player can almost feel the feedback as it is occurring on screen. Feedback is not forced or unnatural within the game play.

- *Inviting*—It's something the player desires to achieve. As the player interacts with the game, he or she wants the feedback and works to get the positive feedback. The player is given just the right amount of power and rewards.

- *Repeatable*—The feedback can be received again and again if the goals, challenges, or obstacles are met.

- *Coherent*—The feedback stays within the context of the game. It is congruent with on-screen actions and activities as well as with the storyline unfolding as the interactions occur.

- *Continuous*—It is not something that the player has to wait for, but occurs as a natural result of interacting within the context of the game environment.

- *Emergent*—It flows naturally from the game; it unfolds in an orderly and well-sequenced fashion. It feels like it belongs within the context of the environment and is not distracting.

- *Balanced*—The player knows he or she is receiving feedback and reacts based on the feedback but is not overwhelmed by it feedback or thinks of it as direct feedback.

- *Fresh*—The feedback is a little surprising contains some unexpected twists, and is interesting and inviting. The surprises are welcomed and congruent with the continuous feedback.

Jesse Schell, a professor at Carnegie Mellon University's Entertainment Technology Center, describes "juicy" simply as "a ripe peach, just a little bit of interaction with it gives you a continuous flow of delicious reward."9

Levels

Games have different types of levels. One is the level- or mission-based structure whereby players progress from one level to the next as they move toward the end of the game. The other concept of level is the degree of difficulty the player chooses when he or she first enters the game. The third level is the level of experience and skills the player receives playing the game. Typically, these three concepts of levels occur simultaneously as the player enters and moves through a game.

Game Levels

Mission-based levels serve several purposes within the design of a game. One purpose is to keep the game space manageable. Developing a game in which a player wanders through one vast level accomplishing hundreds of objectives and interacting with dozens of non-player characters is a daunting programming task and is intimidating for the player. Additionally, attempting to weave a coherent storyline into a game play environment where a player can go wherever he wants in any order can be difficult.

To overcome these problems, game developers add levels to games. In each level the player accomplishes a small set of goals and, when completed, moves on to the next level. A well-designed progression of levels accomplishes three goals. One is that each level helps the story narrative progress. The player learns new information or insights at each level, which keeps her engaged as part of the story unfolds in each level. By unveiling a little bit of the narrative at each level, the player feels compelled to move from one level to the next to find out what will happen and how the narrative will end.

The second is that skills are built and reinforced at each level. At the earliest level of the game, players are taught basic skills such as how to navigate, what elements in the game world are movable or important, and how to use any weapons, special abilities or power-ups. In the early levels, as the players learn about the game world, they typically learn one skill at a time as they move through a level. Also, some levels may simply be a chance to practice a new skill, so no new information or skills is introduced.

Then, as the player progresses and the levels become more difficult, players are required to recall and use skills learned in previous levels to advance. However, at this point the players usually have to perform the skills more quickly or under greater pressure to make the application of the skill more challenging. Toward the end of the game, players typically must combine skills learned from previous levels in unique combinations to win the game.

The third element is that levels serve as motivation. When a player masters a level he or she then wants to progress to the next level and then the next level, and so on until completing the game. The different levels provide small, achievable goals that lead to the player wanting to engage in more and more game activities so he or she can eventually go to the next level.

Playing Levels

Playing a game that is too difficult is not fun. Playing a game that is too easy is not fun either. Therefore, the quandary for game developers is to create a game that is neither too hard nor too easy. But when developing a game for a broad audience with unknown skill sets, the task becomes even more daunting. How do you create a game that appropriately challenges players at multiple levels of expertise and experience? The answer is to create a game that is both easy and hard through the use of different levels of entry into the game. By providing an easy, intermediate, and difficult version of the same game, more players are able to enjoy and partake in the game play.

Create an extremely difficult level designed for more experienced players with faster bad guys, more challenging puzzles, and less time to complete levels. Then create a mode where everything is slower, help bubbles pop up on the screen to provide guidance, and challenges are more manageable. This level appeals to novice gamers who are just trying to learn how the game works and who need simple challenges and basic assistance as they play the game. The novice level provides a comfortable way for new players to acclimate to the game.

The third level created is usually the intermediate level, which is aimed at the middle level of difficulty providing the game space where most players will play. The three levels also increase the replayability of the games. Once someone defeats the game at the easy level, he or she may challenge him- or herself with the hardest level to see how he or she will do under more difficult circumstances.

This concept of creating three different game play levels can be easily transferred to the creation of educational games. When creating an educational game, consider designing three levels of interaction into the game. You can develop an easy, intermediate, and hard level, which can be effective for catching the attention of a wide audience. Designing three levels makes it more accessible to learners and may encourage them to replay the game.

Another three-level approach for an educational game is to create a demonstration, practice, and test mode, with each level providing different information and a different challenge.

If you were creating a game to teach someone how to use a piece of equipment or how to conduct an interview, you might want to create one level where the learner watches a demonstration of the proper procedure or technique. This provides the learner with knowledge and information. In essence, the first level provides the instruction and teaching needed to perform the task. This level would be for someone who was a complete novice.

The next level would be the practice level where the learner is given guidance and feedback on whether or not he or she is performing the right tasks. This mode might provide arrows, hints, instructions, highlights, and advice to the learner as he or she follows the procedure. This level would give enough help to guide the learner toward achieving the goal.

Finally, create a test or "free play" mode where the learners are not given any guidance. They just have to play the game independently and are either successful or not. This would be the level of the most difficulty, but it would also be a chance for learners to apply what they are learning directly to the task at hand in a similar environment to what they would actually be doing on the job or in the classroom laboratory.

Providing different entry levels into one game provides access to players or learners with different knowledge levels, allows players to experience the game at different difficulty levels, and provides a way to make the game accessible to a broad audience.

Player Levels

As a player progresses through a game, he or she is gaining more and more experience. To reward loyalty for playing the game and for progressing through levels, players are often awarded what is known as "experience points," a unit of measurement typically used in role-playing video games to quantify a player character's progression through the game. Experience points are awarded for the completion of quests, for overcoming obstacles and opponents, and for making it from one level to the next higher level. Experience points can typically be accumulated throughout the game and used to achieve special abilities, earn items of value, or sometimes used as currency to be spent on specific abilities or attributes chosen by the player. Players value achieving higher and higher levels and gaining more and more experience points because each level is more difficult and success at the level provides a feeling of mastery and accomplishment.

Storytelling

While not all games have a story narrative behind them, storytelling is an essential part of the gamificaiton of learning and instruction. The element of "story" provides relevance and meaning to the experience. It provides context for the application of tasks. Simple games like Tic-Tac-Toe are not guided by a story. Neither are games like hide and seek, freeze tag, or word searches. But a surprising number of simple games have more story behind them than you may think. Chess uses terms like knight, king, and bishop to evoke a back story of two warring factions, the kid's game Capture the Flag has a similar underlying story, and you can become a king in Checkers. Simple video games like Bejeweled even have a loose story associated with them. The underlying story becomes more evident when you hear the original name of the game, "Diamond Mine," which evokes the story of someone mining away looking for jewels.

Early video games added a thin story layer to make them more interesting and engaging than merely shooting or dodging pixels. Often, just the name of the game and some crude graphics were enough to create a compelling story in the player's mind. Space Invaders conjured up an entire story involving saving the Earth from relentless aliens, and Missile Command made you the commander of a base trying to save cities and your own soldiers from inevitable destruction. Today, video games have huge back stories, complete with complex storylines, plot twists, and surprises. Can you say World of Warcraft or Halo? Even player-driven games like Eve Online have hundreds of underlying stories that have been created by the players themselves. Humans are great at adding story narrative to a variety of situations because stories add meaning, provide context, and guide action.

Stories have been used for centuries to pass information from one person to another and to guide behavior and thinking. The combination of a video game and storytelling provides an interactive story that engages and moves the player forward. Well-designed educational games blend a task-related story with interactive game elements to help the player learn the desired behaviors, actions, and thinking patterns that support the desired outcome within a particular context. Games can provide a visual and narrative context for player performance. A game provides a place for players to practice activities as they directly relate to the narrative of their own jobs or academic learning goals.

Storytelling as a form of teaching or providing lessons is alive and well outside of a game context. One worker tells another a "story" about how to do a job or what to avoid. Learners, students, and employees remember stories more effectively than random lists of policies and procedures. Adding game elements and involving the learner in the story can make the learning even more powerful and memorable. A well-crafted game-based story focused on helping learners to solve problems educates learners and is easily recalled when the actual situation arises.

Storytelling within an instructional game allows learners a vicarious experience through the story which they can apply to their work situation or learning environment. The elements that make this possible are

- Characters

- Plot (something happens)

- Tension

- Resolution

Adding these elements together creates an effective story to accompany the elements of the game. Story elements are not only engaging, but they guide the player through the game as he or she attempts to fulfill story elements and to obtain the goal of the game.

A story within a video game typically unfolds with a character encountering a problem or a situation. The problem builds tension in the story as the character may not know what to do or how to react or, worse, may do the wrong thing. Then a solution is offered in the form of a colleague, a moment of inspiration, or an idea (or even reading a policy); then results are presented in a positive manner. This simple structure can be used for game-based story scenarios to help learners understand what they must do to be successful in their environment. It is as if a wise mentor, faculty member, or co-worker is telling them the best method to deal with a situation.

The Hero's Journey

A common story method in most games is known as the monomyth or the hero's journey.[10] The hero's journey was first described by Joseph Campbell in 1949 and then built upon by Christopher Vogler in 1992. The elements of the journey provide a solid foundation for the unfolding of a story within a game. A visual depiction of the journey appears in Figure 2.2.

The journey works as follows. First, we encounter the hero or heroine as a regular person leading an ordinary, regular life. Then he or she is called to action, as something happens that interrupts his or her ordinary life and seemingly forces him or her into taking some sort of action. However, the hero or heroine is reluctant to spring into action and may refuse the initial invitation to take action. Then some wise figure or mentor causes the hero or heroine to have an epiphany, realizing he or she must act. Then the hero or heroine leaves his or her ordinary life and enters into the adventure or quest. This is often done after another disruptive incident that forces him or her to cross the threshold into the adventure world. At this point, villains and enemies are encountered in minor challenges and the hero or heroine makes some allies and learns how this new world works.

Of course, it is never an easy trip. The next step in the journey is when the hero or heroine encounters setbacks and needs to try something new or learn new skills. Once these new skills are learned, the person encounters the peak of the adventure, facing a life-or-death crisis by confronting the villain in a horrendous battle. For a while it looks like the hero or heroine will be killed but he or she survives by overcoming fear and acting upon the wise counsel received earlier in the journey. He or she reaps the rewards that are part of defeating the villain.

Figure 2.2. The Hero's Journey.

Image reprinted with permission of the artist, Kristin Bittner.

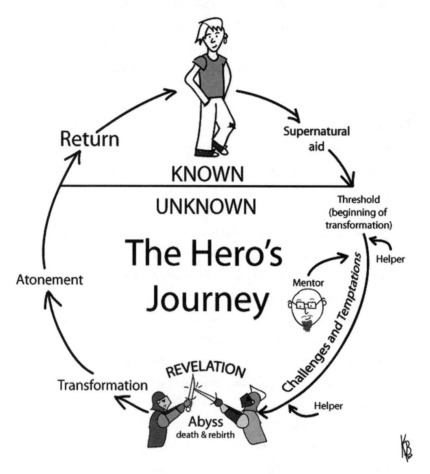

The hero or heroine returns to the ordinary world but, it turns out, all the problems still are not resolved. The villain wasn't really vanquished as the hero or heroine thought. This time the battle/crisis is far greater than the last battle and the hero or heroine must draw on all his or her knowledge and inner strength to defeat the villain; often this is when a solitary hero or heroine realizes that teamwork is a critical element to success and partners with others to achieve goals. At the end the journey is over and crisis is resolved, the villain is gone, and the hero or heroine has improved the lives of others in the ordinary world.

While a story of completing an insurance form properly or closing that epic sale might not be as compelling as a heroine conquering evil and freeing the land from oppression, including elements of the heroic journey and understanding how the heroic journey structure works can transform a rather average case study into a more interesting, engaging, and interactive story.

Curve of Interest

The interest curve within a game is the flow and sequence of events that occur over time that maintains the player's interest. The idea is to purposely sequence events within the flow to grab and hold the player's attention, similar to many educational models, which start with gaining the learner's attention before instruction begins. However, the curve of interest extends the concept throughout an entire experience.

The idea is that the quality of an experience can be measured by the extent to which its unfolding sequence of events is able to hold a learner's attention. As a designer, you can plot the level of interest over time.

The first part of the curve of interest is an entry point—the learner begins instruction. The learner should enter with some level of interest or he or she wouldn't be participating in the learning event in the first place. This probably comes from an externally or internally driven motivation factor, such as, "Hey, I really think this is a great subject for me to know something about" or "Hey, if I don't take this learning, I could get fired." But the designer's job is to take that initial interest and raise it to a new level; Schell calls it "the hook."[11]

This is something that really grabs the learner and gets him or her excited about the learning experience. It is an interesting case study or a description of the danger of not doing the task correctly or it is a mystery or even a series of questions the learner cannot answer.

Once the initial hook is "set," the next step is to settle down to business. If the learning experience is well-crafted, the learner's interest will continually rise, temporarily peeking at different points.

Finally, at the end, is the "climax," and the learning is then over. And, hopefully, the learner leaves the instruction with some interest left over and with knowledge gained by the carefully sequenced instruction.

If you are having learners drop out of your instruction or tune out, go back and check out your interest curve to see whether a re-sequencing might not solve your problem. Interest curves can be very useful when creating a learning experience. By charting out the level of expected interest over the course of a learning experience, trouble spots often become clear and can be corrected. Also, when observing learners having the experience, it is useful to compare their level of observed interest to the level of interest that you, as the designer, anticipated. Then you can see what "works" for your learners and what does not work.

Aesthetics

It might not seem like it, but aesthetics—art, beauty, and visual elements—are part of every game from the symmetry of the Tic-Tac-Toe game space to the clever little Monopoly pieces all the way to the cinematic detail of a video game like Red Dead Redemption with its panoramic views of the American West. Regardless of the game, aesthetics play an important role. Chess pieces require certain aesthetics to distinguish a bishop from a pawn, a knight from a queen, and even to tell one side (white) from the other (black). But beyond those aesthetics, Chess pieces have become a constant source of inspiration for artists who create beautifully handmade pieces or craft an entire board of dinosaurs or Star Wars characters to assume the roles of pawn, knight, queen, and others.

Ignoring aesthetics in the design and creation of a game or the use of gamification techniques reduces the overall experience of the players. The space in which the game is played becomes boring without aesthetics. Appropriate and aligned visuals, attention to detail, simple contrasts, or colorful backdrops create an immersive environment that contributes to the overall game experience. The aesthetics help the players become caught up in the game experience. The artistry, careful mingling of descriptions, and attention to design elements becomes compelling. Even simple elements like receiving a badge in Foursquare or observing the curve of your last run charted on a graph via the exercise-tracking mobile application of NikePlus require attention to detail. Too often educational games and simulations disregard aesthetics, which can cause an experience to be less engaging and less compelling. It is not that good aesthetics will make a bad experience great; they won't. But they can lift a good experience into a great experience.

However, don't confuse aesthetics with realism. A game doesn't need to have photorealistic images to be visually appealing. Games like FarmVille have simplistic and non-realistic graphics but, nevertheless, those graphics add to the game play and dynamics of the experience. It is not the realism of the graphics but the use of the graphics within the game that make them so powerful.

The key is that the cues and small details add to the game environment and convey meaning. When you decide to build an oil-burning power plant in SimCity, the tiny plant puffs grayish black oil smoke into the atmosphere, just as you would expect. This is a small but critical aesthetic that adds to the experience of playing SimCity and supports the underlying story of building a city. In Civilization V, the animation of the farmers cultivating the land in unison creates a sense of people at work, which supports the game's aesthetics.

The game pieces in Bejeweled or Tetris convey meaning visually themselves. You either have the jewels you need in a row or you have a piece that you must fit into a growing floor of blocks. In those games, the visuals are how information is conveyed. In other games, first-person shooters or adventure game visuals convey information to the player within the game interface but not as part of the action of the game. These include meters indicating the level of health of a player or a map image pinpointing his or her location within the game. In some games the color of the player changes if he or she is evoking a special power, such as turning red at times of invincibility.

A caution about the aesthetics of avatars and online characters. Avoid the uncanny valley, the phenomenon put forth by Masahiro Mori, a Japanese robotics scientist noted for his pioneering work on the emotional response of humans to nonhuman entities. The concept of the uncanny valley is that, as a robot or other animated figure becomes more humanlike in its movements and appearance, the emotional response to the figure becomes more favorable, but only up until a certain point. People easily relate to explicitly nonhuman characters like an animated person or animal because when we interact with a highly stylized or abstract avatar we are comfortable. We project attributes onto that character because the details aren't there. At a certain point, however, the animated figure becomes too humanlike to be considered non-threatening but not human enough for us to feel comfortable, and that is the uncanny valley, the area between the cute, stylized character and a full-fledged human. If the character rendering in the game tries to go for 100 percent realistic and doesn't make it, the learner can become "creeped out" by the avatar and be unable to relate.

Replay or Do Over

The "do over" in board or card games and the replay button in video games is an important game element that is often overlooked. The replay button or do over gives the player permission to fail. In games, failure is an option. And it's a good one. Allowing a player to fail with minimal consequences encourages exploration, curiosity, and discovery-based learning. Knowing that you can always restart the game provides a sense of freedom, and players take advantage of that freedom by placing their characters into danger to see what will happen, by using a tactic like running out into the open to learn where the enemies are hiding, or even spending too much on one resource and not enough on another to determine the consequences. Games provide the opportunity to explore a set of rules, to test hypotheses, and to remember which approaches were successful and which ones failed.

In games, unlike many other activities, exploring failure and what it means is a valued approach. Players enjoy failures in a game. or at least use them to progress. The idea of failure is part of the game ethos. No one expects to successfully navigate and win a game the first time he or she plays it. In fact, people expect to fail—and look forward to the lessons learned during the failure process.

Failure adds an additional level of content because it makes the player reconsider his or her approach to a game. The necessity to approach the game differently than originally planned adds to and expands the playability of the game. This is because often two or more approaches are viable to successfully navigating the game, and the player, once made aware of a failed approach, is free to explore multiple options for success.

Many games even have mechanisms built in for overcoming repeated failure. Often these games provide an option to temporarily "level down" to an easier level to complete a mission or provide progressively more prescriptive hints after repeated attempts by a player. These mechanisms are put into place because game designers know that, if a player cannot overcome failure, he or she will eventually quit the game and never return. Failure is only an option up to a point, and then progress is aided by the game itself.

Finally, it should be noted that winning a game without failure or a do over is often a dissatisfying experience for the player. For a player to truly enjoy the game, he or she must feel that something was accomplished and achieved. Failing several times before success instills the feeling of accomplishment once a winning state is achieved. The act of failing multiple times makes the act of winning more pleasurable.[12]

Implications and Importance to the Future of Learning

The game elements outlined in this chapter provide a solid foundation for thinking about the gamification process well beyond just adding a superficial game level of rewards, points, and badges. The concepts of establishing clear, specific goals and a guiding set of rules are areas with which many learning professionals are comfortable and familiar.

Additionally, the idea of using time as a motivator and providing as much feedback as possible are also commonly used techniques. Badges, rewards, and levels as well as storytelling are areas with which learning professionals are not as familiar and are good areas from which techniques can be borrowed.

The use of these techniques along with storytelling and allowing failure can create powerful learning experiences and leverage the elements of gamification to create powerful learning outcomes, resulting in increased retention and application of the learning.

■ ■ ■

Key Takeaways

The key takeaways from this chapter are

- Games are complex systems with many variables.

- Multiple elements are required to make a game an effective learning experience. It is the interplay of the elements that makes for the most effective games.

- Game elements often contain advantages over traditionally presented learning content.

- Game elements work individually and collectively to create the game-playing experience.

- Learning professionals use many of these elements already and can mix in the other elements to create powerful learning outcomes.

Theories Behind Gamification of Learning and Instruction

CHAPTER QUESTIONS

At the end of this chapter, you should be able to answer the following questions:

- What learning theories support the use of games within the instructional process?

- What elements of motivational theory apply to the gamification of learning and instruction?

Introduction

The chapter explores how learning theory supports the use of games for learning in a number of different contexts. The chapter covers operant conditioning and the reinforcement schedules as only one of many elements that make games engaging. Also explored are the concepts of distributed practice, social learning theory, achieving the flow state, scaffolding and game levels, and the power of episodic memory.

Motivation

A key concept of game play is motivation. When looking at the research, it is important to distinguish between internal and external motivation. Is the motivation primarily driven from within the leaner? This is called *intrinsic* motivation. Or is the motivation from some external factor? This is known as *extrinsic* motivation. Understanding these two elements and the research discussing the relationship between the two is critical for the concept of gamification.

Intrinsic Motivation

This is when a person undertakes an activity for its own sake, for the enjoyment it provides, the learning it permits, or the feeling of accomplishment it evokes.[1] Intrinsic motivation is when a learner opens a book and reads for self-fulfillment, not because of some external reward.

When people are intrinsically motivated, they tend to be more aware of a wide range of phenomena, while giving careful attention to complexities, inconsistencies, novel events, and unexpected possibilities. They need time and freedom to make choices, to gather and process information, and to have an appreciation of well-finished and integrated products, all of which may lead to a greater depth of learning and more creative output.[2] Intrinsic motivation is when the rewards come from carrying out an activity rather than from the result of the activity.

Extrinsic Motivation

Extrinsically motivated behavior, on the other hand, is behavior undertaken in order to obtain some reward or avoid punishment.[3] It is when a person seeks to earn something that is not directly related to the activity. The motivation doesn't come from within the person; it comes externally. This can be a high grade, praise from a boss or supervisor, a certificate, badge, reward, prize, or admiration from others. You've experienced extrinsic motivation when someone says something like, "If you wash my car, I'll give you $20." You may not want to wash the car, but you want the money. You may take no joy in car washing but are motivated to do it because of the reward. The same can be said for earning grades, if you are motivated only to earn an A and not to enjoy the learning process along the way, you are extrinsically motivated.

Most motivational models describe elements of both intrinsic and extrinsic motivation, as do the six models presented below. The first model was developed for enhancing learner motivation within a traditional classroom setting. The second was designed to capture the motivation aspects of games. Third is a list of principles for developing motivating instruction. The fourth is The Taxonomy of Intrinsic Motivations for Learning. The fifth is operant conditioning, studied by B.F. Skinner. The sixth is Self-Determination Theory. All models have aspects that are applicable for gamification.

ARCS Model

One way to look at motivating learners is to examine the concept of motivation in games through the four-factor model developed by John Keller. This model is well known in the field of instructional design and is used as a framework in creating e-learning and courseware.[4]

The model, ARCS, represents Attention, Relevance, Confidence, and Satisfaction. The model focuses on designing instruction, but many of the elements have application for the gamification of learning and instruction, and it is easy to see how the elements can be applied to various aspects of game-based learning.

- *Attention.* The first element is to gain the attention of the learners so they are interested in the content. This can be done in several ways. *Perceptual* arousal has to do with gaining attention through the means of specific, relatable examples, the use of incongruity and/or conflict, or the element of surprise. *Inquiry* arousal is the use of stimulating curiosity by presenting a question or problem the learner is interested in solving or providing a role play or hands-on experience for the learner. *Variability* also can be used to maintain learner attention through varying the delivery method periodically.

- *Relevance.* The relevance of the material to be learned should be established using one of three methods: (1) goal orientation: orienting the learner to the importance of the goal by describing how the goal will help the learner now and in the future and by illustrating the importance of reaching the goal; (2) match the motive of the instruction with the motives of the learners, which might be achievement, risk taking, power, or affiliation; (3) familiarity, showing how new knowledge is related to the existing knowledge of the learners, and (4) modeling the results of learning the new knowledge.

- *Confidence.* This is the learners' expectation that they can achieve success. If the learners feel they can learn the material and are confident that they can do so, they tend to be more motivated to proceed. One way to help a learner be confident is to clearly state the learning requirements and expectations in the beginning. If the learners are able to accurately estimate the amount of time and effort they need to put into learning, they are more likely to put forth that effort. If they have no idea what it might take to be successful in terms of time and effort, they tend to be more reluctant. Next, learners like to be successful and success builds on success. Create small opportunities for success so the learner can work his or her way through the instruction by completing small milestones. Create a number of different and challenging experiences that build upon one another. Learners feel confident when they believe they are controlling their own success. Provide feedback and personal reinforcement to help them feel in control.

- *Satisfaction.* Learners need to feel that the learning has value and is worth the continued effort. Provide learners the opportunity to successfully apply their new knowledge and skills in a real or simulated setting so they can "see" what they have learned being applied. Provide positive encouragement and reinforcement of the new learning as a strategy to motivate them throughout the learning process. Try to tap into the intrinsic motivation of the learners. Also, maintain a sense of equity with the learners by maintaining consistent standards and measures of success.

Malone's Theory of Intrinsically Motivating Instruction

In the 1980s Thomas Malone wanted to investigate why games are so much fun and motivational. He conducted a study that looked at a number of games and dissected, as researchers do, the elements of fun. Through this process he developed a model for looking at motivation in games and he determined what made games fun to play, in other words motivating. Based on his findings, he postulated three key elements that make a game motivational: challenge, fantasy, and curiosity.[5]

Challenge. Challenge depends on goals with uncertain outcomes. An environment is not challenging if the individual is either certain to reach a goal or certain to not reach a goal. Ways of making outcomes uncertain include variable difficulty level, multiple level goals, hidden information, and randomness.

Challenge is also flavored by the perception of the learner. If the learner sees a piece of software as a tool, he or she won't want the use of the tool to be difficult. Using a hammer should be easy because the goal is to drive a nail, not figure out how to use a hammer. But if the learner sees a piece of software as a toy, he or she expects and is motivated by a challenge and wants to try to figure out the software. For these learners the game is a challenge. That is why people become frustrated at the complicated process of trying to use a computer program to edit a video to post on a website in time for a wedding but relish the complexity of figuring out a difficult flight simulator game. One is a tool, and one is a toy.

Additionally, goals should be personally meaningful to the learner and should be obvious or easily generated. Malone also calls for the challenge to provide feedback toward progress. He states that the knowledge being learned during the challenge should empower the learners to perform personally meaningful projects they could not otherwise have been able to do. The learning environment should enhance the players' self-esteem.

Fantasy. Malone defines a fantasy as an environment that "evokes mental images of things not present to the senses or within the actual experience of the person involved." He states that the use of fantasies can make instructional environments more interesting and more educational and that fantasy has both cognitive and emotional advantages for designing instructional environments.

He also defines both extrinsic and intrinsic fantasies. An extrinsic fantasy allows the learner to work toward some external fantasy like winning a digital game show or to avoid some external catastrophe like avoiding hanging the character in Hangman. Extrinsic fantasies depend only weakly on the skill used in a game, while intrinsic fantasies are intimately related to the use of the skill.

In intrinsic fantasy, problems are presented in terms of the elements of the fantasy world and players receive a natural kind of constructive feedback. For example, in a fantasy adventure game a player has to actually negotiate with the island natives to move toward the next level in the game. In that case, negotiation is an intrinsic fantasy element because it is embedded into the game and must be mastered to continue. Malone argues that, in general, intrinsic fantasies are both more interesting and more instructional than extrinsic fantasies.

The cognitive advantages of using fantasy are that the metaphors or analogies of the kind provided by intrinsic fantasies can often help a learner apply old knowledge in understanding new things. Additionally, the fantasies provoke vivid images related to the material being learned, thus improving the learner's memory of the material.

The emotional advantages, Malone is a little less clear on; however, he does state that fantasies in computer games almost certainly derive some of their appeal from the emotional needs they help to satisfy in the people who play them. It is fair to say, however, that computer games that embody emotionally involving fantasies seem to be more popular than those with less emotional fantasies.

Curiosity. Environments can evoke a learner's curiosity by providing an optimal level of informational complexity and a novel and exciting environment. He separates curiosity into sensory and cognitive components.

Sensory curiosity involves the attention-attracting value of changes in the light, sound, or other sensory stimuli of an environment. Malone states there is no reason why educational environments have to be impoverished sensory environments.

Cognitive curiosity is evoked by the prospect of modifying higher level cognitive structures and Malone suggests that cognitive curiosity can be aroused by making learners believe their knowledge structures are incomplete, inconsistent, or unparsimonious. The learners are then motivated to learn more, in order to make their cognitive structures better-formed.

To engage the learners' curiosity, Malone suggests that feedback should be surprising and constructive. For surprising feedback, he suggests using randomness. You can also hide things within an environment. A deeper way to do this is to have underlying information and concepts revealed a little bit over time. An example would be the amusement parking building game, Roller Coaster Tycoon. In that game there is a mode where you try to build a park and have one thousand happy customers as a goal. It might seem initially that building the coolest roller coaster and the most food stands that you can possibly build would make the most customers happy. But that isn't true, so maybe you add a few calmer rides. You get closer, but more is needed. You slowly figure out why your customers aren't happy through the process of adding more things until you find the right combination of thrill rides, calm rides, restrooms, trash cans, security guards, maintenance people, food stands, and benches. It turns out that you also need to build restrooms, a number of calmer rides, and place with plenty of benches and trash cans within the park to please up to one thousand customers. Those items aren't intuitive and the unhappy customers cause you to be curious as to why they are unhappy.

Lepper's Instructional Design Principles for Intrinsic Motivation

Another method of looking at motivating learners was proposed by Mark Lepper, a researcher from Stanford University, who proposed a series of design principles for promoting intrinsic motivation in instructional activities to avoid having to rely on extrinsic motivational techniques. Lepper lists four principles.[6]

Control. Provide learners with a sense of control over the learning activity. Let them have some say into when to initiate and when to terminate an activity. Allow the learner to make decisions independent of outside influences. Create an environment that minimizes extrinsic constraints on an activity and decrease any existing extrinsic constraints over time.

If the activity is of inherently intrinsic or of interest, avoid superfluous external rewards and use minimal external pressure. If the activity has little initial intrinsic interest, the use of extrinsic rewards can be initially helpful, but you should withdraw those rewards gradually over time. It is best to try to embed the extrinsic constraints within the activity itself.

Challenge. Create an activity that is continually challenging to learners. This can be accomplished by presenting goals of uncertain attainment and an intermediate level of difficulty. Provide timely feedback regarding accomplishments. If possible, provide multiple goals or multiple levels of goals to ensure the activity provides goals that are at the appropriate level and that the learners can be continuously challenged as they proceed through the instruction.

Curiosity. Appeal to the learners' sense of curiosity. This can be accomplished by highlighting areas of inconsistency, incompleteness, or even inelegance in the learners' knowledge base. Employ activities involving content or problems of inherent interest to the learners.

Contextualization. Present the activity in a functional simulation or fantasy context and, if possible, highlight the functionality of the activity. Use an authentic context and environment to stress the utilitarianism of the learning.

The Taxonomy of Intrinsic Motivation

Lepper and Malone eventually combined their findings into what they called "The Taxonomy of Intrinsic Motivations." The taxonomy was divided into two sections. The first section focused on internal motivation and included:

- Challenge in terms of goals, uncertain outcomes, performance feedback, and self-esteem
- Curiosity in terms of sensory and cognitive inquisitiveness
- Control in terms of contingency, choice, and power

- Fantasy in terms of the emotional and cognitive aspects of fantasy as well as the interweaving of the fantasy and the skills to be learned within the game is important

The second section of The Taxonomy of Intrinsic Motivations deals with interpersonal motivations. This includes:

- Cooperation in terms of players working together to achieve a goal within the game

- Competition in terms of competing against another player to achieve a goal

- Recognition in terms of making achievements available for others to see so the hard work needed to achieve a level of mastery in a game is recognized[7]

Operant Conditioning

Another way of motivating people is the use of operant conditioning. In the 1930s B.F. Skinner looked at the research of Ivan Pavlov and his experiment in which Pavlov conditioned dogs to salivate whenever they heard a tone generated by a tuning fork. Pavlov took an unconditioned response, salivating, and made it a conditioned response by pairing it with a sound. This is known as classical conditioning, the process of creating a conditioned response based on a particular stimulus.[8]

Skinner disagreed with Pavlov's model, in part because it restricted responses to those that are already associated with a particular stimulus, such as a dog salivating when it senses it will be fed. Skinner felt that the important event in changing behavior was the outcome produced by the specific behavior and that he could reinforce the behavior to achieve a desired outcome.

Skinner showed that he could have an organism respond in a particular manner, that he could have an organism do something, manipulate an object, or operate a mechanism that was not part of its function or nature.[9]

It worked like this. A hungry animal is placed into a box and, in the process of exploring the box; it approaches a bar or a button and presses or pecks the button. It is then rewarded with a food pellet. The food pellets are supplied under certain conditions when the bar is pressed, but not others. So when a tuning fork is sounded, pellets are made available when pressing the bar but when the tuning fork is not sounded, no pellets. As a result, after a while, the animal only presses the bar when the tuning fork sounds. The animal only responding when the tuning fork sounds is an example of operant conditioning, as shown in Figure 3.1.[10]

Figure 3.1. Rat Pressing Bar to Receive Food Pellet.

Image reprinted with permission of the artist, Kristin Bittner.

Subsequent studies by Skinner introduced a concept used in many games to keep players engaged for long periods of time, a *variable ratio reinforcement schedule*. This means that reinforcement for a behavior is provided in *unpredictable intervals*. An animal that is rewarded every time it presses a bar is vulnerable to the removal of the reinforcement and stops pressing the bar as soon as it figures out food is no longer being provided. This is known as the extinction of the behavior.[11]

On the other hand, an animal that is rewarded at unpredictable intervals is resistant to behavioral extinction and will keep pressing the bar long after the food is gone. This is not unlike a person putting money into a slot machine and hoping for the occasional payoff or performing an action in a video game and sometimes receiving an extra life or more points and sometimes not. In some games, being rewarded by moving to the next level is a variation on the variable ratio reinforcement schedule; you just never know whether killing that last alien will take you to the next level or you need to kill ten more to reach the next level.[12]

In a variation on variable ratio, an animal receives a food pellet only after it presses a bar or pecks at a button for a fixed number of times. This is called a *fixed ratio schedule*. Typically, the animal will engage in bursts of activity, hitting the bar ten times to receive the pellet. The animal will then again hit the bar ten times to get another pellet.[13]

When games use a fixed ratio, players know that if they collect enough coins, tokens, items, or points they will receive an award. The player collects the requite number, receives the award, and then starts all over again to collect enough items for the next reward. In game players, this reward structure results in a distinct pattern of player behavior.

First, there is a long pause, then a steady burst of activity until a reward is given. This makes sense considering that the very first behavior does not bring a reward, so there is little incentive to initially exhibit that behavior. However, once participants decide to go for the reward, they play as fast as they can to bring the reward quickly.[14]

Another type of reward schedule is to provide the animal with a reward after a fixed amount of time has passed. This is called a *fixed interval schedule*. Regardless of what the animal does, it is only rewarded after a certain amount of time has passed. In this example, the animal will typically wait near the bar but not press it until it thinks enough time has passed and then it will press the bar until reinforced.[15]

Players usually respond to a fixed interval schedule by pausing for a while after a reward and then gradually responding faster and faster until another reward is given. In an example with a magic shield, the player would explore other parts of the game and return later to see whether a new shield had appeared. If not, the player would continue with other aspects of the game and return a little time later. As the time seemed to get closer and closer, the player would check more frequently for the magic shield until he or she received it. The player then would not check for a period of time, knowing that time would need to pass before it reappeared.[16]

Yet another type of reward schedule is the *variable interval*. For this type of reinforcement, the reward appears only after a certain length of time, as in the fixed interval, but the time is not fixed. Sometimes the reward is given within one minute and sometimes its given within five or seven or ten minutes. The variable interval produces a steady, continuous level of activity, although at a slower pace. For the player, there is activity is lower than in a variable ratio schedule because the appearance is not dependent on activity.[17]

Skinner later found out that it was possible to shape the behavior of an animal by rewarding it each time after a small desired behavior. He found he could shape the pecking behavior of pigeons by waiting until the pigeon performed the right behavior and then rewarding it. The schedules and definitions are shown in Table 3.1.

Table 3.1. Operant Conditioning Reward Schedules.

Type of Reward Schedule	Definition	Example
Variable Ratio	Reinforcement for a behavior is provided in unpredictable intervals.	Sometimes receiving a gold coin when hitting a mushroom and sometimes not. Sometimes receiving a reward when stealing a hat from ten elves and sometimes receiving the reward when stealing it from three or fifteen.

(Continued)

Fixed Ratio	Reinforcement is provided after a pre-selected number of times a behavior is exhibited.	Receiving a power-up or reward after collecting one hundred coins or fifty badges.
Fixed Interval	Reinforcement for a behavior is provided after a fixed amount of time has elapsed.	A magic shield always appears fifteen minutes after the last magic shield is destroyed.
Variable Interval	Reinforcement for a behavior is provided after a variable amount of time has elapsed.	The magic carpet appears every so many minutes; sometimes it is every two minutes, sometimes every three minutes, and sometimes up to ten minutes.

Self-Determination Theory

Self-Determination Theory (SDT) is a macro-theory which explains human motivation to perform a task or an activity as being internally driven as opposed to the externally driven theory of operant conditioning.[18] The theory has been used to describe motivation in a broad range of human activities including sports, healthcare, religion, work, and education.

Self-Determination Theory addresses factors that either facilitate or undermine motivation. The theory has several sub-theories including cognitive valuation theory, which proposes that events and conditions that enhance a person's sense of autonomy and competence support intrinsic motivation. And that factors that diminish perceived autonomy or competence undermine intrinsic motivation.

One of the first elements of SDT is autonomy which is the feeling a person has that they are in control and can determine the outcome of their actions. It is the feeling of having control over one's actions and is an integral part of SDT.

Another key aspect of the theory is competence. The concept of competence is defined as a need for challenge and a feeling of mastery. Cognitive evaluation theory proposes that factors enhancing the experience of competence, such as the opportunity to acquire a new skill or the chance to be appropriately challenged enhance perceived competence and, in turn, are intrinsically motivating.

The third major element in SDT is the concept of relatedness. Relatedness is experienced when a person feels connected to others. This can happen most often in an online multiplayer game, but it can also happen when two or more friends are playing a video game together.

Researchers have found evidence that "the psychological 'pull' of games is largely due to their capacity to engender feelings of autonomy, competence and relatedness, and that to the extent they do so they not only motivate further play, but also can be experienced as enhancing physiological wellness."[19]

In fact, in a research study examining SDT and game play, it was determined that perceived in-game autonomy and competence are associated with game enjoyment, preferences, and changes in well-being as a result of game play. Additionally, it was found that competence and autonomy perceptions were related to the intuitive nature of game controls and the sense of presence or immersion participants felt in their game play experience.[20]

In a study of gamers in an online community, it was discovered that autonomy, competence, and relatedness all independently predicted enjoyment and future game play.[21] Crafting a motivational game using Self-Determination Theory and its subcomponents, requires that players feel that they are autonomous and in control of their own actions, that they experience competence in achieving the tasks within the game space, and they feel somehow related to others who either are playing the game with them at the moment or who have played before, for example, a leaderboard or tokens or messages left by previous players. For more discussion on motivating game play, see Chapter Ten.

Distributed Practice

Some games are meant to be played in one sitting without any breaks; other games are too large for one session so the play must be divided among many sessions. At other times, even when a game is played all the way through, it is replayed to accomplish more goals or to obtain a higher score. The space between the times the game is played can be considered *distributed practice.*

In instructional parlance, distributed practice, spaced practice, or spaced rehearsal, as it is sometimes called, is the technique of distributing study or learning efforts over multiple short sessions, with each session focused on the subject matter to be learned. The opposite of this technique is the mass practice technique (or cramming), where a learner studies intensely for one long period of time in an attempt to master all the content at one time. Distributed practice is a robust and powerful phenomenon in learning.[22] Research clearly indicates that distributed practice is a consistent and heavily supported learning phenomenon for long-term retention and recall of content.

Distributed practice helps learners retain access to memorized information over long periods of time because the spacing prompts deeper processing of the learned material. Ideally, the time between the learning events will be greater than twenty-four hours, but shorter time periods have also been found to be effective. Spacing can be accomplished by introducing repetition of the material after a delayed period of time or by interspersing repetitions of the material with the learning of other materials.

The more time between rehearsals of a topic, the better the retention and learning for the student. The effect is robust and appears to hold for verbal material of all types as well as for motor skills As long as eight years after an original training, learners whose practices was spaced showed better retention than those who practiced in a more concentrated time period.[23]

Distributed practice avoids two inherent problems with mass practice. The two problems are that with mass practice the learner can become fatigued and less efficient and mass practice increases the likelihood of interference with preceding and succeeding learning.[24] Therefore, spaced or distributed practice in general results in greater learning than massed practice. For a learner to have long-term retention of the material and to gain the most value, he or she needs the practice to be distributed over time and not provided en mass.

It is important to note that the spacing effect does not result in better immediate learning. It is only after a period of time that the benefits of spaced practice are realized. Since most training programs do not measure delayed learning, this effect would typically not be noticed. Only in long-term evaluation would this advantage be seen.

Games are designed so that players play them again and again. With varying storylines depending on the approach of the player, the different areas open to exploration or the different content that is provided randomly at different times, a well-designed game means the player is not having the same experience twice. This adds to the replayability of the game and encourages players to play it again and again. This means that distributed practice is built into the game experience. The desire to play a game multiple times provides the opportunity to distribute the learning occurring within the game across multiple sessions, helping to make the retention and recall of the learning more effective in the long term.

Scaffolding

Looking at the different levels of some types of instructional games, the movement from one level to another with increasing difficulty and the need to apply more skill to master the new level is similar to the educational concept of "scaffolding."

Scaffolding is a concept built upon the idea of the "Zone of Proximal Development" introduced by Soviet psychologist and constructivist Lev Vygotsky. Vygotsky, speaking of how children learned, stated that the zone of proximal development "is the distance between the actual developmental level as determined by independent problem solving and the level of potential development as determined through problem solving under adult guidance, or in collaboration with more capable peers."[25] In other words, a child tries to solve problems given minimal experience space and lots of adult supervision;

as the child becomes more adept at solving the problems, the adult provides less and less guidance until the child is independently solving problems.

To accomplish that goal, the technique of scaffolding was developed. Scaffolding is process of controlling the task elements that initially are beyond the learner's capacity, so that the learner can concentrate on and complete elements within his or her immediate capability. Once that task is accomplished, the learner is then led to accomplish another goal that builds upon the previous. Scaffolding provides support, functions as a learning tool, extends the range of the learner, and permits the accomplishment of tasks not otherwise possible.[26]

The technique of scaffolding and the use of levels in games provide educational advantages but also maintain interest in the game as a player moves from level to level having different experiences and achieving success as he or she progresses toward the ultimate goal. The levels usually become more difficult and challenging as the players move toward the end of the game, and the skills they exhibit at the final level would not be possible without the experience of playing the preceding levels.

Related to this concept is the idea of progressive disclosure. This is a technique in which a computer program, in this case a game, displays information in small "chunks" a little bit at a time. The technique is used so that a player is not overwhelmed by the amount of information displayed on the screen. As the player becomes more comfortable with the level of display, more information is provided. This is evident in World of Warcraft. A lower-level player has a much less complex user interface screen than a higher-level player.

Combined, the concept of progressive disclosure and scaffolding provide subtle but effective methods for moving players through a game in a manner that is consistent with the skill level of the player. The technique helps provide a customized experience for each person playing the game.

Episodic Memory

Episodic memory is information stored in a person's long-term memory that receives and stores information about temporally dated episodes or events and temporal-spatial relations among those events. In other words, episodic memory contains information about life experiences—information associated with a particular time or place. The information that you were in Philadelphia for New Year's Eve celebrating at Penn's Landing or that you were at your brother's apartment for your surprise fiftieth birthday party is episodic memory.[27]

A person is able to remember certain times and places because they have particular meaning, such as a major sports event, a reunion with lost relatives, or even a particularly compelling instructional event. Episodic memories are stored in such a way that each memory is identified by a personal "tag." Typically, such memories are recalled through association with a particular time or place and tend to be vivid as they are recalled.[28]

With games, the possibility of creating episodic memory is very strong. Many 3D immersive games have the visual and temporal-spatial relations to provide a strong, rich association between what you are doing in the event and your long-term memory.[29] Often it is difficult to remember what was discussed or reviewed in class, but it is far easier to recall the look of the classroom, the position of the instructor's desk, and the location of the door. In a well-designed and vivid game, episodic memory provides the learner with the ability recall the elements of the game, the game board or the game environment, and what was done to solve the problem. Many people remember two important pieces of real estate in the board game of Monopoly—Boardwalk and Park Place. The reason is often because they worked really hard to obtain those expensive spaces to make a lot of money in the game or they kept landing on those two spots and had to pay someone—both powerful and sometimes emotional memories.

With games, the visual cues are established in the mind of the learner, and if the experiences are geared toward real life applications, then the memories of the learner will be strong and properly associated with what he or she needs to do in a particular location. The importance of episodic memory for learning is to provide a schema for the learner that enables him or her to quickly and easily recall information related to the application of knowledge to a particular situation.

Cognitive Apprenticeship

The concept of cognitive apprenticeship is grounded in the theory of *situated cognition*, a theory of instruction that suggests learning is naturally tied to authentic activity, context, and culture.[30] The idea is that the person and the environment in which they are learning cannot be separated in any analysis of learning. They are each part of a mutually constructed whole.

Therefore, the learning must take place in the environment in which it will be applied because the environment and the person's perception of the environment are part of the same learning process.[31] To grasp subjects, learners need more than abstract concepts and self-contained examples; they need to be exposed to the use of the information and cognitive tools in an authentic activity. Authentic activities provide learning opportunities in a way that textbook examples and declarative explanations cannot.[32] The answer to the problem of immersing the learner in an authentic learning experience is to create a *cognitive apprenticeship*.

A cognitive apprenticeship supports learning in a domain by enabling students to acquire, develop, and use cognitive tools in an authentic activity. Cognitive apprenticeship methods try to enculturate students into authentic practices through activity and social interaction in a way similar to that evident—and evidently successful—in craft apprenticeship.

Similar to a traditional apprenticeship, a learner works under a teacher who models the behavior in a real-world context as well as explains the thought processes and actions behind those behaviors. As the cognitive apprentice listens, observes, and models those same behaviors, he or she identifies the relevant behaviors and develops a conceptual model of the processes involved. The apprentice is then given an opportunity to rehearse those behaviors and obtain feedback from the teacher, who provides coaching, tips, and pointers. The idea is that the apprentice learns to solve problems in the context that produced them.[33]

When you play the Uncharted 3: Drake's Deception game on the PlayStation 3, you don't tell Nathan Drake what to shoot, you don't direct him where to go, and you don't give him commands to follow. No, you don't control Nathan Drake because you *are* Nathan Drake. By operating the character in the game, you learn the implicit rules of the world you inhabit. You rehearse the act of jumping from cliff to cliff until you master it. You practice sneaking around undetected and use in-game money to unlock special options. You are serving as an apprentice to the game environment. The environment patiently teaches you how Drake is to behave and what actions and activities are of value within the game environment. Each mission builds on skills and behaviors learned in a previous level, and the game corrects your actions by giving you continuous tips, feedback, and even coaching.

Social Learning Theory

Robert Bandura in the late 1970s articulated the concept of *social learning theory* as a method by which individuals learn from one another in the context of a social situation through observation. Social learning theory is based on the premise that observation and imitation lead to learned behavior. Research in this area indicates that, indeed, human social models can be effective in influencing another person to change behaviors, beliefs, or attitudes, as well as social and cognitive functioning.[34]

Additional research has provided evidence that humans can be socially influenced by automated anthropomorphic agents (avatars), just as they would be by human social models. The use of virtual models to demonstrate desired behaviors can be effective for transferring those behaviors to learners.

Therefore, the use of avatars or agents for presenting the proper model of behavior does transfer learning. There are several advantages to implementing avatars as social models. First, an agent implemented as a social model can be available at any time the learner engages with the game. This means that desired behaviors can be projected whenever and wherever the instruction is needed. Second, the behaviors can be modeled in an environment in which they are desired to occur, as opposed to a classroom space. The game environment allows the creation of an unlimited number of contexts in which the behavior can be modeled.

Third, given the ease of use and "replayability" of games, the learning experience can be replayed many times to aid with retention. Finally, games provide the opportunity for the learner to practice the observed behavior in a safe and secure environment. Video games offer excellent conditions for learning to occur. They simultaneously expose the player to modeling, rehearsal, and reinforcement of the social behavior that is involved in the game's theme.[35]

Flow

One evening you sit down to play a game and you become so involved that you lose all track of time, you are finding and defeating the bad guys effortlessly, you are easily finding the clues, and you are engaged in the challenge. As you play, you are nervous but confident that you can move forward and achieve the goal of this level. Nothing is going to stop you. Four hours later, you suddenly realize you are hungry. You played right through dinner time and did not eat anything—not even a snack. If you've ever had that experience playing a game, working on a hobby, riding a bicycle, or completing a task at work, you've experienced what Mihaly Csikszentmihalyi calls "flow."

Flow is a mental state of operation in which a person is fully immersed and focused in what he or she is doing; it involves full mental involvement and continual engagement in the process of the activity.[36] It is that ideal state between boredom and anxiety or frustration, as shown in Figure 3.2.

Flow is elusive and cannot always or easily be designed into a game. It is even harder to test for flow because it is hard for a designer of a game to get into a flow state with his or her own game. But flow is something game designers want their players to achieve. And while a game designer cannot guarantee a flow state will occur for a player, the designer can create conditions under which a flow state could occur.

Flow is experienced when the challenge facing a person is in almost perfect balance with the person's level of skill and abilities—he or she can accomplish the task, but it will take concentration, blocking out distractions, and a high level of effort. Csikszentmihalyi indicates eight components that make flow possible.

Figure 3.2. Flow, the State Between Boredom and Anxiety.

Image reprinted with permission of the artist, Kristin Bittner.

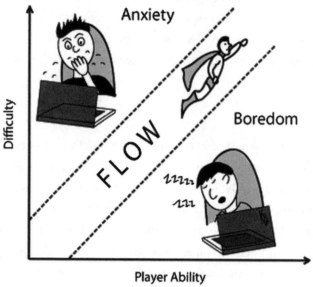

- *Achievable Task*—The person engaged in the task must believe that he or she can accomplish the task with some degree of effort. This doesn't mean the task isn't hard or challenging; just the contrary. It is difficult and, therefore, requires a great deal of effort. If the task is too simple, a person becomes bored and doesn't enter a flow state; if the task is too difficult a person becomes frustrated and gives up. The ideal middle ground is a task that seems achievable but requires a great deal of effort to accomplish.

- *Concentration*—For a person to enter into a flow state, he or she must apply mental and physical energies with intense focus. Outside distractions disappear and the person's actions and thoughts work seamlessly together to accomplish the task.

- *Clear Goals*—Clear goals mean the person knows exactly what he or she needs to do. There is no ambiguity about what is to be accomplished or achieved. The only question is "how" to accomplish the task, not "what" needs to be accomplished.

- *Feedback*—As the person is engaged in the activity, feedback is provided immediately; every action causes a reaction and the person knows whether he or she is doing the right actions or the wrong actions. The immediate and continual feedback helps the person to remain in the flow state.

- *Effortless Involvement*—Because of the high level of concentration, the level of feedback, and the ability to achieve the goal, the person perceives that involvement as effortless. This seems paradoxical when the task is at a level of difficulty that challenges the person, but the level of challenge is the same as the amount of skill and effort the person is able to exert. When in the flow state, no external thoughts enter the mind.

- *Control Over Actions*—The person feels in complete control over what he or she is doing and believes that actions have immediate and purposeful results.

- *Concern for Self Disappears*—In the example at the beginning of this section, the person doesn't even stop to eat dinner. This is common in a flow state where a person is so absorbed in the activity that the only thing he or she is thinking about is the activity.

- *Loss of Sense of Time*—When in the flow state, time doesn't matter. The person sits down to engage in the activity and what seem like a few minutes passing are really several hours.[37]

The ideal goal of game designers is to shape the instructional games they develop so it is possible for players to enter into a state of flow. The game needs to reach a balance between the challenges in the game and the player's skill and ability level. This is a rare occurrence in instructional games. However, the concept of flow serves as a good guidepost for the gamification of learning. If a faculty member, trainer, or instructional designer can provide the environment that encourages flow in the learner, he or she can move closer to putting learners into a flow state.

■ ■ ■

Key Takeaways

For this chapter, Table 3.2 best summarizes the various theories and their impact on the gamification of learning and instruction.

Table 3.2. Theories and Their Impact on Gamification.

Theory	Impact on Gamification Design
Social Learning Theory	Model desired behavior so learner observes and internally processes the desired behavior.
Cognitive Apprenticeship	Setting and environment should be authentic and provide feedback and guidance on the learner's activity.
Flow	Continually adapt to keep the learner at constant state of interest. System adapts to the right challenge level for the leaner, not too difficult and not too easy.
Operant Conditioning	Provide appropriate rewards, points, and badges on a variable basis to maintain learners' interest.
ARCS Theory of Motivation	Grab the learner's attention, contain relevant information, and be aimed at the appropriate level of challenge so the learner is confident he or she will be successful and provide intrinsic and extrinsic motivational elements.
Malone's Theory of Intrinsically Motivating Instruction	Include elements of challenge, fantasy, and curiosity.
Lepper's Instructional Design Principles for Intrinsic Motivation	Include elements of learner control, challenge, curiosity, and contextualization
The Taxonomy of Intrinsic Motivations for Learning	Include internal and external motivational elements such as challenge, curiosity, control, fantasy, cooperation, competition, and recognition.
Self-Determination Theory	Provide the learner with the opportunities for autonomy, a feeling of competence, and relatedness with others.
Distributed Practice	Play out over time to provide spaced repetition of the content within the game.
Scaffolding	Start out providing a great deal of guidance and then provide less and less guidance until the learner is independently solving problems.
Episodic Memory	Evoke learners' emotions to more richly encode the lessons from the game in memory.

4

Research Says . . . Games Are Effective for Learning

CHAPTER QUESTIONS

At the end of this chapter, you should be able to answer the following questions:

- What are the results of studies about the effectiveness of games for learning?
- Do all studies of the effectiveness of games for learning yield the same result?
- What are the limitations of the research in defining the effectiveness of games for learning?
- What game mechanics or attributes have been found to be particularly effective for learning or particularly ineffective?

Introduction

This chapter reviews research describing the effectiveness of games as well as the effectiveness of specific game elements such as the use of avatars and third-person versus first-person viewpoint. The goal of the chapter is to provide support to the argument that game-based learning and gamification are effective for changing behavior and creating positive learning outcomes. This chapter includes studies that build from the theoretical foundation provided in Chapter Three, as well as other areas of research.

The chapter is divided into two sections:

- *Meta-Analysis Research Studies*—a meta-analysis is a study of findings based on the aggregations of finding from many other studies. This section reports on results found through the study of studies on the effectiveness of games.

- *Elements of Games*—examines individual research studies that examine specific elements of games such as reward structures, use of avatars, and player's perspective and how they relate to elements of games.

This examination of research is in no way exhaustive. It is presented to show that games and game elements can be effective in promoting learning and achieving desired outcomes. Games and gamification are tools that, when applied correctly, result in the desired learning outcomes.

Game Research

There are literally thousands of books, articles, and newspaper reports on the effectiveness of games and gamification. Some of the reporting is based on theoretical underpinnings, some of it is based on opinion, and some of it is based on wishful thinking. To separate the conjecture from research-supported evidence, researchers look for empirical studies published in peer-reviewed journals. Research results published in peer-reviewed journals generally need to be clearly reported, easily reproducible, and pass review and scrutiny by fellow researchers.

This narrows the number of articles from which conclusions about the effectiveness of games can be made because peer-reviewed articles provide a level of credibility and scientific research in the reporting of result. Even with this limiting factor, there are still hundreds of individual peer-reviewed studies reporting on the use of games for learning.

To narrow the field even more, researchers periodically conduct a meta-analysis of studies in a particular field. A meta-analysis is an aggregation of a number of research studies to identify trends in the research in order to make evidence-based generalizations that can be used by practitioners to advance the field of practice.

A number of meta-analysis studies have been conducted in the field of game-based research attempting to create generalizable findings that can be used to create meaningful educational and instructional games. This section examines several meta-analysis studies focused on the effectiveness of instructional games. Table 4.1 summarizes the studies and the major findings. An explanation and additional details of each study follow the table.[1]

Randel's Meta-Analysis

Randel and team conducted a review of games and simulations for learning in 1992. They examined sixty-eight studies spanning a time frame of twenty-eight years up until 1991.[2] The team compared of the effect of games and simulations with that of traditional classroom instruction on student performance. Of the sixty-eight studies examined, thirty-eight (56 percent) found no difference, twenty-two (32 percent) found differences favoring simulations/games in student performance, five (7 percent) favored simulation/games but the controls were questionable, and three (5 percent) found differences in favor of more traditional instruction.

The games and simulations studied in the meta-analysis were not corporate related or business games or simulations. The topics covered included social sciences, math, language arts, logic, physics, and biology. It was found that math was the subject area with the greatest percentage of results favoring games.

Table 4.1. Meta-Analysis Studies of Game-Based Learning.

Study	Number of Studies Examined	Major Findings
Randel, J.M., Morris, B.A., Wetzel, C.D., & Whitehill, B.V. (1992). The effectiveness of games for educational purposes: a review of recent research. *Simulation and Gaming, 23*(3), 261–276.	67	56 percent showed no difference between games and conventional instruction and 32 percent favored games, while 5 percent favored conventional instruction. Games are rated as more interesting than conventional instruction.
Wolfe, J. (1997) The effectiveness of business games in strategic management course work. *Simulation & Gaming, 28*(4), 360–376.	7	Game-based approach produced significant knowledge-level increases over the conventional case-based teaching methods.
Hays, R.T. (2005). *The effectiveness of instructional games: A literature review and discussion.* Naval Air Warfare Center Training Systems Division (No 2005–004).	105	An instructional game will only be effective if it is designed to meet specific instructional objectives and used as it was intended.
		Instructional games should be embedded in instructional programs that include debriefing and feedback.
		Instructional support to help learners understand how to use the game increases instructional effectiveness of the gaming experience.
		Instructional designers are needed to design games.

Study	Number of Studies Examined	Major Findings
Vogel, J.J., Vogel, D.S., Cannon-Bowers, J., Bowers, C.A., Muse, K., & Wright, M. (2006). Computer gaming and interactive simulations for learning: A meta-analysis. *Journal of Educational Computing Research, 34*(3), 229–243.	32	Higher cognitive gains were observed in subjects utilizing interactive simulations or games versus traditional teaching methods (although simulations yielded a stronger result).
		Better attitudes toward learning when compared to traditional teaching methods.
		Level of picture realism in the computer program does not seem to have an impact.
Ke, F. (2009). A qualitative meta-analysis of computer games as learning tools. In R.E. Ferdig (Ed.), *Effective electronic gaming in education* (Vol. 1, pp. 1–32). Hershey, PA: Information Science Reference.	65[3]	Effects of learning with games was positive in 52 percent of the studies examined.
Sitzmann, T. (2011). A meta-analytic examination of the instructional effectiveness of computer-based simulation games. *Personnel Psychology, 64*(2), 489–528) and Sitzmann, T., & Ely, K. (2010). A meta-analytic examination of the effectiveness of computer-based simulation games. ADL Research Lab.	65	Confidence with games 20 percent higher.
		Declarative knowledge was 11 percent higher for trainees taught with simulation games.
		Procedural knowledge was 14 percent higher with simulation games.
		Retention was 9 percent higher with simulation games.

The study concluded the following:

- The beneficial effects of games and simulations were most likely to be found when specific content was targeted and objectives precisely defined.

- Games are rated as more interesting than conventional instruction.

- Careful consideration needs to be given to the measures used to demonstrate the effects of games.

- The experimental designs used to evaluate games need to be more rigorous.[4]

Wolfe's Meta-Analysis

Studying only computer-based business games used to teach strategic management, Wolfe reviewed seven studies conducted between 1966 and 1988.[5] The study was published in 1997. The studies all used at least one treatment and one control group. The control groups all used the instructional approach of case-based learning. The studies had the criteria of (1) comparing game use with at least one other instructional approach, (2) having predefined, objectively measured instructional objectives, and (3) having objectively measured learning outcomes.

The study concluded the following

- Every study examined indicated that the game-based approach produced significant knowledge-level increases over the conventional case-based teaching methods.[6]

Hays' Meta-Analysis

Robert T. Hays of the Naval Air Warfare Center Training Systems Division conducted a review of the literature on instructional games in 2005, with a focus on locating empirical research on the instructional effectiveness of games.[7]

He examined 274 documents related to the design, use, and evaluation of games. He eliminated 169 of the documents due to structural flaws in the research, use of opinion instead of statistics, and other reasons. The remaining

105 documents included in the meta-analysis included twenty-six review articles, thirty-one theoretical articles, and forty-eight articles that provided empirical data on the effectiveness of instructional games. He came to five conclusions based on his review of the empirical research on the effectiveness of instructional games:

- The empirical research on the effectiveness of instructional games is fragmented. The literature includes research on different tasks, age groups, and types of games. The research literature is also filled with ill-defined terms and plagued with methodological flaws.

- Although research has shown that some games can provide effective learning for a variety of learners for several different tasks (e.g., math, attitudes, electronics, and economics), this does not tell us whether to use a game for our specific instructional task. We should not generalize from research on the effectiveness of one game in one learning area for one group of learners to all games in all learning areas for all learners.

- There is no evidence to indicate that games are the preferred instructional method in all situations.

- Instructional games should be embedded in instructional programs that include debriefing and feedback so the learners understand what happened in the game and how these events support the instructional objectives.

- Instructional support to help learners understand how to use the game increases the instructional effectiveness of the gaming experience by allowing learners to focus on the instructional information rather than the requirements of the game.[8]

Also included in the report but not called out specifically as conclusions are some other interesting findings:

- The research shows that people can learn from games.

- An instructional game will only be effective if it is designed to meet specific instructional objectives and used as it was intended.

- If the game is not designed to directly support specific instructional objectives related to actual job requirements, much of the learning may be irrelevant.

- Unfortunately, many program managers and game developers do not appreciate the importance of instructional design. It appears that the "instructional gaming" industry does not value the skills of instructional developers.

- Games are not a panacea. Gratuitous use of games or the use of games with no clear instructional goals will probably increase the cost of the instruction without providing the instructional benefit that learners require.[9]

In the end, Hays makes four recommendations:

- The decision to use a game should be based on a detailed analysis of the learning requirements and an analysis of the tradeoffs among alternate instructional approaches.

- Program managers and procurement personnel should insist that game developers clearly demonstrate how the design of a game will provide interactive experiences that support properly designed instructional objectives.

- Instructors should view instructional games as adjuncts and aids to help support instructional objectives. Learners should be provided with debriefing and feedback that clearly explains how their experiences with the game help them meet these instructional objectives.

- Instructor-less approaches (for example, web-based instruction) must include all "instructor functions. These include performance evaluation, debriefing, and feedback.[10]

Vogel's Meta-Analysis

This study was conducted by a team of researchers at the University of Central Florida. Initially the team examined 248 studies but found only thirty-two of sufficient quality to be used for final analysis.[11] For studies to be included in the research, they had to have identified cognitive gains or attitudinal changes as one of the main hypotheses, and it was required that each study report statistics assessing traditional classroom teaching versus computer gaming or interactive simulation teaching.

The team found strong, positive effect sizes of interactive simulations and games in comparison to traditional teaching methods in two areas: cognitive gains and attitude. Although a working or operational definition of "cognitive gains" or "attitude" was not provided in the reported study. The findings included:

- Higher cognitive gains were observed in subjects utilizing interactive simulations or games versus traditional teaching methods (although games, as opposed to simulations, yielded a lower reliability and the results should be considered with caution).

- Games and simulations yielded better attitudes toward learning when compared to traditional teaching methods.

- Level of picture realism in the computer program does not seem to have an impact.

- The effects of games and interactive simulations sustained across people in terms of age and gender and across situations in terms of learner control, level of realism and group and individual usage of the game or simulation.[12]

Ke's Qualitative Meta-Analysis

Fengfeng Ke, a researcher focusing on digital game-based learning, computer-supported collaborative learning, and simulations for instructional use, conducted a review of eighty-nine research articles that provided empirical data on the application and effectiveness of computer-based instructional games.[13] Her goal was to determine the cumulative qualitative and quantitative evidence for using computer games for learning and what factors weigh in on the effective application of instructional gaming.

Ke chose to conduct a qualitative meta-analysis. So, instead of a statistical analysis of the outcomes of aggregated studies, Ke followed the replicable process of analyzing textual reports through a qualitative method to develop new interpretations. She analyzed 256 reports and eliminated 167 for various reasons. Ultimately, she aggregated results from eight-nine empirical studies. She classified the studies into five different areas to examine separate research questions. However, not all eighty-nine studies were applicable to all the research questions, so for some research questions the pool of studies is fewer than eighty-nine.

Key findings:

- The effects of computer-based games on learning are positive. When analyzing research results of the sixty-five out of the eighty-nine studies that specifically examined the effectives of computer-based games on learning, Ke found a significant positive effective for computer-based games as compared with conventional instruction. She found a positive impact 52 percent of the time. She found mixed results reported 25 percent of the time. Mixed results were when an instructional game facilitated certain learning outcomes but not others. She found no difference between the games or conventional instruction reported 18 percent of the time. In only one study was conventional instruction more effective than computer games.

- Instructional support features are a necessary part of instructional computer games and when support is present the studies indicate significant results. In this area seventeen of the studies focused on instructional game design. These studies generally concluded that learners without instructional support in a game will learn to play the game rather than learning domain-specific knowledge embedded in the game. These support features can include elaborative feedback, pedagogical agents, and multi-modal information presentation.

- Instructional games seem to foster higher-order thinking such as planning and reasoning more than factual or verbal knowledge. This conclusion is drawn from studies that looked into cognitive learning outcomes in the areas of basic motor skills, descriptive knowledge, conceptual knowledge, problem solving, and general cognitive strategies.

- Instructional computer games seem to facilitate motivation across different learner groups and learning situations. This is based on studies that looked at affective learning outcomes, involving self-efficacy, attitudes toward subject content learning, and affective feedback toward game use, as well as looking at continuing motivation.[14]

Sitzmann's Meta-Analysis

In 1997, the United States Department of Defense (DoD) developed a department-wide strategy to harness the power of learning and information technologies to standardize and modernize education and training. The strategy was called the Advanced Distributed Learning (ADL) Initiative. Since that time, the ADL has been working with business and university groups to develop consensus around standards for training software as well as associated training services purchased by federal agencies. They strive to advance the state-of-the-art in the science and technology associated with individual and collective education, training, performance support, and assessment.

As part of that mission, the ADL has examined the effectiveness of what they call simulation games, which are "instruction delivered via personal computer that immerses trainees in a decision-making exercise in an artificial environment in order to learn the consequences of their decisions."[15] The term "simulation games" was chosen because Sitzmann, among others, proposes that there are no longer clear boundaries between the instructional methods of games and simulations. She states that often instructional games and instructional simulations contain similar and overlapping elements. And given the similarities, it was no longer valuable to categorize the educational tools as either games or simulations.

To examine the effectiveness of simulation games, the ADL asked the question, "Are simulation games an effective method of providing instruction?" In other words, are simulation games better than traditional instruction?

But even in that simple question, nuances exist. Under what circumstances are games most effective for learning? Where does the use of games fit into a curriculum? Do games have to be "fun" to transfer knowledge? How interactive and engaging does a game need to be to provide effective instruction?

To explore the major research question and the associated nuances, researchers at ADL conducted a study of studies or what is known in research circles as a meta-analysis. The researchers at ADL reviewed sixty-five independent samples and data from more than six thousand trainees.

Fifty-five research reports were examined, including thirty-nine published reports, twelve dissertations, and four unpublished reports. The reports included data from sixty-five samples and 6,476 trainees, with 77 percent of the samples from undergraduate students, 12 percent from graduate programs; employees were in 5 percent of samples and military personnel in 6 percent of samples. The average age of trainees was twenty-three, and 52 percent were male. The majority of the researchers who contributed data to the meta-analysis were in the fields of education (25 percent) and psychology (25 percent), with 12 percent in business, 11 percent in educational technology, 9 percent in the field of medicine, 6 percent in computer science, math, or engineering, 5 percent in science, and 7 percent in other disciplines.[16]

In the study-of-studies, the trainees taught with simulation games were evaluated against comparison groups on key affective and cognitive training outcomes. The outcomes indicate that simulation games are effective for transferring learning in many key areas.

- Trainees' gain higher confidence in applying learning from a training session to their jobs when the training is simulation-game based. The research evidence suggests the use of simulation games to enhance the confidence trainees have in their ability to apply the skills learned in the training to their job. In the meta-analysis, it was found that trainees receiving instruction via a simulation game had 20 percent higher confidence they had learned the information taught in training and could perform the training-related tasks (self-efficacy) than trainees in a comparison group of more traditional methods.

- Trainees participating in simulation game learning experiences have higher declarative knowledge, procedural knowledge, and retention of training material than those trainees participating in more traditional learning experiences. Examining the effectiveness of computer-based simulation games related to comparison groups, it was found that declarative knowledge was 11 percent higher for trainees taught with simulation games than for a comparison group; procedural knowledge was 14 percent higher and retention was 9 percent higher.

- Simulation games don't have to be entertaining to be educational. The research indicated that trainees learned the same amount of information in simulation games whether the games were ranked high in entertainment value or low in entertainment value. There does not appear to be a correlation between the entertainment value of a simulation game and its educational merit.

- Trainees learn more from simulation games that actively engage trainees in learning rather than passively conveying the instructional material. When the majority of the instruction in a simulation game was passive, the comparison group learned more than the simulation game group. However, when the majority of the instruction in the simulation game was active, the simulation game group learned more than the comparison group. These findings suggest that simulation games are more effective when they actively engage trainees in learning the course material.

- Trainees learn more from simulation games when they can utilize the simulation game as many times as desired than when they have limited access to the simulation game. Trainees in the simulation game group outperformed the comparison group to a greater extent when they had unlimited access to the simulation game.

- Simulation games embedded in a program of instruction are better tools for learning than stand-alone simulation games. Trainees learn more from simulation games that are embedded in a program of instruction than when simulation games are the sole instructional method. When simulation games were used as a supplement to other instructional methods, the simulation game group had higher knowledge levels than the comparison group. However, when simulation games were used as stand-alone instruction, trainees in a comparison group learned more than trainees in the simulation game group.

- Simulation games are more effective when they actively involve the learner in the knowledge being taught. It was found that the comparison group learned more than the simulation game group when the majority of the material covered in the simulation game utilized passive instructional techniques. What makes the game effective for learning is the use of engagement within the game. In fact, the meta-analysis found that, depending on the type of comparison, games are most effective when they actively convey knowledge and that some other methods of learner activity are more effective than games. When comparing active forms of instruction, such as computerized tutorials and hands-on practice, games were not as effective for conveying knowledge. In contrast, simulation games were much more effective than assignments, lectures, or reading. Simulation games need to actively engage the learners as they are reviewing the instructional material.[17]

Elements of Games

In addition to the meta-analysis studies cited above, there is a growing body of individual studies that indicate the effectiveness of certain elements games. This section describes findings from several studies that are of particular interest to individuals who are gamifying learning and instruction.

Reward Structures

What happens in the brain? Games are built on reward structures: win the game and get a prize. Accomplish a goal—earn points. One group of researchers carefully looking into the use of rewards for learning are neuroscientists. These scientists are trying to determine what happens in people's brains when they are interacting with a reward structure as presented in games.

It turns out that the relationship between motivation and learning in neuroscience has been studied chiefly in the context of reinforcement learning, a type of learning thought to originally support foraging for food. The release of the chemical dopamine in the midbrain region has been shown to increase when humans are exposed to a variety of pleasures, including food, money, and even computer games.[18] Figure 4.1 depicts a person imagining gamification badges and food items; they both may illicit the same chemical reaction. Some results from the research indicate:

- The value, or size, of an anticipated reward influences the motivational signal sent to the brain only within the context of the reward

Figure 4.1. Gamification Badges and Food: Both May Illicit the Same Chemical Reaction.
Image reprinted with permission of the artist, Kristin Bittner.

system. The maximum signal sent to the brain corresponds with the maximum available reward within that context. This means that if a person played two different games, with one game having a maximum prize of $10 and the other having a maximum prize of $100, the dopamine released by anticipating each prize would be the same. When the player reaches the maximum prize level, dopamine is released in the same amount, regardless of the size of the prize.[19]

- The uncertainty of an outcome influences the brain's response to reward. Uncertain rewards release more dopamine than predictable rewards. In a study of the primate brain, researchers studied reactions to the frequency of rewards by presenting a stimulus with a subsequent reward. In one condition, they provided the reward after the stimulus 100 percent of the time and, in the other, they provided the reward after the stimulus 50 percent of the time. By monitoring brain activity they found that the stimulus associated with the imminent arrival of 100 percent certain rewards generated a similar spike of dopamine activity as the reward itself arriving entirely unexpectedly. But the actual arrival of the reward produced little effect at all because it was an entirely predictable event. They already got excited about receiving the reward after the stimulus and the reward itself did not induce additional dopamine. However, when the stimulus only produced a reward about 50 percent of the time, the stimulus generated a spike in dopamine, and then the dopamine began to ramp up again, reaching another maximum at the moment when the reward might or might not appear. The original spike of dopamine induced by the stimulus and the subsequent ramping up of dopamine while wondering whether a reward will appear or not resulted in more overall dopamine.[20]

- The right level of uncertainty to introduce in games of chance to heighten motivation is 50 percent. It appears that having a 50/50 chance of success keeps players motivated toward achieving the rewards they are seeking.[21]

Putting these findings into an educational perspective are several interesting studies. In the first study, a class of eleven-to-twelve-year-olds in Cyprus, Greece, was asked to practice mental mathematics by playing a simple computer game. Students were given thirty true/false questions (an example of a false answer would be, $13 \times 42 = 564$) with the goal of obtaining the maximum possible score. Before students could answer a question, they were faced with a choice of having the question asked by Mr. Certain or Mr. Uncertain. Both provided the same questions but, if a participant answered correctly, he or she would receive 1 point from Mr. Certain and either 0 points or 2 points from Mr. Uncertain, depending on the toss of an animated coin. The design of the software ensured that each question was presented once, and the order of presentation was randomized for each participant. It was made clear to the children that there was an equal chance of receiving 2 points or 0 points from Mr. Uncertain for a correct answer.

Over the fifty participants in the study, the mean percentage of occasions that Mr. Uncertain was chosen was 61.4 percent, which was a statistically significant preference, and over the course of the game, the preference for choosing Mr. Uncertain increased. Overall, thirty of the fifty participants chose Mr. Uncertain more times than Mr. Certain.

The authors of the study concluded that the results demonstrated a clear preference of primary school children for the incorporation of gaming uncertainty in a mathematical quiz. They add that the preference for gaming uncertainty shown by children in this study and the tendency of this to increase with repetition of the task, concur with current neuropsychological concepts. Gaming uncertainty in reward structures keeps children motivated to play instructional games, and the longer they play the game, the more they utilize the uncertainty elements—they take bigger risks for higher rewards.

Another study by the same researchers looked at how children ages thirteen and fourteen performed in a quiz game answering questions when a game condition was present and then examining how the children discussed the game among themselves. They recorded pairs of children playing the game and the discussions and reactions of the children during the game.

After the children were divided into pairs, they were asked to play the game called "Wipe Out." In the game two animated dice were rolled and the combined score could be won if a subsequent multiple-choice question was answered correctly. If answered correctly, there was the choice of rolling again or passing the dice to the opponent. Rolling carried an inherent risk because, if a single 1 was rolled, all points for that turn were lost. Rolling a pair of 1's resulted in all points accumulated in the game being lost or "wiped out." The first to reach 100 (the team of two players or the artificial opponent) won the game.[22]

The authors of the study indicated that learning was achieved in terms of being able to correctly answer questions that had previously been incorrectly answered, as shown in pre/post-test design. They also observed an intermingling of game talk and learning talk during the game. The authors stated:

> "Fairness was discussed with respect to differences in player–opponent ability but not with respect to losses due to chance (i.e., gaming uncertainty). Such losses produced significant emotional responses but did not appear to deter the players. Indeed, the gaming element appeared to offer hopeful encouragement as a potential means by which to compensate for disparities in player–opponent ability level. During playing of the game, the artificial opponent became personified as something of a 'hate figure.' The game appeared to provide high levels of motivation, but was described as both fun and annoying, echoing a mild form of the dissociation between motivational elements of appetite (wanting) and consumption (liking)."[23]

Gaming uncertainty appeared to subvert the conventional learning discourse and the traditional concepts of classroom fairness (always earning points for correct answers), and the sting of failure was mitigated by the chance to win the game on the next roll of the dice. Failure was attributed to bad luck and big losses the result of chance.

The next natural question is "What about adults?" The same researchers undertook a study with a group of sixteen adults with an average age of twenty-eight. The researchers created an experiment in which the physiological response was measured by electrodermal activity (EDA) when the adults responded to quiz questions, with and without gaming uncertainty. In the gaming condition, the adults played "Wipe Out," as described above. In the non-gaming condition, the adults played a version of the game that removed the gaming uncertainty by having the dice always roll a 3 (so no wipe out condition), turns were automatically alternated between the player and the computer, and there was no final score, the game continued until stopped by player or researcher so no "winning state" existed. The result was that the emotional response in the adults when answering questions was greater when the gaming element was enabled and the rewards were uncertain.[24]

The results of these three studies indicate that gaming uncertainty can transform the emotional experience of learning improving engagement and, more importantly, improving encoding and later recall.[25]

Player Motivation

Intrinsic and Extrinsic Motivation. One of the most typical reward structures in a game designed to motive players is the use of extrinsic rewards like badges, points, and rewards. On the surface, it seems like these are really good ways of motivating people. However, a stronger motivator for learning is intrinsic motivators. In fact, there are a number of problems with pure extrinsic motivation from an instructional perspective.

First, if the structure of the reward is not set up fairly and transparently, and sometimes even if it is, people may feel that they are being manipulated and resent the fact that they have to do something they don't want to do just to obtain a desired reward. In these cases, extrinsic motivation can cause resentment among the very people being motivated.

Second, especially in a learning situation, little or no transfer is likely to take place if the learner is only motivated by the reward at the end. The learner may not even pay attention to the task and, instead, only be focused on the reward. In a study where students were offered a tangible reward for the successful solution of a problem, they displayed less efficient, less logical, and less effective techniques for seeking information about the nature of the underlying concept. Additionally, when those students were later confronted with a similar task under new conditions, they continued to employ less logical and efficient information-gathering procedures.[26] In another study, students who had selected "simpler" problems in an earlier session in which rewards had been offered for correct answers continued later to select less complex problems, even when rewards were no longer available for the correct answer.[27]

Another danger is that, once the extrinsic reward vanishes, so does the behavior, or extrinsic rewards might even interfere with internal motivation. A study of nursery-school children who liked to play with marking pens illustrates the point. A group of children who indicated they liked to play with markers received a promised reward after playing with the makers. Later, when the researchers observed what that group chose to play with, it turned out they played with the markers less than children in the control group who received no reward.[28]

Sometimes the only reason a person does something is because of the external reward. Take away that reward and the behavior stops. Additionally, the learner may become too dependent on the reward and not be motivated in any other way. When this happens, the reward has to increasingly grow and change to be sufficiently motivating to sustain interest over time.

There is a great deal of empirical research focused on examining the impact of extrinsic rewards on intrinsic motivation.

A meta-analysis of 128 studies examined the effects of extrinsic rewards on intrinsic motivation. The study found that the following types of rewards significantly undermined free-choice intrinsic motivation:

- Engagement-contingent rewards—rewards where people have to work on the task to receive the reward.

- Completion-contingent rewards—rewards that are explicitly dependent upon completing the target task.

- Performance-contingent rewards—rewards which are given specifically for performing the activity well, matching some standard of excellence.

The study concluded that when organizations opt for the use of rewards to control behavior, the rewards are likely to be accompanied by greater surveillance, evaluation, and competition, all of which have also been found to undermine intrinsic motivation.[29]

However, out-of-hand dismissal of extrinsic motivation as a tool for motivating learners is not a good idea. In fact, extrinsic motivations are often necessary to produce "learning when the activity is one that students do not find of inherent interest or value."[30] Positive effects of extrinsic motivation can be seen when tasks are of initial low value. It should also be noted that not all forms of extrinsic incentives have detrimental impact on intrinsic motivation. There is research evidence to suggest that, in specific individual situations, extrinsic rewards can be valuable. Research indicates that in some cases extrinsic rewards actually foster intrinsic motivation. In one study focusing on motivation, it was found that performance contingent rewards (found in many games) produced greater intrinsic motivation than the same performance objective and favorable performance feedback without reward.[31]

In another study, it was found that performance-contingent rewards increased students' subsequent expression of task enjoyment and free time spent performing the task, as compared with the receipt of an equivalent performance standard and favorable performance feedback.[32] They also found that "employees with strong performance-reward expectancies showed an increased perception of self-determination concerning how they carried out their usual job activities. This relationship was found controlling for any effects of pay rate, tenure, and performance feedback on perceived autonomy. Reward for high performance appears to strengthen the perception of freedom of action experienced both for college students given novel tasks and employees carrying out their usual job responsibilities."[33] They also found that employees who experienced high autonomy stemming from performance-reward expectancy reported that they felt more active, enthusiastic, and energetic on a typical day at work. There are even a number of studies supporting the concept that making rewards explicitly dependent on creative performance increases creativity.[34] Both of these seem to be because employees felt a degree of autonomy about choosing whether or not to perform a task and a high degree of competence in the ability to perform the task, both aspects of Self-Determination Theory.

Extrinsic motivation is least likely to work and most likely to cause negative effects on intrinsic motivation when the external rewards are functionally superfluous (not needed to engage the learner) and not informative about the student's level of ability or knowledge level regarding the task.[35] Extrinsic rewards tend to focus attention more narrowly and to shorten time perspectives, which may result in more efficient production of predefined or standardized products.[36] When a task is seen as initially having low value, extrinsic motivators do help learners get started.

However, it should be noted that the study of extrinsic and intrinsic motivation is not without its flaws. For example, one widely used scale to measure intrinsic versus extrinsic motivation was created by Harter, who designed a scale with three subscales of intrinsic motivation and one scale of extrinsic motivation.[37] The scale is "designed in such a way that it is not possible for children to report themselves as simultaneously intrinsically and extrinsically motivated. [In fact], a perfect negative correlation between the two scales has been built into the scale."[38] This seems to be a flawed approach, because it is likely that intrinsic motivation is not the polar opposite of extrinsic motivation.

A study found that, when measured separately (not on the same scale with one measure on one side and the other on the side), the relationship between intrinsic and extrinsic motivation were only moderately negatively correlated. This means that children's intrinsic and extrinsic motivation can be viewed as two largely mutually independent constructs rather than the opposite ends of a single dimension.[39] In fact, the researchers indicated that "in the classroom, it seems, intrinsic and extrinsic motivation do coexist."[40]

Harter's scale has been found to be problematic in other ways, for example, "Harter's original scale defined engaging in a task to receive good grades as inherently extrinsic, but the situation is arguably more complex."[41] In the sense intended by Harter's original measure, desiring good grades can indicate that children are engaging in academic behaviors merely as a means to some extrinsic end. In another sense, however, grades can also provide useful information about competence and mastery, and desiring this sort of feedback may reflect an intrinsic interest in the material or activity, rather than an extrinsic orientation.[42]

So are grades intrinsic or extrinsic? By extension then, are points, scores, and certain game rewards informational and, therefore, intrinsic and not extrinsic? Could giving points to someone (as a form of information about competence) actually be intrinsically motivating? The possibility exists. Could giving someone a reward related to a specific achievement give him or her information about level of mastery related to the achievement?

From a practical standpoint, truly separating intrinsic motivation from extrinsic motivation becomes increasingly problematic. For example, a woman studying Cisco Certification may seek certification because it "looks good on a resume" and because it will increase her earning potential when seeking a job and she will receive verbal praise from her friends (extrinsic motivators). But she could also be seeking certification because she is interested in the subject of networking and wants to learn more or prove to herself that she can do it (intrinsic motivation).

It's hard to separate the two. As another example, if I want to beat my last score on Angry Birds today, is that intrinsic motivation (I want to better my own score, I am motivated by the concept of self improvement) or is it extrinsic motivation (driven by the points I earn).

Another interesting consideration brought up in the research is the statement that "one issue not addressed is the development of internalized motivation—those originally external motives that have over time become incorporated into one's personal goal or value systems."[43] There is some suggestion in the literature that internalized reasons do gradually supplant extrinsic reasons for engaging in disliked behaviors and that there are specific teaching practices that facilitate internalization.[44] Which means that extrinsic motivations could eventually lead to intrinsic motivation.

So while intrinsic motivation can be undermined by extrinsic reward structures as indicated above, the important question is when and how and in what cases can learning professionals make use of extrinsic rewards? And how can we create extrinsic reward structures that lead to the internalization of motivation and, therefore, convert extrinsic motivation to intrinsic? This is where Self-Determination Theory (discussed in the last chapter) can provide guidance. Following SDT would encourage the gamification designer to add autonomy, competence, and relatedness to the gamification effort to motivate the player.

This can be done by using extrinsic motivators to provide feedback on performance that is intrinsic, giving the player both a sense of autonomy and competence as he or she voluntarily undertook tasks to improve competence. One such example is the use of points. Points, depending on how they are structured, can provide informational feedback and data on performance improvement and not simply serve as extrinsic tokens. This would give the players a measure of their own competence in performing a task.

For example, in a game you could perform a task of trying to close a sale and, during the process, you could observe what types of selected phrases provided the most points; the closer the answer you select is to the proper closing method, the more points you would score. In that case, the points serve as an indicator of how close the learner is to the right answer. For a learning professional thinking about gamification, points can be an effective method of providing immediate feedback to the learner in a manner that is not binary. A designer can craft degrees of correctness, not absolutes. So in gamification instances where a player is performing meaningless activities just to receive points and there is not much value beyond gaining points, players become bored at best and, in the worst case, they become demotivated. But in games where the points themselves provide feedback on how to improve behavior, then the point system, if implemented properly, guides or informs intrinsic behavior due to the feedback they provide.

A final consideration about the research on intrinsic and extrinsic rewards is that most research on the topic is based on tangible rewards. Gamification typically doesn't have tangible rewards.

Avatars

One commonly used element in many games is the characteristic of a person manipulating a character within the game (sometimes 2D and sometimes 3D). If the player is able to customize the character and make it resemble him or her in some way, the character is called an avatar. This is a recommended strategy for attempting to influence behavior; several studies have been conducted showing the effectiveness of avatars for influencing behavior:

- An experience as an avatar can change a person's real-life perceptions. It was found that negative stereotyping of the elderly was significantly reduced when participants were placed in avatars of old people, compared with those participants placed in avatars of young people.[45]

- Watching an avatar that looks like you performing an activity influences you to perform a similar or same activity in the future. Creating avatars and having a learner perform a task as an avatar influences that person's actual behavior outside of the virtual environment. In one study, users watched avatars that looked like them exercising and losing weight in a virtual environment; the result was that those who watched avatars of themselves subsequently exercised more and ate healthier in the real world, as compared to a control group.[46] A similar study was conducted with three control groups,[47] one where participants were exposed to avatars representing themselves running on a treadmill, the second with avatars running that did not represent the participants, and the third group with avatars representing themselves loitering. Within twenty-four hours after the experiment, participants who were exposed to the avatar that represented themselves running exercised significantly more than those in the other conditions.

- Watching an avatar that resembles oneself changing in some way impacts one's future decisions. When college-aged students observed avatars of themselves ageing in a virtual mirror, they formed a psychological connection to their "future selves" and decided to invest more money in a retirement account, as opposed to a control group.[48]

- Behavioral changes occurring in a virtual environment can transfer to the physical environment. In a study comparing the heights of avatars, it was found that participants with taller avatars behaved more confidently in a negotiation task than participants with shorter avatars; specifically, they were more willing to make unfair splits in negotiation tasks. In contrast, participants with shorter avatars were more willing to accept unfair offers than those who had taller avatars.[49] Research found that the behavior changes originating within the virtual environment transferred to subsequent face-to-face interactions.[50] In the study, participants were placed in an immersive virtual environment and were given either shorter or taller avatars. They then interacted with a human confederate for about fifteen minutes. In addition, the authors found that participants given taller avatars negotiated more aggressively in the subsequent face-to-face interaction with the confederate than participants given shorter avatars.[51]

- It is better to have one "expert" avatar and another "motivational" avatar in a learning environment, rather than having one combined "mentor" avatar. In multiple studies with avatars of different gender and race, evidence indicates that students learned significantly more and had significantly greater motivation when working with one motivator avatar and a different expert avatar, as compared to working with just one mentor avatar. This can be explained by the fact that it was easier for students to figuratively compartmentalize the information from the avatar when it was delivered by two distinct sources.[52]

Player Perspective

Research has found that a person is more likely to adjust his or her self-concept to match a desired behavior if that behavior is imagined from a third-person observer's perspective rather than a first-person experiencer's perspective. The research strongly suggests that the idea of "picturing yourself" performing a desired behavior may, in fact, be an effective strategy for translating "good intentions into practical actions."

In one study before the 2004 U.S. presidential election, researchers asked registered voters in Ohio to picture themselves voting in the election from either a first-person perspective (looking through their own eyes) or a third-person perspective (observing themselves as if in a movie).[53]

The individuals who pictured themselves voting from a third-person perspective adopted a stronger pro-voting mind-set; they indicated they were more likely to vote. Those people who pictured themselves voting in third-person were significantly more likely to vote in the election than those who pictured themselves voting in first-person.

Other studies in autobiographical memory shows that the visual perspective people use to picture a past event affects their present emotions, self-judgments, and even behavior. Perspective matters when visualizing activities and translating those visualizations into changes.[54] Additionally, the changes in behavior are even stronger when photographs are used to depicting the desired behavior. It is believed by researchers in the field of autobiographical memory that manipulations of perspective in a 3D game environment should work like manipulations in mental imagery, perhaps even better, as in the game environment you could more carefully control the image, whereas with mental imagery you are relying on people maintaining the perspective you instruct on their own.[55]

Translating this concept to a game environment, many games allow the player to experiences the game from a third-person perspective. Often in these environments, the learner is looking over his or her own shoulder. That perspective may lead to more behavior change than asking the learners to witness their activities in first-person as is often in the case in a traditional classroom environment when people role play, where they are naturally seeing the event in first-person.

■ ■ ■

Key Takeaways

Based on the findings from the various meta-analysis studies on games and the additional research studies, the following conclusions can be drawn:

- The beneficial effects of instructional games were most likely to be found when specific content is targeted and objectives precisely defined.

- Instructional games can provide effective learning for a variety of learners for several different tasks in the domains of higher declarative knowledge, procedural knowledge, and higher retention.

- Instructional games should be embedded in instructional programs that include debriefing and feedback so the learners understand what happened in the game and how these events support the instructional objectives.

- Providing learners with unlimited access to the instructional games improves learning.

- Instructional support to help learners understand how to use the game increases the instructional effectiveness of the gaming experience by allowing learners to focus on the instructional information rather than the requirements of the game.

- Games and simulations yielded better attitudes toward learning when compared to traditional teaching methods and seem to facilitate motivation across different learner groups and learning situations.

- The level of visual realism in the computer program does not seem to have an impact, and instructional games do not need to be entertaining to be educational.

- Instructional games seem to foster higher-order thinking such as planning and reasoning more than factual or verbal knowledge.

- The value, or size, of an anticipated reward influences the motivational signal sent to the brain only within the context of the reward system.

- The uncertainty of an outcome influences the brain's response to reward; uncertain rewards release more dopamine than predictable rewards.

- The right level of uncertainty to introduce in games of chance to heighten motivation is 50 percent.

- An experience as an avatar can change a person's real-life perceptions.

- Watching an avatar that looks like you performing an activity influences you to perform a similar or same activity in the future.

- Watching an avatar that resembles yourself changing in some way impacts future decisions. Behavioral changes occurring in a virtual environment can transfer to the physical environment.

- Better learning outcomes for instructional games may be the result of including instructional designers in the game development process.

- Gaming uncertainty can transform the emotional experience of learning improving engagement and, more importantly, improving encoding and later recall.

- The extrinsic reward structures of engagement-contingent rewards, completion-contingent rewards, and performance-contingent rewards all undermine intrinsic motivation in most cases.

- Extrinsic motivation is least likely to work and most likely to cause negative effects on intrinsic motivation when the external rewards are functionally superfluous (not needed to engage the learner) and not informative about the student's level of ability or knowledge level regarding the task.

- Extrinsic rewards tend to focus attention more narrowly and to shorten time perspectives, which may result in more efficient production of predefined or standardized products.

- A reward that seems to be extrinsic only, such as points, can have intrinsic value if it provides feedback to the player/learner.

- When a task is seen as initially having low value, extrinsic motivators do help learners begin.

- Strive to include both intrinsic and extrinsic motivational aspects in the gamification effort.

5

Leveling Up: What Gamification Can Do

CHAPTER QUESTIONS

At the end of this chapter, you should be able to answer the following questions:

- What types of content can be taught through gamification?
- What are the different ways gamification impacts behavior?
- What are some uses of gamification?
- What research exists that indicates certain types of knowledge can be taught through gamification?

Introduction

Most people only think of gamification as an effective tool for motivating behavior. But it can also be used for teaching problem solving, improving hand-eye coordination, and even helping people lose weight. The concept of gamification can be applied to a wide range of activities and outcomes.

Gamificaiton has been used to teach everything from psychomotor or physical skills to cognitive skills—and even for influencing attitudes. Gamification can teach memorization to higher order thinking and every cognitive level in between. It can also be used for assessing learner's abilities, knowledge, and skills.

Problems can be even be solved with game-like interfaces and interactions. Several organizations are using game mechanics and techniques for group problem solving. Additionally, elements of games are being used to motivate people to take action and perform proper behaviors.

In some cases, gamification has even impacted how teachers and professors take attendance and interact with students. The military uses gamification to replace typical slide-based briefings with more impactful presentations. This chapter explores various usages of gamification from a performance improvement perspective, examining everything from helping people gain knowledge and skills to changing attitudes, solving problems, assessing performance, and motivating learners.

Improving Surgeon Hand-Eye Coordination

One of the first places to look for gamification to make a meaningful difference is hand-eye coordination. From the activity of button mashing on controllers and viewing the results on the screen, it makes intuitive sense that hand-eye coordination improves through gamification. And, indeed, research supports the conclusion that videogames improve hand-eye coordination. Several studies indicate that reaction times of gamers are faster than those of non-gamers and that playing games for as little fifteen minutes can improve a person's hand-eye coordination.

Research has shown that videogame players tend to be faster at searching for and identifying stimuli presented in the visual periphery than non-videogame players. It seems that visual attention, the set of mechanisms by which relevant visual information is selected while irrelevant information is suppressed, can be made faster through videogame playing. Studies have established improvements in groups of non-gamers after giving them experience playing games. The games that seem to have the most beneficial effect on attention are fast-paced, embodied visuomotor tasks that require divided attention. Examples of such games are Metal of Honor, Halo, or Call of Duty.[1]

In terms of spatial abilities, research has shown that videogame play is related to the ability to mentally rotate or arrange objects. Playing Tetris, a videogame in which the player mentally rotates and fits a variety of shapes together to gain points, is related to heightened spatial abilities.[2] Participants who performed well playing the videogame The Empire Strikes Back and then were asked to complete a spatial rotation task (paper folding) performed significantly better on the task compared to those who did not perform well at the game.[3]

Studies of videogames indicate that people who play electronic games have[4]

- Faster reaction times[5]
- Significantly faster eye-hand coordination[6]
- Heightened spatial visualization skills[7]
- Increased capacity for visual attention and spatial distribution[8]

Applying those hand-eye coordination skills to a practical application, a study found that surgeons who played videogames in excess of three hours a week had 37 percent fewer errors and 27 percent faster completion of laparoscopic surgery than non-videogamers. Laparoscopic surgery is surgery performed with the assistance of a video camera and small media instruments. During the procedure, small incisions are made and plastic tubes are inserted. The camera and instrument are then used to perform the procedure. The surgery procedure is a lot like playing a videogame.

The study found that surgeons who were active videogame players made 32 percent fewer errors, performed 24 percent faster, and scored 26 percent better overall (time and errors) than their non-playing colleagues. The research also indicated that videogame skills and past videogame experience are significant predictors of demonstrated laparoscopic skills. The study indicated that training curricula that include videogames may help reduce the technical interface between surgeons and screen-mediated applications, such as laparoscopic surgery.[9]

In another example, National Public Radio reported that a study by researchers at the Banner Good Samaritan Medical Center in Phoenix, Arizona, showed that trainee surgeons who played Nintendo's Wii before going into surgery performed more effectively in simulated surgery. The trainees played Wii games that required precise hand movements like Marble Mania, which involves guiding a virtual marble around a 3D maze. The Wii players did almost 50 percent better than other students when it came time for the virtual scalpel.[10]

Solving Problems

Solving complex problems is important for human progress, but problems are increasingly complex. Chapter One discussed how the U.S. military is crowdsourcing the Somali pirate issue though the development of a multi-player game to address different strategies and approaches for dealing with the violent pirates, but that's not the only large-scale gamification process being used to solve problems. Here are several other examples:

Researchers at the University of Washington in Seattle have created an online game environment that allows non-scientists to work at the incredibly difficult task of folding proteins into 3D structures. Players work against each other to pack the protein—making it as small as possible; hide the hydrophobics that don't like water (orange sidechains), and expose the hydrophobics that like water (blue sidechains); and finally, clear the clashes—don't fold a sidechain so that two sidechains are too close together. In other words, avoid the red spiky balls or your score will go down a lot.

Scores that are used to determine player levels are based on biochemical measures of how well the players' final structure matches the way the protein appears in nature. The game is called Foldit, and the goals go way beyond those of typical videogames. The website for Foldit explains:

> "For protein structure prediction, the eventual goal is to have human
> folders work on proteins that do not have a known structure. . . . The
> more interesting goal for Foldit, perhaps, is not in protein prediction

but protein design. Designing new proteins may be more directly practical than protein prediction, as the problem you must solve as a protein designer is basically an engineering problem (protein engineering), whether you are trying to disable a virus or scrub carbon dioxide from the atmosphere."[11]

By playing the game, the players are actually predicting protein sequences and even designing brand new proteins. If all goes well, the players will design new vaccines and make enzymes for repairing DNA in diseased tissues and create proteins that work in flu vaccines. A player can work alone or as part of a team. The evolver rankings are for people who have worked on solutions shared with other people and improved them. The soloist rankings are for people who have worked on their solutions alone. Players are assigned global points based on their ranks in solving a protein puzzle.

A similar project dealing with DNA called Phylo describes itself as "a human computing framework for comparative genomics, but don't let the fancy name scare you; really, it's just an interactive game that lets you contribute to science." Through playing the game, players are helping researchers identify sections of DNA that are similar across species and that contribute to traits such as hair color—or medical conditions such as diabetes.[12]

By pinpointing these DNA sections, scientists hope to trace the source of certain genetic diseases. In the game, the goal is to align rows of colored blocks that represent the four letters of the genetic code (A, C, G, T) from two organisms. The game play arises because it is not always possible to create columns with the same color. Sometimes players have to put different colors in the columns. When that happens, a player is penalized. More importantly, the player will also typically need to create "gaps" (unoccupied positions in the grid). The gaps are unavoidable in the game but are strongly penalized—so the fewer the better. The goal is to find the best tradeoff between aligning color and creating gaps. Game players are given a time limit to come up with the best match. When alignments of DNA are made, the information is analyzed and stored in a database to be studied. Studying the alignments of DNA allow scientists to infer shared evolutionary origins, identify functionally important sites, illustrate mutation events, and trace the source of certain genetic diseases.

Teaching Higher Order Skills

Gamification is not just for solving problems; it can actually be used to teach the problem-solving process. Videogames present players with one problem after another; in fact, you can't get to level two in a videogame if you can't solve the problems in level one. Determining what route to take, how to balance variables, and which actions bring the most return for the effort are all problem solving variables that can be easily presented with the use of a game. A videogame environment is a great place for immersing a learner in a problem and allowing him or her to practice different problem-solving techniques.

Consider the game Civilization V which is a turn-based strategy game where players attempt to lead a civilization from prehistoric times into the future on a procedurally generated map, achieving one of a number of different victory conditions through research, diplomacy, expansion, economic development, government, and military conquest. A player wins by achieving the highest-scoring civilization. Players allocate limited resources, plan movements in advance, improve land, maintain roads, develop culture, determine what technologies to research, engage in diplomatic exchanges, determine the cost of waging war, and even bribe city-states to obtain loyalty.[13] The skills required include the higher order problem-solving skills. While playing the game, the player must:

- Think strategically about positioning, analyze opponent strengths and weaknesses, plan how to achieve game goals, and execute those plans;

- Master resource management—managing people, money, food, and natural resources—and learn to acquire and apply force multipliers such as knowledge and technology;

- Interact with systems and understand the interaction of variables;

- Multi-task, manage complexity, respond to rapidly changing scenarios, and make decisions;

- Learn compromise and tradeoffs in satisfying the needs of diverse constituencies.

- Manage complex relationships; and

- Exercise leadership, team building, negotiation, and collaboration.[14]

All skills and talents are required to lead and manage projects and co-workers. Such skills are being taught in the best business and law schools in the country, but they must also be taught to as many individuals as possible so that organizations and institutions can remain competitive.

The skills taught by videogames are not lost on many. An article in the *Harvard Business Review* pointed toward using massively multi-player online (MMOs) games as incubators for growing leadership talent. The authors assert that effective leaders in the future will exhibit many of the skills that leaders in online games exhibit today. These skills include:[15]

Quick Decision Making. A lot happens in a short time within games. For instance, the authors explain how a hastily formed team in-world decided who would lead an assault, assessed the strengths and weaknesses of rivals from another team, crafted an attack strategy, and coordinated battle assignments, all in less than one minute. Leaders also need to know when ultra-quick decision making needs to trump team consensus. These skills are practiced and honed in online games.

Risk Taking. Trail and error are key components in succeeding in a game task. Failure, instead of being viewed as career limiting, is actually just another tool used to find out information, move closer to goals, or help solve a problem—it is a necessary antecedent to success. In real life, however, fewer risks are taken; in fact, often a type of paralysis sets in and people won't take action because they are afraid to fail.

Grabbing and Releasing Leadership. In MMO games, it seems that leadership is not a role assumed by a player but simply a task that needs to be accomplished. Leadership can then switch to the person most capable of leading the next task. The idea of temporary leadership seems foreign in many organizations, but with the focus on project-based organizations, a person might lead one project but serve in a supporting role in another. Leaders in the future will need to understand leadership as a task and not a position.

Thinking the Unthinkable

One advantage of games is that they can create an environment filled with unreal elements, concepts, or ideas. Many games are based on a fantasy world and use fantasy as a backdrop for the story and actions. This has been found to be highly entertaining from a leisure perspective. But it can also be used to help people think through problems and situations they might not otherwise imagine.

In the 1970s the large oil conglomerate BP created a board game called Offshore Oil Strike. The goal of the game was to create an oil empire by drilling offshore oil and, naturally, players encountered hazards such as blowouts and oil spills and cleanup costs. Hazards were presented as cards with phrases like "Blow-out! Rig damaged. Oil slick cleanup costs. Pay $1 million."[16]

Then forty years later in 2010 the Deep Horizon oil platform had a blowout and leaked oil into the Gulf of Mexico for three months. The similarities are frightening, but the lessons that can be learned from the gamification of disasters is important. Games provide the license to think outside of normal parameters, to add a little bit of fantasy or surrealism, and to force people to think in different ways. Once the new ways of thinking are opened up, people can safely consider worst-case scenarios and then think about contingency plans.

Imagine if BP executives and managers were encouraged to go through game-like scenarios on a frequent basis, trying to develop contingency plans, worst-case scenarios, and clean up efforts to react to a spill that "most likely will never happen." The act of playing a "game" can open up thinking processes that might not be considered in normal day-to-day operations but become apparent when one player is trying to "outmaneuver" another. Translate those lessons learned into activities and the spill might have been prevented, or at least the cleanup efforts might have been better coordinated.

The same type of thinking went into the board game called Worst Case Scenario Survival Game. The game provides a situation such as "What do you do if you are attacked by a shark?" and then gives three possible responses. The person has to choose the best response. The idea is to cause the players to think about situations and scenarios they may not consider in the normal course of events, such as what to do if you receive a tornado warning. Players can learn what the experts recommend and then implement that advice if they are ever in the actual situation.

The same technique can be applied to strategizing about competitors, thinking about obstacles to growing a business, or any other activity in which you want to carefully think through contingencies and possible obstacles. Making the content into a game will help players think in ways that are outside of normal everyday consideration but, when the games starts, those extraordinary events become part of the discussion.

Thinking Like Your Opponent

In the 2008 Bowl Championship Series football game, number two ranked Louisiana State University (LSU) defeated (some would say humbled) number one ranked Ohio State in a 38 to 24 victory. In addition to all the strength training, conditioning, and opponent film watching, one other technique used by LSU was to battle their opponents on a videogame screen before facing them physically.

The LSU offensive coordinator used a custom-made videogame to help his quarterbacks learn to read defenses. LSU put their offensive plays into the game and then entered in their opponent's defenses to give their quarterbacks a chance to get accustomed to the different defensive formations they would encounter during the game.

The videogame allows the coaches to make the virtual opponents as difficult and fast as in real life and even faster to hone the quarterback's understanding of the different defensives schemes and potential blitzes. This forces the quarterback to make decisions quickly. It helps him to make the right reads and get to the right spot. The game provides immediate feedback; instantly, the quarterback can see the results of a decision, an interception, or a touchdown or something in between.[17]

Another group adding opponents into a videogame for training purposes is the U.S. military. Playing a videogame where players can assume the role of terrorists is something that the U.S. Army not only understands, but actively develops and plays on a regular basis. There is a military unit tasked with using videogame tools and techniques to help soldiers and commanders understand how to not only train smarter, but also to understand how their enemy thinks. Part of that mission is occasionally playing the role of insurgent in a videogame environment.

The adaptation of videogame tools is done under the Joint Training Counter-IED Operations Integration Center (JTCOIC). So now they use videogame technologies to re-create battle situations and then "play" the battle from different perspectives to learn what the enemy was doing and where they were located at the time of the engagement.

The team takes a scenario—whether based on actual events or invented by a trainer—and using a variety of software, creates a 2D or 3D virtual training event of that scenario. With this technology and interface, during training sessions, the warfighters are put into the heat of the battle.[18] Instead of briefings with a slide deck, briefings can take place in a 3D environment and the warfighters being briefed can change perspectives to see multiple views of an engagement, as in Figure 5.1.

The training is based on actual locations, villages, and events. The geographies are accurate and, more importantly, the activity is accurate. An article in *Wired* sums up the ability of the JTCOIC team in creating a version of a recent battle in theater.

> "There was a five-vehicle convoy. The first vehicle turned the corner . . . and got hit by 400 pounds of deep-buried explosives . . . . following that, there was a complex attack: Insurgents to the east . . . north . . .and south on top of a building, attacking. We produced this product, created the terrain . . . everything . . . and had it done in four days. . . . it was amazingly powerful because what we did was create a transition from the real world of photographs and reports into the virtual world's polygons . . . now we can see what the bad guys [were] doing and what their point of view was."[19]

This information is invaluable for decision-makers and warfighters; it allows them to play the role of the insurgent and see what the insurgent saw and then consider ways to counter that activity. The game elements added to the reproduction of battles and events to provide extra

Figure 5.1. Seeing the Battle Through the Eyes of the Enemy.

Image reprinted with permission of the artist, Kristin Bittner.

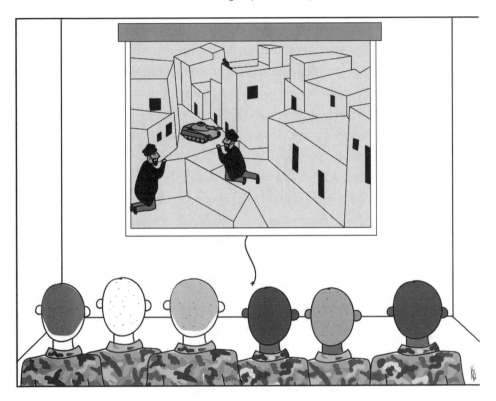

knowledge and capabilities that would not be available in typical 2D slide presentations.

Engaging Learners in a Live Classroom

Professors, high school, middle school and elementary schools teachers are finding that they can employ simple devices to receive immediate feedback on student understanding, visually display that feedback, and see a quick comparison of learning among students simply by using an audience response system. The system adds game-like elements to classroom instruction and can drive motivation, participation, and learning.

Audience response systems (ARS) allow 100 percent engagement in a class. A teacher can ask a question and immediately know whether a concept was understood by everyone. Additionally, many of the ARS can be tied directly to a student so that an instructor can, at the end of class, check which students had trouble understanding the material and pull them aside for remediation. Research indicates that students rate lectures as more interactive, interesting, and entertaining when an ARS is used. Additionally, students who participate in ARS instruction performed significantly better on exam questions concerning the lecture, compared to another group of students who did not use the ARS.[20]

The devices can be used to have groups compete against each other or can be used more collaboratively. They can even be used with images whereby instructors can ask students to identify a figure, event, or issue from a photograph. One instructor at a vocational school teaches custodial maintenance and uses photos to identify tools, safety methods, and proper usage, asking questions such as, "In the event of this, what tool would you use?"

ARS are also great for class discussions on controversial topics, asking students if they are for or against issues, and reviewing serious issues. This can be done without students having to necessarily state their views publicly. Using an ARS to gamify the classroom includes techniques like:[21]

- Assigning point values to questions instead of simply setting them as right or wrong
- Using point values to award attendance and/or participation points
- Use a "count down" timer to add a sense of urgency to responding
- Track performance of teams on questions
- Create a leaderboard
- Visually display opinions and ideas
- Provide the class immediate feedback by visually displaying the distribution of responses

Helping People Lose Weight

Games have been around longer than electricity. So it is no surprise that one of the first human activities to experience gamification is that of physical exercise. Humans have created all kinds of competitive sports to challenge each other with clear goals, immediate feedback, scores, and engaging activities. Gamification of exercise helps people lose weight, run that extra mile, and get into shape.

One modern example is the television show "The Biggest Loser." In that show contestants compete against one another to see who can lose the most weight. Instead of points as a method of keeping score, the game uses weight. Every week contestants who lose the most weight are able to remain on the show; the contestant who loses the least amount of weight must leave the show. Players can earn immunity by competing in mini-games throughout the week. Mini-game winners are exempt, even if they don't lose weight that week. The winner of the game is the person who has survived the longest on the show and who loses the most weight.

Other versions of the gamification of weight loss and exercise can be seen in a variety of game/exercise interfaces. An often-cited example is the NikePlus product. The NikePlus product is a sensor that you put in your shoe that tracks your running and reports the results back to a website so you can track progress. But NikePlus does more than just record your run. It provides incentives and motivations to encourage more exercise. First, the run is graphically displayed on the website to give you visual feedback on your run progress. Each mile is marked and pace and distance are displayed.

Next, there are levels in NikePlus. You start at the yellow level (beginning) which is between 0 to 49 kilometers and then at certain milestones you level up. The next level after yellow is orange which is from 50 to 249 KM, through various levels all the way to black which is 5,000+ KM. As you move up to different levels, the interface changes colors to reflect your new level. Other gamification elements include the ability to create goals and measure yourself against them. There are also opportunities to challenge friends and foes to see who can run the most miles and even the ability to customize an avatar based on awards that you receive by moving from one level to the next. NikePlus is the gamification of running.[22]

The credit for the gamification of dancing goes to a videogame called Dance Dance Revolution (DDR), a game where a player or players stand on a mat or dance platform and step on an arrow on each side of the platform pointing up, down, left, and right with their feet, attempting to match musical and visual cues shown on the screen. Players are scored by how well they time their dance moves to the moves presented by the music and on the video screen.

The latest game has a dance-off mode that allows players to take turns while playing. They can see themselves dancing on the screen through a camera attached to the videogame console. The player who is able to step and dance more accurately will gain more points and will be the winner. There is even a club mode that allows players to play four to twenty songs consecutively. The difficulty level varies depending on how well the player is dancing. If the player changes the options to non-stop, he or she can keep dancing until the dancing gauge is empty.

DDR has even been credited with helping people to lose weight. Several individuals from high school to college students claim to have lost from sixty to 150 pounds playing Dance Dance Revolution.[23]

Adding to the use of videogames in weight loss and exercise is the change in interface between people and games; no longer is the controller the only way to interface. It is now possible to use your body to control movements within the game. The Xbox Kinect and the Sony EyeToy both promote player movement by integrating actions the players perform with results shown on the video screen through full body motion capture. A player is literally able to interact with objects on the screen as his or her body moves. Players track their heart rates on screen in real time, calories burned, and progress made toward reaching fitness goals. The Nintendo Wii allows for wireless movement with a simple controller and add-ons like the Wii Fit exercise mat that tracks movements and helps with balance and body control. These programs provide instant feedback on activities, with activities like dodging balls, boxing with opponents, or jumping over obstacles.

With all the innovations in computer controllers and sensing devices like the NikePlus, it is safe to say that the act of exercising is experiencing gamification. The addition of progress reports, goals, rewards, levels, engaging activities and other game elements has transformed almost any physical activity into a game.

Making Physical Therapy More Enjoyable

The wireless controller of the Nintendo Wii game platform has had so much interest from the rehabilitation community that some have started to use the term "Wii-habilitation" The use of the Wii as a therapeutic device has been used to help encourage movement and activity in both adult and youth populations that are impaired. The advantage is that it engages patients in an interesting and sometimes competitive activity while repeating motions used in rehab.

In one case, researchers have developed a therapeutic videogame to teach children who suffer from hemiplegic cerebral palsy, a condition that can partially paralyze one side of the body, to use the muscles on the weaker side of their bodies to improve their motor function. The game helps the children practice their motor functions outside of therapy sessions.[24]

For older people who have had strokes, the Wii has been used to motivate them to do exercises that strengthen their arms. After playing active Wii games, stroke victims with weakness in their arms could reach out and grab objects more easily and more quickly than before, after only two weeks of playing.[25]

Influencing Pro-Social Behavior

Many organizations want to change the attitude of employees, students, or even customers. Sometimes they want employees to have better attitudes toward quality or safety; sometimes they want students to have better attitudes toward each other and their teachers; sometimes organizations want members to have better attitudes toward giving to the less fortunate. Marketers want potential customers to have better attitudes toward their products. All types of organizations are interested in influencing attitudes, but it can be difficult and possibly time-consuming. Each year companies spend thousands of dollars on safety training. Charities spend money on brochures and advertisements to change attitudes.

So the question arises, can videogames influence attitudes? For example, can playing a videogame make someone "nice"? That was a question posed by a pair of researchers from Germany and the United Kingdom.[26]

The answer, it turns out, is "yes." Actually, the question the researchers investigated was a little more nuanced: "Does playing pro-social videogames cause pro-social behavior and pro-social thoughts?" To find out the answer the researchers conducted a number of interesting experiments placing the subjects of the experiments in positions to assist others or not assist them after the subjects had played a pro-social videogame. In every instance, the subjects who played a pro-social videogame were more willing to help than were the other experimental control groups.

The first experiment was designed to examine the impact of pro-social, aggressive, and neutral games on spontaneous, unrequested assistance. The researchers used a method that is commonly used as a measure of spontaneous, unrequested assistance; they would "accidentally" spill pencils on the floor and observe whether or not the subjects assisted in picking them up.

First, the researches randomly assigned subjects ranging in age from nineteen to forty-three to one of three videogame conditions. The pro-social game was called Lemmings. In that game the object is to help a group of animals, lemmings, get to safety. The basic objective of the game is to guide the lemmings through a number of obstacles to a designated exit and save the required number of lemmings to win.

The aggressive game was Lamers, the exact opposite of Lemmings. In Lamers, the player has an arsenal of weapons and attempts to destroy as many lamers as possible so they do not reach their intended destination. If enough lamers are destroyed, the player wins. The neutral game was Tetris, a puzzle game with a number of random shapes the player manipulates to complete a solid row of blocks.

After a subject played a videogame for eight minutes, the researcher came into the room, acted as if he were reaching for a questionnaire, and spilled a cup of pencils. The researcher then waited five seconds to see whether the subject would help. The subjects who played the pro-social videogame were more likely to help pick up the pencils than those who had played the neutral or aggressive games. In total eighteen subjects played the pro-social game and twelve (67 percent) helped to pick up pencils; eighteen subjects played the neutral game and six (33 percent) helped with the pencils. Of the eighteen subjects who played the aggressive game, five (28 percent) helped pick up pencils.[27]

In the second experiment, the researchers did not include the aggressive videogame condition. They just wanted to compare subjects who played the neutral game with those who played the pro-social game. They wanted to see whether playing a pro-social game would make subjects more willing to volunteer time to help the researchers. After the subjects, ranging in age from eighteen to fifty-six, played either the neutral game or pro-social game for ten minutes, they were asked whether they would be willing to assist in further studies and how much time they would devote. It turns out that all twenty subjects who played the pro-social game, Lemmings, were willing to help. Only 68 percent of those who played Tetris (neutral game) were willing to help, and those who played the pro-social game were willing to volunteer more time than the people who played Tetris.

In a third experiment, the researchers wanted to take into account two variables that may have confounded the earlier experiments. First, they wanted to eliminate the possibility that not all pro-social games fostered pro-social behavior. Maybe just Lemmings was an effective pro-social game. So they switched the Lemmings game with another pro-social game called City Crisis to see whether that would make a difference. City Crisis is a helicopter simulation wherein players assume the role of a rescue helicopter pilot. The object of the game is to save civilians from fires that spring up around the city.

Second, picking up pencils or volunteering time are two activities that are low risk to the individual. The researchers wanted to see whether subjects would react in a pro-social manner if they were in possible physical danger, so they upped the stress level of the experiment.

In the experiment, thirty-six students, ranging from nineteen to forty-three, were assigned randomly to one of two groups. The one group played the game City Crisis for eight minutes and the other group played Tetris for ten minutes. Each of the groups was overseen by a female researcher. After ten minutes a male researcher came into the room posing as the female researcher's boyfriend. The researcher/boyfriend proceeded to enter the research area, ignore the subject, and approached the female researcher. He then said, "Ah, there you are! I was looking for you in the whole building! Why do you ignore me like that? Why do you do that to me? Now you have to talk to me!" The researcher/boyfriend talked loudly, then shouted and kicked a trash can, and finally he pulled the arm of the female researcher to force her to leave the room with him.

Meanwhile, the female researcher, playing the part of the girlfriend, reacted reservedly and passively. She always repeated the following sentences with a low voice: "Shush, be quiet please. I have to work in here, I cannot talk to you. You are disturbing the experiment. Please do not be so loud."

The researchers wanted to see whether or not the research subject would intervene. An intervention could be saying something to the female researcher ("Do you need help?") or saying something to the boyfriend/researcher ("I think you need to leave"). In the group that played the pro-social videogame, 56 percent intervened (ten out of eighteen); in the group that played the neutral videogame only 22 percent helped (four out of eighteen).[28]

The researchers concluded that playing videogames with pro-social content is positively related to increases in different kinds of pro-social behavior. Participants who had played a pro-social videogame were more likely to help researches pick up spilled items, were more willing to assist in further experiments, and were more likely to help an individual being harassed.

The conclusion that pro-social games have an influence on pro-social behavior has been repeated in other studies. In a study led by Douglas A. Gentil from Iowa State University with researchers from around the world, the findings indicated that videogames in which game characters help and support each other in nonviolent ways increase both short-term and long-term pro-social behaviors.[29] The research team reported on three studies conducted in three countries with three age groups. In a correlational study, Singaporean middle-school students who played more pro-social games behaved more pro-socially. In two longitudinal samples of Japanese children and adolescents, pro-social game play predicted later increases in pro-social behavior. In an experimental study, U.S. undergraduates randomly assigned to play pro-social games behaved more pro-socially toward another student. These similar results across different methodologies, ages, and cultures provide robust evidence that pro-social games can positively impact pro-social behavior.

In another study, researchers wanted to see whether a person's empathic reactions to social issues could be influenced by playing an interactive digital game. The study focused on a game called Darfur Is Dying. It is a narrative-based game wherein the player, from the perspective of a displaced refuge, negotiates around forces that threaten the survival of his or her refugee camp. It is meant to highlight the plight of people who have been displaced by the fighting in the Sudan region of Africa. Two experiments were conducted.

The first experiment demonstrated that playing the Darfur Is Dying game resulted in greater willingness to help the Darfurian people than reading a text conveying the same information. The second experiment added a game-watching condition. It was found that game playing resulted in greater role taking and willingness to help than either game watching or text reading. The study provides empirical evidence that interactive digital games are more effective than non-interactive presentation modes in influencing people's empathic reactions to social issues.[30]

Testing Knowledge and Performance

Not only can gamification techniques be used for instruction, as is most common, but they can also be used to assess performance. In one case, a 3D simulation game was designed as an assessment to help certify energy professionals by assessing movements of candidates through a virtual house as they conducted a combustion analysis.[31] Home energy efficiency is a relatively new industry and there is a growing need for trained professionals to conduct home analysis. It is critical that the individuals who enter the homes to do the analysis are skilled and knowledgeable in the standards and guidelines required.

This poses a difficult situation because energy efficiency certification requires an understanding of a complex safety issue that is challenging to teach and test due to the wide number of variables that could affect an outcome in each scenario. To try to "simulate" this amount of complexity with field training is expensive and prohibitive; but the training is essential and must be carried out. As the industry moves to scale, this skill set will become the cornerstone of safety standards and a longer-term solution was needed.

Although a written test for combustion safety is fairly standard to administer, the field test is challenging for a number of reasons. It is expensive due to the fact that an experienced field proctor must administer the test in a "volunteer" home. In addition, the volunteer home is often logistically difficult to manage, so some of the training companies that offer the testing have resorted to buying homes and setting them up as test homes. The test homes are effective, but they cannot be easily reconfigured to assess multiple scenarios, and only so many houses can be purchased for assessing competences of the inspectors.

To address this issue, Interplay Energy, in partnership with the Residential Energy Services Network (RESNET), created a simulation that measures applied knowledge and the resulting behaviors that are the heart of the field test using the 3D simulation software called Thinking Worlds. The 3D simulation of the house accomplishes this while ensuring consistency and testing control across the numerous training/testing companies.

The assessment simulation takes approximately one hour to complete and takes place in a virtual two-story home. The test conditions were linked into an administrative control panel and can be set differently prior to each test to keep test-takers actively engaged.

The testing environment assesses the learner's ability to work in a number of areas, including proper equipment usage, gas line leak detection, ambient CO testing, unvented appliance testing (ovens and stove top burners primarily), and other related required tests.

Each of these areas is tested as the trainee walks through the virtual house troubleshooting problems and conducting the inspection. The testing system is set up so that the administrator of the exam can configure a large number of scenarios and situations and then track the tester's time on tasks, movements through the house, sequence of performing steps, sequence of using equipment, and amount of danger he or she places him- or herself into during the inspection.

Having this level of standardization and consistency in combustion safety analysis certification tests provides a measure of assurance that the people who are certified can apply their knowledge in the field and that the assessment data is available to ensure that the people who are able to apply their knowledge correctly are certified.

Good for Young and Old

It appears that playing games can benefit both young and old. Results from a study of 180 third-graders, sixty-one male and fifty-four female, in a school district in Taiwan found that computer-based videogame playing not only improved participants' fact/recall processes but also promoted problem-solving skills by helping the third-graders recognize multiple solutions for problems.[32]

A slightly older group of forty non-gamer adults in the Urbana-Champaign, Illinois, community, with an average age of sixty-nine, were randomly divided into two groups. The lucky group was asked to play the real-time strategy game Rise of Nations Gold Edition (RON). RON combines the speed of real-time gaming and the complexity of turn-based strategy games. In the game, the players had to build new cities, improve city infrastructure, and expand their national borders. The game has several ways in which victory can be achieved. One is through conquering others via military might, but other paths to victory include building a set of world wonders, diplomacy, and technological victory. A series of cognitive tests was administered to track executive control and visuospatial skills.

The second group, the control group, only took the cognitive tests and did not play the game. The purpose of this group was to provide a standard of comparison.

The results indicated that the group that played Rise of Nations improved significantly more than the control participants in executive control functions such as task switching, working memory, visual short-term memory, and reasoning.[33]

■ ■ ■

Key Takeaways

The key takeaways from this chapter are

- Gamification can be applied to a wide range of activities and subjects.

- Gamification involves methods of adding various game elements to different types of content.

- Gamification can be used not only for instruction and learning but to elicit outcomes such as problem solving.

- Games and gamification can help influence people to exhibit pro-social behavior.

- Gamification can help with learning physical skills and mental skills.

- Games have positive impact on young and old alike.

Achiever or Killer?

Player Types and Game Patterns

CHAPTER QUESTIONS

At the end of this chapter, you should be able to answer the following questions:

- What are the different player types?
- How do player types interact with a game? With each other?
- What are the different patterns of play in games?

Introduction

Not everyone plays a game the same way. Some are ultracompetitive—they play to win. They don't like losing and become emotionally upset when they lose. Others play games because of the challenge; they want to achieve the goal, whatever it may entail. Others play for the social aspect. Still others want to explore the elements of the game and determine what they all mean.

Types of Play

Not all games have the same type of interactions, goals, or playing styles. In some cases players work together; in other games, they battle one another. In many games both cooperation and individual achievements are necessary for ultimate success. Sometimes, the players just like to have an opportunity for self-expression.[1] When thinking about player types, consider what players of games like to do.

The most obvious is probably competing. Players compete against the game or others to achieve goals. First-person shooters or their close cousin, first-person thinkers, often involve a player working against non-player characters created by artificial intelligence within the game. A first-person thinker game involves moving around an environment encountering obstacles, but not using violence. A good example might be a sales negotiation game wherein a person within the game attempts to negotiate a sale by moving from office to office.

Other times the competitive situation might be against other people who are assuming the role of another character within the game environment. This is the classic player-versus-player game mode, where two or more players compete against one another until one player loses. It can be a sports game, military game, racing game, or even a game of Chess. The idea is that one person or one group of people competes against another person or group of people.

Another type of game play is cooperative play. In these types of games, players work together to help each other and share resources to achieve mutually desirable goals. Sometimes this is referred to as the cooperative game play or co-op mode. Some games such as MMORPGs are specifically designed so that players may work alone to accomplish some goals but cannot reach the final stage of the game without working with others. Eve Online and World of Warcraft are two such examples aimed at adults, but kids' games such as Disney's Toontown Online involve cooperation and teamwork as well. In Toontown, a person can play as a cartoon animal and then customize that animal within certain parameters. The Toons then battle against the Cogs.

The Cogs have transformed Toontown into a dark place so the Toons use "gags," silly pranks based on slapstick routines from cartoons. These include such elements as pies to the face, banana peels so people slip, anvils for dropping on people, and even squirting flowers. Teamwork is encouraged within the game and as many as four Toons can team up to battle Cogs. One example of teaming up is that a "Toon-Up," which heals a player who has been injured by a Cog cannot be used on yourself. You need another Toon to administer the Toon-Up.

Another good example of cooperative play is the social game FarmVille, which leverages aspects of the social network Facebook to encourage interaction and sharing among players. In this game players start with a blank tract of land and attempt to grow a successful farm with crops and animals. Along the way, the players can invite Facebook friends to be their neighbors, allowing them to perform actions on others' farms by dropping in for a visit. Neighbors are able to send gifts and supplies to each other, help each other with crops, and even join together to grow a certain amount of a certain crop.

The company that created FarmVille, Zynga, also creates other social games that require cooperative play. One such game is CityVille. In CityVille, you first clear your land and then place road pieces to activate buildings, deliveries, and the flow of citizens. Players also construct houses, businesses, and community buildings like post offices and schools. Players' friends can become involved by allowing the establishment of franchises in each other's cities and by trading with each other.

A third type of play is often not considered play but is a critical element in many games—self-expression. Some games are played simply to provide players a chance to express themselves and exercise their creativity. One good example of this is the classic version of Minecraft, a game that focuses on creativity and building. The game allows players to build constructions out of cubes in a 3D environment. In the classic modes, players are given an unlimited supply of blocks with which to build. The structures created range from giant snowmen to castles to billboards with cartoon characters to giant teddy bears and even the USS Enterprise.

Another example of a game based on creativity and self-expression is Spore. The game involves creating a creature and guiding that creature through five stages of evolution. The phases are the cell phase, creature phase, tribal phase, civilization phase, and space phase. Each phase exhibits its own style of play and the outcome of one phase impacts the initial conditions the player faces in the next phase. During the game, players can create custom buildings, vehicles, and even spaceships. A major feature of the Spore game is the user-generated content. The game has many different types of content editors ranging, from a creature editor to a music editor used to create a national anthem, clothing editors, and even an editor for customizing an entire planet. This allows the players of the game to create completely unique in-game content and to express themselves as much as they would like.

While each of these three play types can be used to support the creation of a game and the gamification of learning and instruction, most often gamification involves a combination of these three elements. It is difficult for any one of these elements to stand independently. When considering what type of play to use for the creation of gamified content, keep in mind the blending of competition, cooperation, and self-expression. Allowing all three of these elements will encourage the most engagement and activity with the gamified content. It is also important to consider that, when combining these three types of game play, one will be the dominate form. The other two will be subservient. When thinking about gamification, consider these three elements and which type of game play would primarily appeal to the targeted group of learners.

Player Skill Levels

In considering player types, the various skill levels of current and future players must be considered. The approach taken to motivate and attract a new or novice player needs to be different from the approach used to hold onto players who consider themselves masters of the game.

For a novice, an important first step is to guide them into the game gently but with a great deal of attraction and interest. Many successful games provide a simple method of slowly getting into the game. Most of the time the first task, quest, or mission is nothing more than walking over to a particular area. Once the player reaches the area, he or she receives a reward or token—immediate reinforcement.

Meanwhile, the walking requirement teaches basic navigation and interface controls. The teaching happens seamlessly. The next step might be manipulating objects within the environment. One task after another slowly brings the player up to speed so he or she can be fully engaged in the game. But the ramp up elements are not separate and distinct from the game; they are an integral part and provide rewards and feedback immediately, rather than waiting until the player reaches a high level of competence before activities are rewarded or reinforced—activity first, competence second.

Once players have reached competence in the game play, they have reached the expert level. This is the level where they have all the skills they need to competently engage at a high level of game play. They can interact with the content and game environment for long periods of time and achieve success after success. A player can remain at this level for an extended period of time because well-designed games continue to provide fresh activities, content, or challenges to keep the expert players coming back to experience more of the game. At the expert level, players want to gain access to rewards, items, and levels that are not accessible to novice players.

The highest level of player and the level rarely reached is the level of a true master. At the master level, the player has accomplished every task in the game and has a high level of knowledge about the game play, sequence, and mechanics of the game. The masters are a great resource if you can convince them to give back to the community. They are looking for things like status, exclusivity, and special perks to keep them interested in staying with the game.[2]

Bartle's Player Types

There are many ways to look at different types of game players and how they interact within a game environment. One often-cited classification of player types was created by Richard Bartle, a well-known figure in the gaming industry.[3] This classification works best when considering multi-player games that have either text or audio chat capabilities, although some of the characteristics described can be seen as people interact with single player games as well.

In 2010 at the Game Developer's conference, Bartle was the recipient of the first ever Online Game Legend Award, in part because of his pioneering of online games more than forty years ago. Bartle and fellow programmer Roy Trubshaw created the first multi-user dungeon game online in the late 1970s.

A multi-user dungeon game, or MUD as it is commonly called, is a real-time virtual world described entirely in text. MUDs were one of the first virtual environments in which people could interact online. The term "dungeon" was used because these text-based games were an extension of the board games in the genre of Dungeons and Dragons. The characters, rooms where chats took place, topics, and environment were similar to the Dungeons and Dragons games.

While Bartle was the senior administrator for a commercial MUD, a heated debate broke out concerning what people actually wanted from the MUD experience. The online debate comprised of several hundred bulletin-board postings, some of considerable length, describing what the players liked, what they didn't like, why they played, and changes they would like to see to "improve" the game.

The result was that Bartle was able to identify that people mostly liked the same types of things within the game, but opinions were divided into four subgroups. Based on his impromptu analysis, he named and classified the four types into Achiever, Explorer, Socializer, and Killer. Every person tends to exhibit traits from all four types when playing games, but many people tend to lean more heavily toward one of the types. Understanding these types provides insights into the elements that are best included during the gamification of learning and instruction.

Achiever

These players want achievement within the context of the game. They want to be at the top of the leaderboard. They want to know how they can gain status and then show everyone the status they have achieved. They strive to accomplish the goals of the game. Their primary enjoyment is the challenge. These players give themselves game-related goals and vigorously set out to achieve them.

Achievers regard gaining rewards, gathering points, and moving from lower levels to higher levels as their main goal. They tend to only engage in other activities if they can be used to move them toward their goal of achieving victory.

They find exploration necessary only to find new sources of rewards or points. They socialize with others in a large part only to learn about methods others use to gain levels or to earn more points. They engage in aggressive behavior or "killing" of opponents only when they become obstacles to achieving the goal of gaining more rewards, points or levels. The social capital of achievers is that they have accumulated a large number of points and are good at the game. Achievers tend to think and say things like:

- "Sorry, I can't help you. I'm busy right now."
- "Yes, I will help you, but let's negotiate." or "What do I get out of it?"
- "What is the trick to this level?"
- "Only three more levels to go."
- "I've got to get 2,400 gold coins quickly."
- "What do I need to do to get to the next level?"
- "What are the objectives of this level?"
- "Can you tell me the fastest way through this level?"

Explorer

Explorers try to find out as much as they can about the game environment. They want to understand the breadth of the game and learn all the nooks and crannies. These folks are looking for the surprises (Easter eggs) hidden within the game. They enjoy the discovery of learning new things about the game that others don't know.

To explorers, the act of scoring points may be necessary to explore new locations or gain access to new, unexplored levels or mini-games. They will experiment with all types of aspects of the game to see what happens. One time they might be a little more aggressive to gage the results and at other times they may be a little more social. They socialize because it can be a source of new and interesting information and because they can share their knowledge of the environment with others. They really like to discover the parameters of the game and enjoy finding new and interesting elements both purposefully placed into the game and those that are actually bugs or programming errors within the game.

These folks are similar to what Malcolm Gladwell calls "mavens" in his book *The Tipping Point*. These are the information specialists who accumulate knowledge and enjoy sharing it with others. Their social capital is based on knowing the ins and outs of the game. An explorer will say and think things like:

- "I wonder what's over here."
- "If I click on that door, what happens?"
- "If I click on the ceiling, what happens?"
- "Did you know that walking three steps to the north and then one step to the east will teleport you to a strange room?"
- "Ha, you don't know the quickest route to the golden treasure."
- "Let me show you how to get there."
- "I know how to beat the game. Want me to show you?"
- "You don't need to spend your time doing that, instead. . . ."

Socializers

These players are interested in relationships with other players and in organizing players. They enjoy connecting with others through the game environment. To the socializer, the game is merely a backdrop in which they can enjoy the company of others. These are the folks who like to greet new players, establish subgroups within the game, and use the communication tools to speak with others and set up relationships. In a multi-player game, these are the first people to send you a friendship request. These players enjoy empathizing with others, having engaging conversations, and helping other players achieve success.

They explore to see what others are talking about and to learn of new places to socialize or discuss with other game players. They achieve points on occasion to purchase items to adorn their avatar or because others have achieved the same level or number of points. Killing is something they rarely do, but if a friend is unjustly attacked or killed, they will often seek revenge or social justice within the game environment. Their social capital is that they know a lot of people within the game. A socializer will say and think things like:

- "Hello, and welcome."
- "Hi, how are you doing today?"
- "Would you like to meet my friends?"
- "What are you looking for?"
- "Oh, right, Juan knows the answer to that question."
- "Let me introduce you to. . . ."
- "Let me tell you what happened to me today."
- "Where did you get that great hat?"

Killer

In many games, the name represents exactly what this player does. He or she is interested in defeating others by killing them any way possible. The goal is not to win the game but to kill as many other players as possible and cause as much disruption as possible.

But this isn't the only way to look at this player type. It might be best to think of these players as putting themselves into a position to impose themselves on others. In some cases, this can be someone who is overzealous to help a fellow player. They impose their ideas or will on the other player, they are trying to be helpful but are overbearing. One can also look at a killer as someone who engages in player-to-player activities and gages his or her impact on other players as more important than their engagement with the game.

But for the most part, the killer is someone who enjoys the ability to anonymously defeat others and relishes being able to cause frustration to others. They want to conquer and/or destroy. These players will answer a question wrong to see whether it results in mayhem. In multi-player environments such as Second Life, killers are often referred to as "griefers." They want to know what are the craziest or strangest things they can do in the game. Their social capital is that they are very powerful within the game and others fear them. A killer will say and think things like:

- "I am going to kill you."
- "I will destroy that person."
- "Get out of my way."
- "Let's battle."
- "Die."

To place these players into the world of the game, Bartle created a graph indicating where the player types might fit. On the X-axis is a continuum of interaction from interacting with players to interacting with the world of the game. The Y-axis stretches from interacting to acting. Together they form the space of a game. Achievers are interested in acting on the world. Explorers are interested in interacting with the world of the game. Socializers are interested in interacting with players. Killers are interested in acting on other players.

Bartle came up with an easy way to remember the four player types. Think of a deck of cards and consider each suit as one of the player types. Achievers are Diamonds because they're always seeking treasure; Explorers are Spades

Figure 6.1. Player Types and How They Interact.

Image reprinted with permission of the artist, Kristin Bittner.

because they dig around for information; Socializers are Hearts because they empathize with other players; Killers are Clubs because they hit people with them. Figure 6.1 shows the four player types and how they interact within the game world.

Caillois' Patterns of Play

Roger Caillois was a French writer and philosopher who studied different types of play and games as they existed in society. In the late 1950s and early 1960s, he developed a taxonomy for organizing different forms of games. In his book *Man, Play, and Games*, Caillois builds upon and expands Johan Huizinga's work *Homo Ludens*, in which Huizinga attempts to define games within the primary lens of competiveness. The Latin word for "play" is ludus, from which Huizinga derived the title of his book.[4]

In response to Huizinga, Caillois developed a framework for thinking about games expanding well beyond the concept of competitiveness. Caillois proposed a division of four types of games. He purposefully sought terms to identify each type of game that did not carry meaning in the contemporary language. He did not want prior understanding or common usage of a term to interfere with the concept he was trying to convey.

Agôn (Competition)

This is the concept of competition when one person or group of people attempts to defeat another. In Agôn you have winners of the game who have defeated, in some way, an opponent. Caillois identified games like football, billiards, or chess as games of Agôn. He describes the concept in philosophical manner:

> "It is therefore always a question of a rivalry which hinges on a single quality [speed, endurance, strength, memory, skill, ingenuity, etc.] exercised with defined limits and without outside assistance in such a way that the winner appears to be better than the loser in a certain category of exploits . . . the search for equality is so essential to the rivalry that it is re-established by a handicap for players of different skills . . . the point . . . is for each player to have his superiority in a given area. That is why the practice of agôn presupposes sustained attention, appropriate training, assiduous application, and the desire to win."[5]

Alea (Chance)

Caillois borrowed the term Alea from the Latin name for dice as the name to describe games of chance. Alea are games in which the outcome is based on decisions that are independent of the player such as the roll of the dice or the flipping of a coin. In this list he included games like roulette and playing the lottery. He describes alea as:

> "destiny is the sole artisan of victory, and where there is rivalry, what is meant is that the winner has been more favored by fortune than the loser. . . . Here, not only does one refrain from trying to eliminate the injustice of changes, but rather it is the very capriciousness of chance that constitutes the unique appeal of the game. The player

is entirely passive; he does not deploy his resources, skill, muscles, or intelligence. All he need do is await, in hope and trembling, the cast of the die . . . alea negates work, patience, experience and qualifications . . . alea is total disgrace or absolute favor."[6]

Mimicary (Simulation or Role Play)

This is the concept of pretending or make-believe. It is the temporary acceptance of an imaginary universe. In mimicary players assume the role of others or a role they do not currently poses. Caillois identified a child waving his arms pretending to be an airplane or imitating an adult. He also points to the spectacle of theater. The concepts of a MMORPG or a flight simulator are appropriate examples of mimicary. He describes the concept:

> "All play presupposes the temporary acceptance, if not an illusion . . . then at least of a closed, conventional, and, in certain respects, imaginary universe. Play can consist of not only deploying actions or submitting to one's fate in an imaginary milieu, but of becoming an illusory character oneself, and of so behaving . . . he forgets, disguises, or temporarily sheds his personality in order to feign another."[7]

Ilinx (State of Dizziness and Disorder)

This is the pursuit of vertigo and trying to momentarily destroy the stability of perception. In ilinx players purposefully attempt to disorient themselves through movement. He includes activities like children spinning around, mountain climbing, and skiing as games of ilinix. Riding a rollercoaster or skydiving would also fit into this category. He describes ilinix thus:

> "an attempt to momentarily destroy the stability of perception and inflict a kind of voluptuous panic upon an otherwise lucid mind . . . in a parallel fashion, there is vertigo of moral order, a transport that suddenly seizes the individual. This is readily linked to the desire for disorder and destruction, a drive which is normally repressed."[8]

It is important to note that Caillois does not view these game types as mutually exclusive. He points out that games like Dominoes, Backgammon, and most card games combine agôn and alea. And that agôn contains elements of mimicary, especially when spectators view a sporting event. He states that identification with a sports champion constitutes mimicry. The combination of timing of one skier against another in a competition is a combination of ilinix and agôn. It could also be argued that participation in a first-person shooter game is the definition of the "vertigo of moral order" combined with the completion of agôn.

According to Caillois, each of the four types of games exists on a continuum. One side is the sense of spontaneous play. It is the freewheeling activity of an infant laughing at the rattle he or she is holding, a child doing a summersault, or an adult jumping up and down for joy. He named this end of the continuum paidia. Caillois defined it as the spontaneous manifestation of the play instinct.[9]

On the other end of the continuum are structured activities with rules and what Caillois called a "gratuitous difficulty." These are formal contests, highly regulated sporting events, and structured games like Chess, boxing, and roulette. He called this end of the continuum ludus; a disciplined approach with rules, standards, and conventions.

Using both the four types of games and the two ends of the continuum, it is possible to plot certain play and game activities into a grid. Table 6.1 shows the two ends of the continuum and some games and activities that fit under each of the game types. As indicated earlier, often a game type can cross from one to another. For example, a massively multiplayer online role-play game contains elements of agôn. alea, mimicry, and ilinx. Table 6.1

Table 6.1. Relationship Between Degrees of Freedom in Play and Different Game Activities.

	Agôn (Competition)	Alea (Chance)	Mimicry (Simulation)	Ilinx (Vertigo)
Paidia (Freewheeling/ Spontaneous Play)	Two kids racing on the playground	Tossing a coin	Virtual social world	Moving your body wildly to music
Ludus (Standards/ Rules/Procedures)	Football game	State lottery	MMORPG/ simulation/first-person thinker	Dance competition/ first-person shooter

illustrates the relationships between degrees of freedom in play and the different game activities.

When considering the types of games to create to foster learning, a consideration of where you want to place the game on the Paidia-Ludus continuum and which type of game will be the primary focus of player activities will help to frame the design and development of the activity.

Game Interactions

One other way to think about games was proposed by Chris Crawford, who some call the "grand old man" of computer game design. He founded and led the Computer Game Developers' Conference, which became the much respected Game Developers' Conference for many years. He sold his first computer game in 1979 and spent many years working for Atari. He is author of the first edition of *The Art of Computer Game Design* and has published well over a dozen computer games he designed and programmed himself.[10]

His take on game types is that they should be driven by the types of interactions the designer wishes to illicit from players. He indicates that a common mistake among novice game developers is that they think of a new game in terms of the topic they want to include in the game and not the interactions driving engagement.

He gives the example of a young game designer approaching him with the concept of a King Arthur game. Crawford is puzzled because the topic of King Arthur is so broad. The topic can be covered in a serious manner with earnest knights or it can be handled in a lighthearted farcical manner. as was done in "Monty Python and The Holy Grail." The content can focus on Arthur or Sir Lancelot or even Queen Guinevere. With all of the various notions of King Arthur floating about, it doesn't seem to make sense to define the development of a game solely on its content.

Crawford recommends that, when launching a game project, focus on the core of the game, its interaction. Defining the interactions that will occur within and drive the game is the first step in building a successful game. Interactions are a clear way of looking at the type of game you want to create.

Ask yourself whether the game is going to be a matter of quickly identifying enemies or obstacles. Is it going to be about deep strategy, complex logic, human insight, chance, competition, self-expression, or cooperation? How will the interactions of new players be balanced against the interactions undertaken by masters? Can you include activities that appeal to killers and achievers as well as explorers and socializers? Do you want to?

Crawford contends that once these sorts of questions are answered, then you can ask yourself what topic or treatment of the topic best serves these goals. Since interaction is a major driver of game play, then understanding player and game types is critical to the gamification of learning and instruction.

■ ■ ■

Key Takeaways

The key takeaways from this chapter are

- Gamification can be applied cooperatively or competitively or can allow self-expression. Typically, all three elements are included in a quality experience.

- Different types of people have different styles of playing games. What one person enjoys in a game environment is not necessarily what someone else will enjoy.

- Different levels of players need different types of attention. You can't treat a new player the same as an existing player, and master players need special attention to keep them engaged.

- Consider the concepts of agôn. alea, mimicry, and ilinx and how they fit into your design. Also consider how the interplay among these concepts will influence the interactions within the game you create.

- When designing a game, consider the continuum from freewheeling play to heavily structured rules and standards. Determine where on the continuum you want your game to exist.

- Prior to considering the treatment of the content within the game, consider the types of interactions that will drive the game play. Relate the interactions back to player and game types.

7

Applying Gamification to Problem Solving

CHAPTER QUESTIONS

At the end of this chapter, you should be able to answer the following questions:

- What are the parameters for designing a game to teach problem solving?

- What are the differences between internal knowledge structures of experts and the knowledge structures of novices?

- How do you gamify the problem-solving process?

- When is gamification of work processes appropriate?

Introduction

Problem solving occurs when an employee or student is confronted with a previously un-encountered situation and applies prior learning or knowledge to address the problem. The capacity to solve problems depends on prior knowledge. Individuals cannot solve problems if they don't have the requisite factual, conceptual, or procedural knowledge. Additionally, prior experience helps to solve the problem, as does the ability to properly frame the problem. In fact, research indicates that experts and novices frame problems in different manners.

Keep in mind that problem solving in this context does not necessarily mean a difficult or troubling situation. Problem solving can also involve the creation of a business case for a new product, launching a social media advertising campaign, figuring out protein sequencing, or the generation of ideas during a brainstorming session. This could be considered the common notion of true innovation. Problem solving is any activity that involves original thinking to develop a solution, solve a dilemma, or create a product.

The ability to problem solve adds value. There is little competitive advantage for an organization to know factual knowledge about an industry. Everyone in that industry has access to the same set of facts. Even conceptual knowledge is commoditized. In the manufacturing industry the fact that excess inventory costs money is widely known, and lean manufacturing concepts have been commonly known and practiced for decades. Companies considered best in class have tackled those issues, but so have the mediocre companies.

The difference is that the best in class manufacturing organizations continue to innovate, overcome shifts in the market, and find new ways of streamlining processes and procedures. Best in class companies incorporate known customer desires and anticipate future customer needs in the development of new products. These companies solve problems every day and don't just follow rote procedures.

This is true in all industries, from retail to logistics to consulting firms and biotech organizations. Even colleges and universities that want to stay competitive have moved beyond teaching facts, concepts, and procedures. Many innovative institutions of higher education actively encourage student entrepreneurship and innovation. They move out of the classroom and into realistic situations. The skill of effectively solving problems faster than competitors is one of the last sustainable competitive advantages left in a flat world.

But organizations don't solve problems; people solve problems. In the fast-paced global competitive landscape, organizations need knowledgeable people who grok situations and problems. Grok? The term "grok" coined by Robert Heinlein in his novel *Stranger in a Strange Land.* Grok means that a person understands something so thoroughly that he or she has become one with it and even loves it. To grok something means to move from intellectual understanding to intuitive understanding. It is a profound understanding beyond intuition or empathy (although those steps are required along the way). It comes from experience, intuition, and a little bit of wisdom. It can also come from gamification.

To explain how gamification can help with grokking and problem solving, this chapter describes how game elements can be integrated into game-based simulations, virtual worlds, and augmented reality to provide knowledge based on information needed to solve problems as well as building the knowledge base within the person who is solving the problems. This chapter also discusses how integrating game-type mechanics into the design of workflow and everyday objects is critical for engagement with customers and employees.

Differences Between Novices and Experts

In comparing the knowledge structure of experts with the knowledge structure of novices, differences have been observed in both the nature of their knowledge and their problem-solving strategies. For experts, the knowledge structure represents phenomena in the domain in relation to higher-order principles. In other words, experts represent problems at deep structural levels in terms of basic principles within a domain; novices represent problems in terms of surface or superficial characteristics.

For example, in physics, an expert arranges knowledge around higher-order principles like Newton's laws of force, while a novice organizes knowledge around the behavior of individual objects such as inclined planes.[2] A novice learning professional focuses on determining which delivery method is best for instruction, while an expert considers whether or not the situation described by the manager can actually be solved by a formal learning intervention. A novice salesperson focuses on "making the sale"; an expert develops a relationship with the client.

Additionally, in the minds of experts, knowledge is organized in the form of a problem schema that includes procedures for solving relevant problems and content knowledge. This means that, when an expert views a problem, he or she is able to see both the problem set and possible procedures for solving the problem; a novice views domain knowledge and problem-solving knowledge separately.

So when confronted with a problem, the expert applies his or her knowledge problem schema by working forward from the information given to solve the problem. Experts tend to work from the known to the unknown. The expert has solved many similar problems and recalls schemas easily. The novice, on the other hand, tends to work backward. He or she begins with the unknown in the problem and tries to use trial and error or incomplete schemas to solve it.

Another difference is that novices often have inefficient use of short-term and long-term memory because knowledge is not stored in a single bundle or schema but, rather, is spread out in different related but not grouped domain areas. An expert is more efficient in searching his or her memory because large portions of content are "bundled" or "chunked" for easy retrieval.

In a pattern recognition task with Chess, novices and experts are asked to recall the placement of pieces on a board, which is shown to them in a mid-game configuration. A Chess master has access to over 50,000 configurations of Chess pieces on a board and remembers the mid-game position of pieces within the context of one of those configurations (matching the pattern to an existing pattern masters already know).[3]

A novice attempts to memorize and hold in short term memory the position of each individual piece, and eventually this is unsuccessful because of the number of pieces that need to be memorized. In other words, the expert groks the Chess board and pieces; the novice tries to memorize them. As Brett Bixler, lead instructional designer and educational gaming commons evangelist at Penn State University, indicates, experts often take shortcuts in their thought process, where novices proceed step-by-step. It seems that experts have chunked groups of steps together and automatized them.

Finally, novices tend to lack awareness of errors and omissions and the need to continually check solutions and assumptions. Experts use strong self-monitoring skills that include testing and fine-tuning solutions and challenging assumptions.[4]

Turning Novices into Experts

Gamification has been shown to improve the ability of learners to problem solve. The key is to design the game-based learning environment in such a manner that it encourages higher-order thinking skills. Certain elements in the game should exist to encourage problem solving. Not all games can help novices transform into experts; however, games that contain the following components tend to provide a rich environment in which learners can gain knowledge and work toward expertise. The games can be individual one-on-one game-based simulations or can be part of a virtual world learning experience or can occur within a classroom setting.

John W. Rice, a school technology director in Texas, has spent several years researching instructional gaming. His doctoral dissertation focuses on predictors for student success in educational video games. Since 2007, he has chronicled research in the field on his blog at edugamesresearch.com, presented at major conferences on the topic, and written several intriguing papers, including "Assessing Higher Order Thinking in Video Games," which appeared in the *Journal of Technology and Teacher Education*.[5]

In the paper, Rice presents a rubric designed to measure the probability an educational game will convey higher-order thinking skills to players. The tool is called "The Video Game Cognitive Viability Index" and it presents a series of components necessary to help ensure a game is teaching higher level skills.[6] Every component doesn't need to be present to encourage cognitive processing, but the more components present, the higher the probability that the game will encourage higher-order thinking. The components can also be used as a guideline for developing a game that teaches higher-order thinking skills such as problem solving, synthesis of information, and decision making. This list is presented as a guideline for creating a game that teaches higher-order thinking skills.

Some modification to the original list has been undertaken, but the fundamental elements of Rice's design remain. Here is a look at each component.

Assume a Role

To foster higher level skills, the player should assume a role during the game and not just play. Assuming a role means the learner must actively think about his or her actions, decisions, and choices from a perspective other than him- or herself. As Educational Gaming Commons Evangelist Bixler indicates, a player has to have a stake in the outcome for the game to be meaningful.

From a social learning context, allowing the learner to mimic or role play desired behavior influences future behaviors of the learner. A role play provides a framework for the learner to practice what he or she needs to do in a safe and secure environment.

A role play places the learner into a learning situation closely resembling the real-life environment in which the desired behavior will be exhibited. Situating the learner in as realistic a situation as possible increases on-the-job recall, knowledge transfer, and reinforcement of appropriate behaviors. Rice states that "role playing often forces users to engage in analysis, in which they must interpret elements in the game according to the role they are playing; synthesis, in which they must apply concepts to a new setting (the role they are playing within the game's environment); and evaluation, in which they must constantly evaluate whether actions taken within the role they are playing assists them in meeting the goals of the game."[7]

Since role plays can occur in a classroom setting, e-learning modules or in a virtual 3D environment, it is important to consider advantages and disadvantages of each. In a classroom, the instructor can oversee the event and make sure it follows the necessary flow. However, it is sometimes difficult to persuade students to volunteer for a face-to-face role play; and if the students veer off in an unanticipated direction, the instructor needs to step in. The biggest drawback is that the role play typically takes place in an environment dissimilar to the actual environment in which the actions are to be undertaken. Sitting in the front of a classroom is not typically where the desired behavior being learned is going to be exhibited. The classroom context is artificial.

One solution to that problem is to deliver the role play in a pre-scripted, self-paced, branching e-learning module. Using an e-learning module, images of the desired environment can be taken and put into the program, graphics can be designed to look like the location where the behavior is to be exhibited; and the learner can move through the content at his or her own pace. This can be effective for novice learners who are trying to understand the right sequence and general statements to say, but for learners who have intermediate or high-level experience with the content, a branching e-learning role play is unsatisfying. The typical complaint is that the options for answering a role-play question are too limited and the learner would never say any of the choices given. The problem is that the branching is limited. It is only possible to program in a limited number of choices or decisions. Another complaint is that no instructor is available to offer customized assistance.

Using a 3D virtual world can remedy both of those issues. One advantage of a virtual world role play over a pre-programmed role play is that the number of branches is unlimited. In a virtual 3D environment there is an actual person operating the avatar so that any question posed by a learner can be responded to appropriately by an instructor. The presence of the instructor also allows for unanticipated questions. Another advantage is that the learner is immersed into the environment. The space inside the 3D virtual world can look like the space where the skills are to be applied. If uniforms are needed, the avatars can don the appropriate apparel.

Problems with virtual world role plays include the fact that the instructor cannot see body language, which may play a key part in a person-to-person role play. Additionally, the added "layer" of having an avatar may allow the learner to be more bold and aggressive in the virtual environment than he or she might be in the real-life situation.

Regardless of the environment in which the role play takes place, the concept of immersing a learner in a role to mimic a real-life activity in order to learn skills is an effective method of engaging higher-order thinking skills. Properly designed role plays can prove to be invaluable for practicing key interpersonal skills.

In one example, the Department of Public Welfare in a Northeastern state is using a virtual office building to teach caseworkers how to interview potential and existing welfare clients. The role play in the gamified environment, complete with avatars, wall posters, and pencil holders on the virtual desks, provides a realistic environment in which caseworkers can practice their interviewing skills. The caseworks take applications, walk the client to the proper location within the office, and hone their skills of listening to the needs of the clients.

Meaningful Dialogue

To gain something out of the game, the player has to engage in dialogue that is meaningful as part of the game and to the learner. As mentioned in Chapter Six, meaningful interactions are a core part of a game for learning. Rice clarifies this point by stating, "Meaningful interaction is important because it offers additional opportunities for thinking. It is possible to have a complex environment in which users wander about but have little meaningful interaction within the environment."[8] It takes time to write an effective script and to develop the right tone and approach, but the time is worth it.

Whether it is non-player characters (NPC) providing thought-provoking dialogue to learners, a scripted role play in a 3D virtual world, or discussion about key elements of content while playing a game face-to-face in a classroom, the interactions have to be realistic, meaningful, and focused on the learning objectives to be accomplished. Dialogue that seems stiff, superfluous, or forced will break the learner out of the immersiveness of the game play. If the player is interfacing with non-player characters, make sure the non-player characters maintain the pace of the dialogue, initially create the illusion that they are aware of the learner, and then maintain that illusion over the time span of the game. For more information on how this can be done, see pages 207 through 211 in Chapter 7 of my book *Gadgets, Games, and Gizmos for Learning*, which outlines how Jellyvision has created a realistic human/computer dialogue process.[9]

Complex Storyline

Stories, as indicated in Chapter Two, are an important element in games and are critical for fostering higher-order thinking skills. But it is not the outcome of the story where the learning occurs; it is through the process of the story unfolding. As the leaner journeys through the story, the decisions that are made, the objects chosen, and the questions asked or unasked are moments of opportunity for learning. A well-designed story places the learners into a case study they are not passively reading, they are an integral part of the action.

The inclusion of the learner as a character in the story allows him or her to examine, first hand, the variables involved in the situation. Learners don't have to wonder what they would do in a certain situation; they are now forced into the situation and need to make a choice.

The story must be complex enough to address the instructional objectives and rich enough to engage the learner in the process. If the story is interesting enough and the design appropriately interactive, the learner almost forgets that he or she is external to the story and becomes part of the story, which internalizes the learning at a much deeper level than watching, as indicated in the study reported in Chapter Five about how playing the game Darfur Is Dying was more likely to result in a willingness to help the Darfurian people than reading text or watching another play the game. Game playing is a rich experience that ties to emotions and interactivity; the more complex the story, the more learners will become involved.

Of course, the complexity needs to be purposeful and related to what the learner will need to do in the real-life situation. Complexity without purpose will not be effective. But if done well, the complexity of the story will foster increased thinking and cognition. A purposeful story embedded in reality helps learners with their understanding of the underlying factors influencing the outcome of a situation and in developing alternative solutions. Immersing the learners in a well-designed story and having them live the events and actions leads to the learning of higher level skills.

Challenges the Learner

Working hand-in-hand with the complexity of the story is the amount of challenge provided to the learner. Unless a learner is overcoming challenges, no higher level learning will occur. The game must place the learner into a situation in which he or she will be challenged. The challenge can be introduced by the tasks in the game, the other players seeking the same reward, or by machinations of the NPCs. Whatever mechanism or combination of mechanism is used; the player must feel the game is at an appropriate challenge level.

To encourage learners to enter a flow state, the game must be difficult enough to challenge the learner but not so easy or simple that the learner becomes bored, as discussed in Chapter Four. Players improve quickly, and what was challenge fifteen minutes ago is now boring. To reach higher level skills, the game needs to use the concept of scaffolding, also discussed in Chapter Four. The player must be leveled up over time so that he or she is increasingly challenged to use higher level thinking skills.

Immediate Immersion

Immerse the learners in the situation immediately when they enter the game. Traditional instruction does not immerse learners in the environment in which the skills need to be practiced; games provide that opportunity and should be leveraged. Traditionally, how problem solving is taught in a classroom is to list all the elements that need to be learned and then include a case study or role play two-thirds of the way through the instruction. Instead, start with a problem for which the learner is playing a critical role. Then provide guidance and assistance when the learner encounters an obstacle. Create the need for the learner to seek or require the information you want them to acquire from NPCs in the game, from the game environment or from other players if it is multiplayer. This creates motivation and helps with retention.

In a recent consulting project for a large financial organization, I was asked to reconfigure their investigator training program so that it would be more engaging. Several gamification techniques were employed. To start with, the original course was presented in the traditional instructional design fashion. The objectives were presented to the students as they arrived for class, the instructor reviewed the model for conducting an investigation, the learners memorized the parts of the model and, toward the end of the class, the students were presented with two small case studies and then more lecture and a wrap-up slide.

The first step was to flip the class. As soon as the students entered the classroom, they were broken into teams and given a case study, even before the objectives were presented. They had a job to do—determine whether the case was worthy of investigation. (It wasn't) The learners had a chance to explain why they thought it was or was not worthy of investigation and then determine, on their own, what criteria should be used to classify a case as eligible for investigation. The learners received immediate feedback on whether or not they determined the correct criteria.

Next, students were given an initial complaint for another case. The students determined whether or not to investigate. After determining that it meets the criteria for investigation, they proceed with the case. The instructor reveals different facts and information throughout the course of the class as requested by the learners. A story unfolds that becomes increasingly complex as the learners uncover more and more information. During the course of the day, they develop interview questions, conduct role-play interviews, review documents, and determine what charges need to be filed against parties involved in the indiscretions. The entire time, learners are given instant feedback by the instructor on whether or not their assumptions and suggested actions are correct. This gamification doesn't have points or a reward structure, but it does have the elements of story, feedback, levels as the students move from one fact pattern to another, and even emotion as the learners are drawn into the story and attached to their ideas of who is accountable and who is not.

Manipulating Variables

Rice states that "readjusting variables causes users to readjust their understandings, resulting in increased cognitive functions."[10] This is also how learners assimilate new ideas and information. It is also an effective method to show gaps in the learner's understanding. The cause-and-effect nature of variables is a good way to show cause-and-effect relationships within complex systems or within systems where inputs don't result in immediate feedback in reality, like allowing substandard material into a production line and not realizing it until the product fails at the client site.

Encouraging variable manipulation causes the learner to weigh options and make tradeoffs. In the game SimCity, for example, players make decisions based on a fixed budget and must decide how to allocate that budget among different needs within the city, including military, health, manufacturing, education, and leisure. Players must also weigh taxation against the mood of the citizens. Working with multiple variables causes the players to consider cause-and-effect relationships, weigh multiple options, and prioritize efforts. One caution, as pointed out by Bixler, is to constrain the over-manipulation of variables. It is important to constrain players so they do not attempt to randomly manipulate a large set of variables at one time. This is a key problem in some games and simulations.

Lifelike Avatars and Third-Person Perspective

Chapter Three explains why lifelike avatars are important to learning and promoting behavior change. When avatars look like the players, the likelihood of meaningful behavior change increases. When an avatar looks like the learner being represented, research indicates that the player is more likely to exhibit the behavior displayed in the game in the near future.

As discussed in Chapter Four, perspective matters. Viewing yourself performing actions in the third person seems to have a larger impact than viewing yourself in the first person. As Rice indicates, complex three-dimensional environments afford users additional opportunities for cognitive processing. Multiple views and camera pans enhance the interaction opportunities within three-dimensional environments. Additionally, as co-author, Tony O'Driscoll and I explained in our book, *Learning in 3D*, a 3D environment provides a sense of presence, an embodiment of learners, and the chances to realistically encode situations into our memories.[11]

Interaction with Game Environment

As indicated before, meaningful interactions are important, but they just can't be player-to-player or player-to-non-player; interactions also have to take place between the player and the environment. In real life people interact with their environment, and the same affordances need to be available in a game environment to foster higher-order thinking. As Rice points out, games should allow the learner opportunities to "hold," examine, manipulate, and interact with objects in the game.[12]

Just clicking around a screen doesn't require much cognitive activity, but being asked to look for specific items or combine one or more virtual elements to create a third or fourth element requires sequencing and problem-solving skills. The goal is to develop the type of environment that fosters additive learning through the direct manipulations of items within the game. Rice states that "a game requiring users to understand the proper sequence and combination of certain compounds in order to develop powerful weapons or tools . . . even if the interface for the game is simple and intuitive" is the right sort of game to foster higher-order thinking.[13]

Synthesis of Knowledge

Knowledge can be a difficult type of element to incorporate into a game. But synthesis is a higher-order skill that is valued in many situations. The ability to proper synthesize information and make predictions or recommendations or pursue a course of action is a valuable skill. Games that foster synthesis develop higher-order thinking skills.

As indicated in the discussion of novices and experts, the ability of a person to synthesize domain knowledge with problem-solving ability is one of the differences between an expert and a novice. The expert has synthesized domain knowledge and problem-solving knowledge, while the novice has not.

In game design, strive to create tasks, missions, and activities that force the learner to synthesize knowledge from several sources. Research indicates that the structure of knowledge that a person accumulates may have important implications for subsequent problem solving. Therefore, carefully consider what type of higher-order problems you want the person to be able to solve in the future and structure the synthesis requirements around those types of problems.

Authentic Environment

This is a caution against trying to use simplistic games to teach higher-order thinking skills. While simplistic games do have a place in the learning hierarchy for teaching facts, higher-order skills are best taught with games that have large elements of the real world. This becomes especially important when you consider the transferability of learning from the game environment to the actual situation. Strive to create games that closely represent situations the learner will encounter in the real world.

For example, touring a nuclear power plant training facility I had a chance to see the room where operators are trained. It was an exact replica of the actual operations room in the real plant right down to the same ambient sounds. The training that took place in that room mimicked the actions and events that occurred in the live control room. The advantage of the training room was that all types of what-if games could be run and the employees could test their skills in a safe environment.

When visiting a large teaching hospital, I was invited to take part in a simulation involving a patient heart attack. The actions taken by myself and others occurred in a simulated hospital room using the same equipment found in any actual hospital room. When pilots train, they use a flight simulator that acts and reacts just like a real aircraft, complete with hydraulic movements to simulate actual responses of the plane.

When lives are on the line, the learning process is studied, calculated, and formalized to a degree of realism as close to 100 percent as possible. In these life-and-death training situations, the actions of the individuals involved in the training are timed and measured against objective standards. If you don't administer oxygen within the prescribed time frame in the simulation, you know about it as you watch a recorded and timed version of your actions as an instructor provides feedback. The fidelity between the environment in which the performance is required and the environment in which it is trained and practiced is extremely high.

Immediate and instructive feedback loops, established standards, and prescribed activities are all critical to the success of the learner in nuclear power plants and hospitals and while flying planes. The training replicates the real world. Learning and expected behaviors are not left to chance, actions are parsed, best practices studied, conclusions drawn from data and the experience of experts. This is because the difference between a radioactive disaster and successfully generating electricity is authentic practice in a realistic environment.

So if you want a highly trained individual capable of performing his or her job to the highest standard, create a game that takes place in an authentic learning environment. Anything less is not as effective, and the performance will not be guaranteed.

Without realistic environments, if someone does something right, it is most likely by chance. Do we really expect a person to effectively sell product in a retail environment without ever having been in that environment? Do we expect a customer service employee to provide excellent customer service and use the computer system to look up critical information when the training is delivered in a classroom environment nothing like the actual environment in which he or she is asked to perform. We need to make our learning events as authentic as we can possibly make them. The higher the fidelity, the better the performance in the actual situation.

Do we expect college students in an economics class to understand entrepreneurship without ever having run a business? Do we expect managers or leaders to effectively operate in a crisis situation when they've only read about the five steps needed to operate in a crisis? Or discussed it in a chat room?

High-fidelity games and simulations have always made sense in medical, military, and aviation situations. Now they make sense for factories, call centers, retail stores, and other "work" environments because of the relatively low cost of the technology and the ability to create immersive environments.

Replayable with Different Results

Games that are complex and have multiple routes to completion tend to require a great deal of higher-order thinking skills by the players. Decisions need to be made, options considered, and compromises made as they proceed to win the game. A good example of this is the commercial game created by Rockstar Games called Red Dead Redemption. In the game, which takes place in the American West, the player assumes the role of John Marston, a former outlaw trying to live the straight and narrow. He is confronted by some government officials and is sent off on an adventure.

The environment is an open world in which the player can follow the main storyline or choose to go on side adventures and take part in random events as they occur. Players can even engage in an activity such as shooting animals and selling their pelts for money. Players can choose to do good deeds and be known as heroes or to commit crimes and be known as criminals. Based on decisions the player makes for John Marston, the non-player characters in the game react differently. If he is an outlaw, they treat him differently than if he is law-abiding. The ability to choose between "good" and "bad" behaviors, the chance to take part in random and planned side adventures, and the non-sequential order of the game all make for a high level of replayability because the results are highly variable.

Preparing Firefighters

Putting the design principles above into practice results in creating dynamic and engaging learning experiences.

Fighting Fires

Firefighting is a dangerous job, and even practicing firefighting can be dangerous. One way to help make the practicing of firefighting a little less dangerous is to add game elements to a simulation and allow novice firefighters to tackle online fires where no one gets hurts.

This project was created by a company called Designing Digitally, a games and simulation company. The simulation role-playing game walks new firefighters through the REVAS (rescue, exposure, ventilation, attack, and salvage) process while encouraging him or her to employ higher-order thinking skills like problem solving, decision making, and information synthesis.[14]

The player is immediately immersed in the role of the firefighter, and that role is continually reinforced throughout the experience. This occurs in several ways. First, the person is dressed in the uniform of a firefighter, a visible manifestation of the role. Second, the player does actions that firefighters perform, such as responding to a burning house fire, riding on the fire truck to arrive at the home, and finally selecting and using firefighting equipment. Third, the player is spoken to in the language of firefighters; the introduction and the non-player character firefighters use terminology that is familiar and common among firefighters. Fourth, the NPCs treat the player like a firefighter. They expect the player to act and behave as a firefighter. They trust that the player is a competent firefighter and treat him or her accordingly. Figure 7.1 illustrates the concept by showing the fire truck the learner is riding in while responding to the fire call.

The fact that the NPCs treat the player as a firefighter means that the conversations they have, the dialogue they present, and the information they share are all relevant and meaningful. The player must think of how to respond, what the NPCs are saying, and how they need to react. The game includes the ability to communicate with artificial intelligence within the gaming engine that reacts to the decisions players make as they choose the steps required to fight the fire.

Adding to the experience is the fact that player enters into the environment as an avatar and must maneuver in three dimensions. This means players can approach an object from different directions. They must be aware of

---

Figure 7.1. Riding a Fire Truck to Respond to a Call.

the environment on all sides, and they gain a perspective similar to actually being in a burning building. As Figure 7.2 illustrates, the learners must even be careful climbing ladders because they may fall.

Entering a burning build is a complex proposition. There are multiple dangers, and every room is a potential deathtrap. This complexity mirrors the real-life scenario. Throughout the experience, players are required to choose the necessary steps to put out the fire without endangering themselves or the other firefighters involved. The complexity challenges the learners to think quickly and to make the right decisions.

The game is used in conjunction with traditional classroom training methods in a blended approach. The interactive scenario provides new firefighters with a safe and effective way to learn about each step in the process by putting them into dangerous life-like scenarios.

The scenario provides the opportunity to utilize real variables such as current temperature, time of day, and even the location of the realistic burning home. The learner interacts with the computer-generated non-player characters, fellow firefighters and victims in the home. The trainee must work with the virtual players to coordinate activities and make sure everyone is safe and that the fire causes minimal damage. A wrong move

---

Figure 7.2. Climbing the Ladder to Reach the Fire.

and the player's firefighter could be injured or killed, as could fellow fire-fighters or the residents of the home. The learner must determine what steps need to be taken at key points within the experience. The player can replay the scenario multiple times and have different results based on the choices made.

The only element missing from the list of design concepts for teaching higher-order thinking skills is the fact that the player doesn't openly manipulate any variables. However, every game that is created to foster higher-order thinking skills doesn't require every element. It is possible to leave out a few elements and still reach the level where the learner is actually solving problems and making critical decisions.

Gamification of Problem Solving

It is one thing to teach someone how to solve a problem using gamification techniques; it is another to actually have people work on the problem itself. This is where gamification problem-solving projects like the U.S. military's game platform for generating multiple ideas for defeating the Somali pirates, FoldIt, and Phylo come into play, as discussed in Chapter Five. Each of these gamified platforms has several similar components that can be employed when creating large scale gamification problem-solving efforts.

In these cases, instead of turning novices into experts, the idea is to create a gamified constraint system that lets the novices behave as experts. Examining the concepts behind these efforts provides insights into how to create these types of problem-solving games.

Create a Shared Purpose. The stated goal of the problem-solving effort is obvious: well-articulated and serves humankind. The players of these games aren't just killing time; they are contributing to a larger good with examples like fighting real-life pirates, creating potential vaccines, and aligning DNA of the human genome to map diseases. The component is critical to the involvement of the players, and it is compelling. More than 100,000 people have downloaded Foldit. When considering the creation of gamified problem solving, appeal to a larger good.[15] Figure 7.3 depicts the collaborative shared purpose people have when solving large but critical problems.

Figure 7.3. Everyone Is Working on the Problem with a "Shared Purpose."

Image reprinted with permission of the artist, Kristin Bittner.

Celebrate Accomplishments. While appealing to the larger good is compelling, it only gets you so far. You need to establish leaderboards, scoring mechanisms, player profiles, and recognition of outstanding players. Achievers need a way to show off. The Foldit game has contests within the greater context of the game. Different proteins need to be folded and discrete contests are established, so that it is possible to have different winners in different categories. Once a person wins, he or she is celebrated.

Allow Individual and Team Efforts. In the massively multiplayer war game, individuals can choose to work together to rescue hostages, coordinate humanitarian aid, attack pirate ships, and invade pirate camps. Or a person can work individually. Some people want to solve problems as part of a team and some want to work together. In Foldit, you can be an evolver, working with others to fold the protein, or a soloist, working by yourself. Both categories have leaderboards, points, and rewards. This appeals to the socializers and appeals to the relatedness concept from Self-Determination Theory discussed in Chapter Three.

Carefully Consider the Point System. To enable thousands of individuals to work on shared problem solving, the goals need to be clearly defined and the point system well-defined. There can be little ambiguity about the definition of success. This can be emphasized by the rules of the game and how points are awarded. For example, in Phylo, gaps in the sequence you create are highly penalized because a gap in the actual DNA sequence results in less favorable genetic characteristics being aligned. This thought process also involves a careful consideration of how players will interact with the problem. In the war game, interactions will be monitored to make sure things aren't too unrealistic and, therefore, negate the possibility of transferring ideas generated in the game to the actual pirate situation.

Additionally, as discussed in Chapter Four, consider how much emphasis you want to place on extrinsic motivation. Helping to solve a problem of significance is a fairly intrinsically motivated activity. Adding too many extrinsic badges, points, or rewards may undermine your efforts.

Use a Variable Interface. The initial interface to the game should be easy and straightforward. The icons should be labeled, and there should be plenty of screen "real estate" for the player to navigate. But after a short amount of time, after the novice player has been on-boarded to the game, he or she wants to have more options. Perhaps he or she wants to see the dynamically changing leaderboard as he or she goes head to head with a rival or perhaps see a map, the interaction icons, the chat window, and the leaderboard all at the same time. Allow the player to add windows, customize views, and create the problem-solving dashboard to fit his or her playing style and not the preconceived notion of the game developer.

Be Transparent About Shortcomings. Gamifying problem solving is not easy, and issues are bound to arise. Sometimes game play will need to be sacrificed to maintain the integrity of the problem-solving process. Sometimes elements will seem boring to players, and sometimes technical glitches will interfere. When these problems are brought to your attention, be transparent about them. Offer work-arounds or explain why changes cannot be made. Being defensive or dismissive of issues will not be helpful. Let everyone know what is happening.

Create a Community Around the Game. The social aspect of crowdsourced problem solving is attractive to many players. Foster that community. Include bulletin boards within or outside of the game. Recognize players and encourage player-to-player interactions. The more people are drawn to the community and game, the more time and effort will be spent on solving the large problem.

■ ■ ■

Key Takeaways

The key takeaways from this chapter are

- To teach problem solving, design a game where the learner:
  - Assumes a role
  - Partakes in meaningful in-game dialogue
  - Navigates a complex storyline
  - Feels challenged
  - Immediately is immersed in the environment
  - Manipulates variables within the game
  - Assumes a lifelike avatar with a third-person perspective
  - Interacts with the environment of the game
  - Is forced to synthesize knowledge
  - Enters an authentic environment
  - Replays the games with different outcomes
- To create a game that solves a problem:
  - Create a shared purpose
  - Celebrate accomplishments
  - Allow individual and team efforts
  - Carefully consider the point system
  - Use a variable interface
  - Be transparent about shortcomings
  - Create a community around the game

Applying Gamification to Learning Domains

At the end of this chapter, you should be able to answer the following questions:

- What are the differences between facts, concepts, rules, and procedures?
- What gamification techniques and mechanics are appropriate for conveying factual knowledge?
- What gamification techniques and mechanics are appropriate for conveying rules and conceptual knowledge?
- What gamification techniques and mechanics are appropriate for conveying procedural knowledge?

- What gamification techniques and mechanics can be used for reinforcing elements of the affective domain, such as attitudes and beliefs?

- What gamification techniques and mechanics can be used for reinforcing elements of the psychomotor domain, such as movement and hand-eye coordination?

Introduction

Learning to solve problems and using higher order thinking skills are not the only types of instruction that occurs in businesses, schools, colleges, and universities. People need to know facts, concepts, rules, and procedures. These are all different types of knowledge and, therefore, each requires a different type of game design technique to effectively convey that knowledge. One problem organizations run into is trying to teach different types of knowledge using the same techniques. The knowledge that needs to be taught should dictate the design techniques and game mechanics used for gamification. One-size-fits-all doesn't work.

Experts have developed classification schemes for defining knowledge. These schemes help match the design of instructional interventions with the type of knowledge to be taught. Typically, declarative or factual knowledge is deemed to be the first level of the hierarchy because without factual knowledge higher knowledge levels, like problem solving, cannot be obtained. Once facts are learned, then concepts can be understood; when two or more concepts are put together they form a rule, and multiple rules form procedures. The combination of all those types of knowledge is brought to bear when a person is problem solving.

Consequently, gamification techniques need to convey the appropriate level of knowledge. Learners who lack an understanding of the basic concepts needed to perform a procedure cannot be immersed in a gamification event focused on teaching those procedures; they don't have the requisite knowledge. Subsequently, the learner will become frustrated and upset. To avoid this frustration, the right game mechanics and thinking have to be developed at the right content level.

Gamification can contain multiple levels such as a mini-game and other techniques and mechanics to bring a learner from a lower place in the knowledge hierarchy to a higher place. A gamification effort can start teaching basic facts and then progress to concepts and rules.

Additionally, because higher-order learning doesn't always need to be conveyed to learners, it is possible to use simple or casual games or gamification events to convey knowledge. Elaborate 3D games are not the only gamification that can be beneficial to an organization. Simple games help to save both time and money and are easier to develop and, in some cases, more impactful for a particular type of learning than elaborately developed complex learning games. This chapter explores different types of knowledge and provides methods of matching gamification technique to learning requirements.

Declarative Knowledge

Declarative knowledge, also known as verbal knowledge or factual knowledge, is any piece of information that can only be learned through memorization. It is an association between two or more items that are linked through memorization. The fact that ADDIE represents the words analysis, design, development, implementation, and evaluation is declarative knowledge. Facts, jargon, terminology, and acronyms are some of the most common factual knowledge found in organizations. Every field and discipline is filled with declarative knowledge that must be known, in many cases to just understand a conversation between two people practicing in a certain area such as engineering. It is no accident that most instructional lessons begin with vocabulary so everyone knows the basics before proceeding.

Most organizations have numerous acronyms and jargon so declarative knowledge is key, especially for new employees, new product introductions, and new markets. Facts, jargon, and acronyms are important knowledge that must be learned to be successful in any career and within any organization or within any academic discipline. Creating games to help learner acquire this knowledge provides a strong foundation for future learning.

Several types of gamification techniques and mechanics can be used to teach facts. First, it is important to understand some of the methods of teaching facts to understand the appropriate game techniques to use.

Elaboration. This is the process of linking the new information with prior relevant or even irrelevant information, showing the learner the context of the new fact and its relationship to a known knowledge structure. For example, one technique some people use to remember a grocery list is to mentally place the items to be purchased around a familiar room in their house and then they "walk" around the room remembering the items to purchase—a rather involved elaboration technique, but elaboration none-the-less.

Organizing. Organizing involves placing facts into logical groupings. This can be tables, diagrams, lists, models, and even mnemonics. ADDIE is a mnemonic. The term "chunking" or categorizing is often used to convey the idea of organizing.

Association. This term means linking a word to an image or linking a term to its definition. At the image level, show a picture of a defective part and provide the name of the type of defect underneath the part. On the text level, match the word with its definition.

Repetition. Repeating content over and over again is actually a good method to memorize a fact. It is how most people remember their phone number or home address.

Translating these techniques into game mechanics can be beneficial from a motivational perspective and from an instructional strategy perspective for helping learners master the facts. Some game techniques related to facts are the following:

Stories. "Researchers have found that the human brain has a natural affinity for narrative construction. People tend to remember facts more accurately if they encounter them in a story rather than in a list; and they rate legal arguments as more convincing when built into narrative tales rather than on legal precedent."[1] This picks up on the elaboration technique embedding facts into a known context of the learner and is a key element in games as described in Chapter Two. The story element of a game can help to encode the content more richly in the learners' brains and help them recall facts when needed.

One implementation of this is a simple game in which the learner becomes an inspector who identifies potential problems within a manufacturing environment, as shown in Figure 8.1. The game, created by Kaplan-EduNeering, provides a story in which the learner must inspect the work area so that production can proceed. As the learner explores the environment looking for potential problems, he or she learns the names of the equipment and machinery within the environment and learns about potential problem areas. Rather than being handed a list of the machinery and names with no context or images, learners encounter the names within the natural setting in the story.

Sorting. These are games where a learner needs to place content into the right slot or location. At the factual level, the learner doesn't need to be able to understand the different categories or sorting requirements; he or she just needs to identify what goes where. In fact, these kinds of games are good for having multiple levels; once the learner sorts correctly at the factual level, the next step might be to have him or her sort by conceptual relationships instead of by identification.

Matching. These games require the learner to link an image or idea to another image or idea. Any game that requires matching fits into this category. These types

Figure 8.1. Learning Facts Through a Story-Based Interface.

of games can also be used to teach concepts using the same leveling up approach as described above.

As an example, young adults who are learning to drive often do not appropriately identify road hazards and therefore don't exercise the right amount of caution. To help overcome that obstacle, a course was created to teach them to identify various road signs and obstacles. In this mini-game, the learners are asked to match the appropriate items with a work zone. The learner identifies the right items and drags the items onto the work zone linking the visual of the item with the idea of a work zone, as shown in Figure 8.2.

Replayability. When teaching facts, it's a good idea to make the game replayable so that the player repeats it again and again. This doesn't mean the content has to be exactly the same, but having similar content presented over and over

---

Figure 8.2. Drag and Drop of Road Safety Signs for Learning Facts.

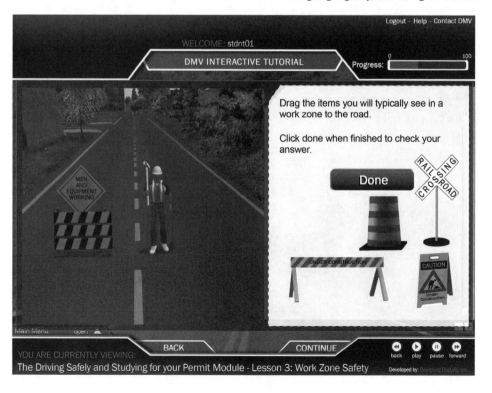

helps with memorization. While almost any game can be played again, the trick with declarative knowledge games is to keep the content fresh but still related to the knowledge that needs to be memorized. When considering the creation of games to teach facts, consider how you can get the learners to play it again and again.

Trivia. Trivia is nothing but facts and declarative knowledge. A trivia game like "Who's Smarter Than a Fifth Grader" doesn't really show how smart a fifth-grader is; instead, the game shows how much useless information (read trivia) is taught in fifth grade. But trivia-type games are not all bad. For repetition, association, and organizing, trivia games work very well (not for proving you are smarter than a fifth grader).

One example is using a trivia game to reinforce product knowledge among salespeople. A trivia game was developed to help salespeople to memorize the features of new product so they could intelligently discuss them with customers. The game was played on a daily basis, and each morning the salespeople would receive an e-mail with a link to the game. The game presented them with five questions related to the product they would be launching in a few weeks. The goal was to take advantage of distributed practice and provide repetition for the learners. The questions were drawn from a pool of questions, so the likelihood of an exact repeat of a question was small.

The scores were tallied each week on a leaderboard that could also be viewed from e-mail. At the end of a five-week period, the salespeople with the highest scores received a prize. An image of the trivia game is shown in Figure 8.3.

Conceptual Knowledge

A concept is a grouping of similar or related ideas, events, or objects that have a common attribute or a set of common attributes. Concepts such as quality, customer service, and organizational security are all important to the effective operations of an organization. Students learn the concepts of free markets and mathematical proofs. Employees must understand the concepts

Figure 8.3. Trivia Game Interface.

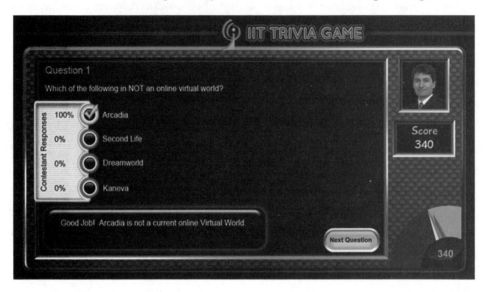

related to the effective operations of the enterprise. Employees in financial organizations must understand the concept of compound interest, while employees in a retail organization must understand the concept of product display. Students must learn the concepts related to their disciplines and understand how those concepts contribute to the fields they are studying. Several types of game techniques and mechanics can be used to teach concepts. First, it is important to understand some of the methods of teaching concepts.

Metaphoric Devices. This technique provides a link between the known elements within the metaphor with the unknown concept to be learned. This can include the use of analogies and comparisons of the familiar with the unfamiliar. The presentation of the content can be in verbal or visual format. For example, you could describe the inventory within an organization as a creek with unknown problems covered by the water and you could show a diagram of a creek with no rocks exposed. As the water in the creek is lowered, the problems are exposed, just as rocks would be exposed as you reduce the level in the creek. You could now show a picture of lower water in the creek with rocks sticking out. This would represent how lowering inventory in an organization exposes problems that can then be addressed.

Provide Examples and Non-Examples. Knowledge of a concept can be attained by providing the learners with several examples of the concept and then providing them with non-examples of the concept. If the concept is "safety," for example, the learner can observe a series of incidents where a worker is acting in a safe manner. Then examples of unsafe behavior can be shown, and learners can be asked to make comparisons. This allows learners to identify safe behaviors and unsafe behaviors.

Attribute Classification. Concepts are defined by their attributes. All concepts have attributes that, when taken together, define the concept. For example, the concept of money is defined by assigned value, the ability to trade it for tangible goods, and the ability to earn it through effort. Concepts also have irrelevant attributes that vary from example to example. An irrelevant attribute might be roundness, color, or even markings. Some money is round, but it can come in many different shapes and colors and even common markings like the portrait of a famous person doesn't always define money. Some money has symbols or artwork instead. Salient attributes define a concept. Categorizing information based on its attributes is a key method of teaching concepts.

Translating the techniques above into game mechanics can be beneficial from a motivational perspective and from an instructional strategy perspective for helping learners master the concepts. Some game techniques related to concepts follow.

Matching and Sorting

As mentioned under factual knowledge, it is possible to create a matching or sorting game that requires learners to think at the conceptual level. This would be when a learner must apply knowledge of the attributes of the concept and either place content into the right location or try to match one concept with another.

An example, first explained in my book *Gadgets, Games and Gizmos for Learning*, provides a good illustration of using a matching/sorting game to teach concepts attributes. The idea is based on the popular children's game "Whack a Mole" or "Bop the Fox." In the physical world, the player tries to hit as many animals as possible with a rubber mallet as they randomly pop up. The animal receiving the hit may change, but the concept is the same: score points by bopping as many animals on the head as possible. This game can be modified for teaching concepts by attaching a trait or concept to each animal as it appears. The learner then identifies the correct information by "bopping" the animal with a mouse click.

For example, in a bop-the-fox game used to teach the attributes of acids and bases for lab technicians, foxes are labeled as "acid" or "base" and the learner clicks on one of the choices based on the attribute provided. Figure 8.4 shows an example where the learner must correctly classify an item as an acid or base depending on a particular trait of either the acid or the base.

This game can be used to classify any type of information or list any attributes or characteristics of a concept. The learner determines the proper categorization by clicking on the correctly labeled object. The game can be programmed to provide either examples or non-examples, and the graphics can be changed to be appropriate for the audience playing the game.

Figure 8.4. Teaching Facts with a Simple Matching Game.

Experiencing the Concept

Another method of teaching concepts is to immerse the learners in the concept and let them experience it. It is possible to place the learners in an unsafe environment and allow them to identify all the attributes that make the environment unsafe; learners could experience the consequences of the unsafe environment by observing what happens to their avatars in the environment, all while safely behind the keyboard.

This immersive process allows the learners to experience a concept first-hand and can be used to provide both examples and non-examples of the concept in action. This could include the concept of an angry customer, the concept of driving under the influence, the concept of situational awareness when sitting in a virtual tank, or the concept of tradeoffs when forced to choose between funding a power plant or funding a local community development project in the game SimCity.

The immersion doesn't have to be 3D. Learners could be involved in a data-driven immersion where they are in the position of having to make decisions based on their understanding of a concept, such as supply and demand or understanding the type of category into which a customer's claim should be placed.

In Chapter One where Emanuel is looking at his inventory stacking up in front of his work station on the lean manufacturing game board is an example of letting a player experience a concept first-hand.

A game that combines examples and non-examples and allows learners to experience a concept is UnitedHealthcare's Appeals and Grievances (A&G) You Bet! The online game was created to help UnitedHealthcare customer care call center professionals appropriately recognize, differentiate, and categorize calls. Calls that may be a customer appeal or grievance can sometimes be related to a life-and-death medical situation, so it is crucial for customer care professionals to easily and quickly identify verbal cues and categorize and resolve the calls appropriately. A screen capture of the game is shown in Figure 8.5.

The learning objectives of the game include the following:

- Recognize typical triggers or verbal cues that should be used to categorize a call.
- Classify a scenario based on triggers/verbal cues.

Figure 8.5. Helping United Healthcare Call Center Professionals Recognize, Differentiate, and Categorize Call Types.

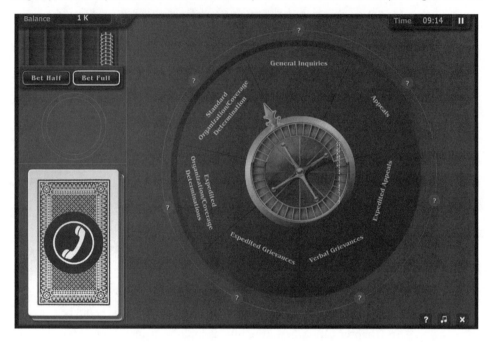

- Identify relevant categories.

- Explain the rationale behind categorizing a particular call.

The game allows the learners to experience randomized call summaries, which include common verbal clues, and then choose which category is most appropriate. These are the same categories they'll use in their desktop systems when processing calls. For a learner, confidence can be built by betting only portions of the available cash or by splitting the bet across categories if the learner is unsure.

More points are gained for a higher, more sure bet; but learners feel safe enough to take a chance. In all cases, each selection is followed by detailed feedback on the correct categorization and the rationale and clues so that next time the learner receives a similar call, he or she is likely to improve. The game may be played multiple times and generates several new scenarios in different sequences, which gives it the feel of a new attempt.

The game was built as part of a larger learning solution, which included team communication huddles, web-based training, instructor-led training, an assessment, and the game. UnitedHealthcare found that by having customer care professionals play the game after training but before the assessment, overall assessment scores improved.

Rules-Based Knowledge

Rules express the relationships between concepts. Rules provide parameters dictating a preferred behavior with predictable results. A common rule of language is "i before e except before c," a rule that provides predictable results. Common representations of rules are "if/then" and cause and effect constructs. If the employee arrives late for work, then his or her pay is docked. If the paperwork is not completed properly, it may cause a delay in filing the claim. One area within organizations that contains a great number of rules is compliance training. There are lots of compliance regulations in every industry, and those rules and regulations need to be followed to keep people safe, to comply with government regulations, and to remain operational as an organization.

Game techniques and mechanics can be used to teach rules. First, it is important to understand some of the methods of teaching rules to understand the appropriate game techniques to use.

Provide Examples

Illustrating the rule in action is a good method of conveying cause-and-effect or if/then relationships. Examples help to clarify the rule and show learners how it is applied. A good idea is to show the rule being applied in several different ways with several different examples. The various examples help learners to generalize the rule and create knowledge structures that help to reinforce the rule in the learners' minds.

Role Play

To teach a rule, have the learners role play situations in which they have to apply the rule. Application helps to convey the if/then or cause-and-effect aspects of the rule. The role play can be with another person or it can be a simulation where learners have to apply the rule to specific situations or pieces of equipment. For example, a learner might turn up the temperature on a piece of equipment, which causes the vibrations to increase illustrating the relationship between temperature and vibrations. Or it might be a rule about completing a proposal for a client and rules for responding to specific client requests.

Translating these techniques into game mechanics can be beneficial from a motivational perspective and from an instructional strategy perspective. Some game techniques related to rules are described next.

Experience Consequences

Allow the learners to practice applying the rules in situation in which they are timed or where points are kept for correct or incorrect analysis of the rules. A game-based simulation allows the learners the opportunity to apply the rules and, if a game is designed for replayability, it is possible to experience applying the rules in different ways and observing the impact. Practicing the application of rules in a virtual game environment that looks authentic situates the learner in the right context for learning and provides visual, audio, and spatial cues for future recall and application of the rule.

An example of this type of game is one designed to teach employees the rules related to sexual harassment. Sexual harassment has if/then implication, that is, if a person says this, then you should do or respond in what way? Or it has a cause/effect implication in that moving too close to someone in an apparent intimate gesture may cause the person to feel uncomfortable.

Games of this sort have multiple perspectives and allow learners to experience the situation from both the "offender" and the "victim" viewpoints. Once the learner is presented with the scenario, he or she is prompted with options that allow them to change the outcome. This gives them multiple chances to play the scenario to observe when the rules are applied properly and when they are not. The learner experiences the consequences of his or her actions, as shown in Figure 8.6.

In the game shown in the figure, the system prompts the learner with questions on how to handle the given situation and what to do when

Figure 8.6. Ethics Instruction Using Game-Based Mechanics.

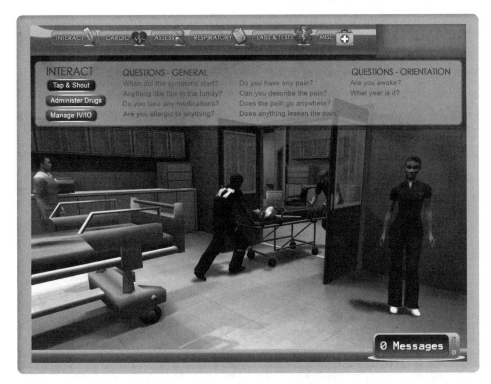

confronted by this person in the future. The game was programmed to track the user's progress, bookmark where the user left off, and track his or her score to ensure the staff at each location was effectively trained on the human resource policies.

Board Games

Online board games are a convient structure for teaching rules. A board game can allow the learner to apply rules through the use of well-crafted multiple-choice questions asking the learner to predict and/or apply rules in certain situations. One approach is to write short scenarios on quesiton cards, have the learner answer the questions, and then, based on the answer, determine how many spaces a learner's piece is eligible to move. The goal here is not to have an absolutely wrong answer but to have shades of gray so that, for 100 percent correct, the player moves four spaces but for an answer that is adquate but not completely correct perhaps the learner only moves two spaces. The design is to teach the learner to really think through the rule and all its applications. The difficulty is in writing the questions eloquently enough to have various feasible but still incorrect options as well as a "most correct" option.

One of the nice things about using a board game as a frame for game play is that most learners understand the basic premise of a board game. They understand the concept of spaces on the board, they know they have to use a spinner or roll some dice to progress; and they realize they need to draw cards for information and instructions. An example is shown in Figure 8.7.

Figure 8.7. Using a Board Game as a Familiar Convention.

Procedural Knowledge

Procedures are step-by-step instructions for performing a particular task. A procedure is a series of steps that must be followed in a particular order to reach a specific outcome. Organizations literally have thousands of procedures that must be learned and followed on a regular basis, from computer procedures to procedures for handling client questions, answering the phone, and even locking up the building for the evening. Learning proper procedures is an integral part of the efficient functioning of an organization. The more quickly and effectively employees can learn procedures, the better run the organization, so it is important to understand some of the methods of teaching procedures to understand the appropriate game techniques to use.

Start with the Big Picture. Provide an overview of the entire procedure. Learners need an understanding of the context in which the procedure is applied and they need to know how all the parts of the procedure work together. Often a flowchart or a diagram is an effective method for providing an overview. A good sequence for teaching procedures is to provide an overview of the procedure for the learner and then allow them to practice each individual part of the procedure. They have them perform the entire procedure from start to finish.

Teach "How" and "Why." Provide the "why" as well as the "how" of the procedure. If you don't provide the "why", learners won't be able to deal with anomalies or changes because they will only have memorized the steps in the procedure and not understand why the steps are being performed. It is important that learners understand the concepts behind the procedure as they learn. Understanding underlying concepts helps with trouble shooting, performing meaningful workarounds and adapting to procedural changes.

Translating these techniques into game mechanics can be beneficial from a motivational perspective and from an instructional strategy perspective for helping learners master procedures. Some game techniques related to procedures are listed below.

Software Challenges

Software programs are nothing but codified procedures; therefore, one of the areas that receives the most attention in terms of teaching procedures is learning how to use software. Software training is typically boring. The learners traverse through the screens and enters the data as required; occasionally the system instructs them on how to fix their mistakes and then the learners continue. Occasionally, these exercises are timed or the learner works through a scenario. But there is another alternative that adds game elements and incentives to work through the procedure.

UnitedHealthcare has developed a game called Data Miner: The Claim Game to teach medical claim examiners the process of reviewing information received on a medical claim in a system in which medical claims are received and dropped into queues when errors are detected. The game, as shown in Figure 8.8, is an interactive web-based experience that takes place in a digital

Figure 8.8. Teaching Call Center Representatives the Process of Entering Claims Data.

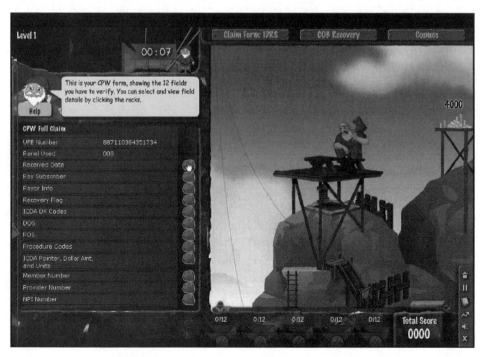

medieval world of miners and jewels. When the learner enters the game, he or she must use the company's data verification process procedures, which are the same as the live systems, to earn mined jewels and points. The better the learners understand and apply the procedure, the more jewels they are able to mine.

Claim and system data are creatively displayed so learners can compare the data and determine whether the system information correctly reflects the claim information. The game randomly generates scenarios within three levels, including a timed option, and the ability to generate a score, which provides hands-on practice with the system without directly impacting live claims. The Claim Game is used in new hire training and also as reinforcement to employees who are experiencing quality concerns.

Another variation of teaching software procedures is to provide an "impossible" challenge for the learners to try to solve. Adding the game element of challenge can inspire learners to work though the challenge to see whether they can solve it. Often, when presenting lessons in a training session, we provide easy and simple procedures so the learners can understand the content easily. However, we rarely challenge the learners with the types of variations and twists and turns they typically encounter on the job.

For example, an order entry clerk might not know what to do if a customer is over his or her credit limit but is challenging a charge. Can the customer place the order? What size order? So create a game out of trying to solve the challenge.

Tell the learners that they have an "ultimate challenge" and, based on all the cunning and knowledge they have learned during the lesson, they need to solve the impossible scenario. By trying to solve the challenge, learners will think through unusual or infrequent applications of the procedure. At the end of the game session, they'll have more confidence because they've dealt with an "impossible" procedure. This method forces learners to move beyond memorization of keystrokes to cognitively processing procedural information.

Practice

Game environments are great for allowing learners to see a procedure demonstrated and then allowing them to practice it with some guidance. Finally, the environment can be used as a testing ground to see whether the learners really understand the environment. This can be done with a virtual bank, where learners have to lock up for the night. Learners must understand the proper steps in the proper order or be penalized. This sort of process can be used with paperwork procedures also. It can even be used when training someone how to use a piece of equipment.

Think like a video game developer and create different levels of instruction so that learners at different levels of proficiency can utilize the instruction. It provides a great progression to move learners from novice state of learning to an expert and, eventually, perhaps even to master. The four levels to consider adding to a procedural game are

- *Demonstration*—the game demonstrates what needs to be done and the learner just observes.

- *Tutorial*—the learner is in control of actions and activities but the game offers helps and suggestions. Many video games have the feature of having the player go through the first level with guidance and assistance from the game itself. This is even better than the demonstration mode because learners are activity involved.

- *Play Mode/Test*—this is the mode with no guidance or assistance from the game. The players move through the environment, making decisions and interacting, and at the end they are assessed on their efforts or they simply progress to the next level.

- *Free Play*—sometimes a learner just wants to explore an environment without having to worry about assessment or being walked through step-by-step. Consider placing a free play mode in the game where there are no formal instructions, assessments, or goals or objectives. The player can just move around the environment and explore.

This process is effective for teaching procedures because it provides an overview of the procedure for the learners and then allows them to break the procedure into the various parts, learn the procedure, and then reassemble the procedure by practicing it in the play mode. It gives the learners complete autonomy to further explore the elements of the procedure without any strings attached.

Soft Skills

Soft skills, sometimes called principles, are non-sequential guidelines for dealing with social interactions. These include negation skills, leadership skills, and selling skills. The idea is that you learn a set of guidelines and apply those guidelines as needed in a situation, but they are not followed in any particular order. For example, you might be in a leadership role, and sometimes in that role you must make quick decisions without asking for consensus, but other times it makes more sense to gather the group together to reach a mutual decision. To truly understand leadership, you need to know when to apply one approach over another. Understanding the methods used to teach soft skills can help frame a game for teaching soft skills.

Analogies. When the guidelines being taught are unfamiliar to the learners, an analogy can help them link the new knowledge with existing knowledge. Analogies provide a framework for applying guidelines.

Role Playing. Immersing people in a leadership or negotiation role helps them to practice the skill and to become better at using the guidelines within the social situation. Translating these techniques into game mechanics can be beneficial from a motivational perspective and from an instructional strategy perspective. One particularly effective game technique that works well for soft skills is social simulation.

Social Simulator/Game. A social simulation immerses the learners in an environment and allows them to practice skills associated with it. The environment can be realistic, as in a flight simulator, or it can be more fantasy-based. An example is World of Warcraft as a social simulator for teaching leadership skills. It is a safe environment in which the skills can be practiced, but the learners still must understand when to apply which leadership skills. Sometimes a leader makes a split-second decision and may need to reach group consensus about how to divide up captured loot.

Affective Domain

The affective domain deals with attitudes, interest, values, beliefs, and emotions. While most of the time we do not think of teaching attitudes, organizations like Habitat for Humanity and the initiative behind the Darfur Is

Dying game mentioned in Chapter Five are trying to change people's attitudes about specific humanitarian issues and helping the less fortunate. Advertisers attempt to change attitudes and feelings about products, and public awareness groups teach attitudes toward smoking, drugs, and unsafe sex.

Researchers who have tested pro-social games have found strong evidence to support the use of games for positively influencing behavior through use of the following techniques.

Encouraging Participation. Research has shown that if a person can be encouraged to perform an important act that is counter to the person's own attitudes, a change in the person's attitude can occur.[2] This was evident in the research on the Darfur Is Dying game, indicating that people who played the game were more willing to help the Darfurian people than others who read about the plight or who watched someone else play the game.

Showing That Success Is Possible. When people think a goal is unobtainable, they are less motivated to work toward that goal. If they know it is possible, they are more willing to work for it. Often, if people are convinced that a goal is achievable they will accomplish the goal.

Celebrity Endorsement. If you don't think people are influenced by celebrities, then you haven't watch Oprah. Companies, politicians, and charitable organizations all recruit celebrities to endorse what they are doing. This is because, like it or not, people's attitudes and behaviors are influence by people perceived as well informed or whom they personally identify with.

Translating these techniques into game mechanics can be beneficial from a motivational perspective and from an instructional strategy perspective for helping learners master procedures. Some game techniques related to procedures are discussed below.

Immersion. Place the learner in a position to help others or make the goal of the game to perform the task that you want the learners to perform. If you want them to help others, provide a game design where helping others is necessary for winning. Immerse the learners in the desired activity within the game. When players are performing a desirable behavior in the affective domain, they are likely to exhibit that behavior outside of the game.

Providing Success. Since part of impacting the affective domain is helping a person realize success is possible, the game should provide the opportunity for the learners to achieve success. If an affective outcome is desired, the game should allow for success more often than not. But don't make it too easy, if it is too easy, the game will be boring and the success will seem contrived. A good idea is to provide multiple paths to success. In Rise of Nations, for example, a player can win by building wonders, capturing territory, through advanced technology or through diplomacy. The player has the option to chose the path to victory.

Provide Encouragement from Celebrity-Type Figures. When you successfully complete a running level in NikePlus, a video of a well-known runner appears and speaks about the accomplishment and encourages you to strive toward the next level. This short celebrity appearance provides motivation. Within a game, when a learner is moving from one level to the next, consider having an executive within the company provide a message, or at a college have a well-known campus personality present a message of encouragement, or go outside of the organization and choose someone to provide a message. If you can obtain a video message from an actual person, consider using a hero within your game structure to provide the encouragement to the player. In-game characters can act as mentors as effectively as a video of a live person.

Psychomotor Domain

The psychomotor domain is the intersection of physical skills—holding a scalpel or clicking a mouse or pushing down on the throttle—and the cognitive space, thinking about how deep to make the cut for this type of surgery, whether to double or single click and how pushing down on the throttle will impact the plane. Many jobs require mastery of the psychomotor domain.

Understanding the following methods used to teach within the psychomotor domain can help you frame a game for influencing the psychomotor domain.

Observe. Observation involves watching someone perform the skill so that you can see what he or she is doing. It provides an overview of the steps. This is important because it give the learners a chance to see the sequence of actions. An example is when the soccer coach says to a new player, "Let me show you how I do it first. Then you try."

Practice. Psychomotor skills cannot be learned without practice. No matter how many times you explain to someone how to double click on a mouse, he won't really understand how to do it until he places his hand on the mouse and attempts to double click. Practice is at the heart of learning any psychomotor skill.

Translating these techniques into game mechanics can be beneficial from both a motivational and an instructional strategy perspective for helping learners master psychomotor skills. Some game techniques related to psychomotor skills are described below.

Demonstration. Game environments can provide the opportunity to demonstrate how a psychomotor procedure is to be done. This could be an opening sequence where a character walks through the demonstration. It could be an automated sequence the learner watches. The advantage of watching the sequence in a game environment is that the learners can then practice that sequence, at least cognitively within the environment itself. Even if the learner can't physically touch the machinery, she can learn where the knobs and buttons are and become familiar with the physical elements of the skill to be learned.

Haptic Devices. A haptic device is a computer-person interface that works through a sense of touch or movement. The Wiimote is an example of a haptic device. As an example, a medical device company has created a haptic device to allow surgeons to practice implanting the device. With computer devices like Xbox Kinect and the Wii controllers, affordable haptic interface devices may allow psychomotor skills to be more easily gamified in the future. For example, surgeons learn to perform surgery by watching a patient on a large screen and manipulating a pen that acts like the scalpel. The pen moves, resists, and gets caught in a manner similar to the actual medical instrument.

In Table 8.1 the domains of learning are listed with key instructional and game techniques for teaching those domains.

Table 8.1. Domains of Learning and Associated Instructional and Gamification Techniques.

Type of Knowledge	Definition	Instructional Strategies	Gamification Elements	Examples
Declarative Knowledge	An association between two or more objects. These are typically facts, jargon, and acronyms. Content must be memorized.	Elaboration, Organizing, Association, Repetition	Stories/Narrative, Sorting, Matching, Replayability	Trivia, Hangman, Drag and Drop
Conceptual Knowledge	A grouping of similar or related ideas, events, or objects that have a common attribute or a set of common attributes.	Metaphoric devices, Examples and non-examples, Attribute classification	Matching and sorting, Experiencing the concept	Wack a Mole, You Bet!
Rules-Based Knowledge	A statement that expresses the relationships between concepts. Rules provide parameters dictating a preferred behavior with predictable results.	Provide examples, Role play	Experience consequences	Board games, Simulated work tasks
Procedural Knowledge	A series of steps that must be followed in a particular order to reach a specific outcome. Step-by-step instructions for performing a task.	Start with the big picture, Teach "how" and "why"	Software challenges, Practice	Data Miner, Software scenarios

(Continued)

Table 8.1. *Cont'd.*

Type of Knowledge	Definition	Instructional Strategies	Gamification Elements	Examples
Soft Skills	Non-sequential guidelines for dealing with social interactions. These include negation skills, leadership skills, and selling skills.	Analogies, Role playing,	Social Simulator	Leadership simulation
Affective Knowledge	Knowledge about attitudes, interest, values, beliefs, and emotions.	Encouraging participation, Believing success is possible, Celebrity endorsement	Immersion, Providing success, Encouragement from celebrity-type figures	Darfur Is Dying
Psychomotor Domain	The intersection of physical skills and the cognitive knowledge.	Observe, Practice	Demonstration, Haptic devices	Virtual Surgery Simulator

■ ■ ■

Key Takeaways

The key takeaways from this chapter are

- To teach declarative knowledge, design a game where the learners:
  - Encounter the facts, jargon ,or terminology within a story.
  - Sort items or information based on identification of the item or information.
  - Match items or information based on identification of the item or information.
  - Are able to replay the game over and over again, encountering the same or highly similar items or information.
  - Play a trivia game against a computerized or human component.

- To teach concept knowledge, design a game where the learners:
  - Must sort and match items or content based on the attributes or traits of those items or content and not purely based on memorization.
  - Experience the concept they are learning about.
  - Experience examples and non-examples of the concept within the framework of the game.
- To teach rule-based knowledge, design a game where the learners:
  - Experience the consequences of not following the rule.
  - Play a board game that outlines and provides the rules that must be learned.
  - Must sort and match items according to rules they are learning.
- To teach procedural knowledge, design a game where the learners:
  - Are presented with a challenge they must overcome in following the procedure.
  - Practice following the procedure under difficult circumstances.
  - Can experience the procedure in various modes such as: demonstration, tutorial, play mode/test, and free play.
- To teach soft skills, design a game where the learners:
  - Practice applying the guidelines in various sequences.
  - Make guideline-related decisions under difficult circumstances.
  - Can experience the impact of applying the guidelines themselves.
- To teach in the affective domain, design a game where the learners:
  - Are immersed in the value, belief, attitude, or behavior you want to influence.
  - Have opportunities to achieve success within the game environment related to the affective elements you want to teach.
  - Hear from celebrities that are outside of the game environment or a celebrity or key player from within the game environment.

- To teach in the psychomotor domain, design a game where the learners:

  - Have opportunities to practice the mental aspects of the psychomotor domain.

  - Have the opportunity to observe a player within the game conducting the psychomotor activity.

  - Are able to use a haptic device to mimic the steps and receive tactical feedback on the activity within the psychomotor domain.

9

Managing the Gamification Design Process

CHAPTER QUESTIONS

At the end of this chapter, you should be able to answer these questions:

- What are the differences between the ADDIE and Scrum models for developing a game?

- What belongs in a gamification document?

- Who should be on the game design team? What role does each person fill?

Introduction

Your boss is playing Angry Birds on her iPhone and it looks simple. It has basic graphics, an easy-to-use, intuitive interface, and she thinks, "Hey, we need to do a simple learning game." She pulls everyone together and tells them she wants to gamify the content for completing an expense report and she'd like the finished game in a few weeks. She puts you and one other person on the job. The last thing she says is "Keep it simple and uncomplicated like Angry Birds; that was a basic game probably done in somebody's garage, and look where it is today."

Your boss is wrong and you are in trouble. You don't have enough people or time to build a game like Angry Birds. What your boss doesn't know is that building even a "simple" game like Angry Birds is not a casual or haphazard undertaking.

To put it in perspective, the Angry Birds development project was a purposeful project created by a game development company with lots of experience. Rovio, a game company located in Finland, had previously published fifty-two other games and created sixteen original games. The success of Angry Birds was not a accident. The twelve-person team spent eight months carefully studying the iPhone application ecosystem and developing the game.[1]

They wanted to make sure they knew what would work and what would not work. As part of the process, they refined the game many times before it was released. It took a great deal of research, engineering, and prototyping to make it a success. It wasn't random that Angry Birds was successful.

The gamification of learning cannot be a random afterthought. It needs to be carefully planned, well designed, and undertaken with a careful balance of game, pedagogy, and simulation.[2] The design process must consider creating extrinsic reward structures that do not negate intrinsic rewards, instructional objectives, and playability.

Based on the research, theory, and practice presented early in this book, this chapter brings together the various elements into one design process, combining the best practices to create the best possible outcome. We'll start by providing a high-level overview of the process and then looking at each step in more detail. This chapter will examine project management structure options, who should be on the design team, how the instruction goal should be developed, developing ideas for the game, prototyping those ideas, the development process, testing the game, and ultimately deploying it within an educational, corporate, or other setting. Finally, we'll discuss evaluation.

Development Process: ADDIE vs. Scrum

There are two prevailing methods for developing gamification efforts. The one most familiar to learning and development professionals is the ADDIE process. This involves a linear, waterfall approach consisting of discrete steps of analysis, design, development, implementation, and evaluation. In reality the process is less linear than it seems. In contrast, a Scrum approach is based on iterations.

ADDIE

ADDIE is a process model for creating instruction based on five individual and semi-discrete steps. The five steps are analysis, design, development, implementation, and evaluation. Occasionally, it will be referred to as the MADDIE model with the inclusion of project management. ADDIE is usually associated with the creation of instructor-led classroom materials or e-learning modules. It is used by many instructional design and e-learning development firms.

In the analysis phase, the type of problem to be solved by the instruction is analyzed to ensure that the problem is indeed a lack of knowledge requiring instruction and not a problem due to another issue like a poorly designed process. Analysis also takes into account the type of content to be learned, determining, for example, whether it is declarative knowledge or problem-solving knowledge. The analysis also looks at the learners to see their prerequisite skills and dispositions, as well as the technology available for the delivery of the learning solution.

Once the analysis is completed, the next step is design. In the design phase, the instructional objectives are written, typically using behaviorally measurable language (that is, "the learner will be able to identify. . . ."). The appropriate instructional strategies are selected, such as using examples and non-examples. Assessment items are created to match the behavioral objectives. One outcome of this process is typically a fairly robust design document with a content outline, details on instructional strategies, a list of embedded and summative assessment items, and storyboards. Usually, a client signs off on the design document so that the developers can begin and not have to worry about any unexpected changes.

The development stage is where the programming and creation of the instruction occurs. This involves adding any necessary links, creating interface items for the instruction, or using a preexisting template. It also involves creating and loading images and sound files that may be used to accompany the instruction. At points throughout this phase, a formative evaluation process takes place whereby the instruction is viewed by learners and stakeholders. If changes need to be made, the process might go back to the design phase or the changes incorporated directly into the development phase.

Once development is completed, the next step is implementation. This is the actually rollout of the instruction to the learners. It usually involves making sure the instruction can run on any required computer systems or that instructors using the materials understand how they are to be utilized.

Evaluation actually runs throughout the module and is divided into two types. With formative evaluation that occurs during the design and development, materials are reviewed, feedback is presented to the team, and changes are made as needed. Summative evaluation occurs at the end when an assessment is made of the utility of the instruction.

Management or project management is sometimes listed as an element of the model. This typically means that a project manger oversee a team of an instructional designer, graphic artist, programmer or developer, and a subject-matter expert who provides input on the content.

Scrum

A scrum is agile development methodology for working with complex, unpredictable projects using an iterative approach. Scrum is usually associated with large scale software development projects and is used by many large massively multiplayer online game development companies to update and maintain their products. Scrum is not an acronym; the word comes from the sport of Rugby, where the ball is handed from one person to another as the entire team moves down the field.

The scrum process starts when a stakeholder, a product owner or developer, is handed a vision or idea for a new product or update. The product owner represents the business or the client as the voice of the customer.

From that vision or idea, a list of requirements is created, known as a product backlog. The list of product backlog items is incomplete due to emergent requirements that will appear during the lifecycle of the project. However, rather than try to define all possible requirements in a design document up-front, as with ADDIE, the process accounts for the emergent requirements by allowing them to enter the project in one of the many iterative cycles called sprints. The product owner is responsible for the prioritization of the product backlog items. He or she decides in what order the items should be addressed based on estimates provided by the scrum team who are going to be working on the product.

The concept is illustrated in Figure 9.1. The teams are cross-functional and there are no official roles, although in an instructional game environment you'll need people who have knowledge in programming, instructional design, artistic development, animation, and even music, which makes it a little harder to have a truly cross-functional team. Most scrum teams are seven individuals, but teams can scale up or down one or two people as needed. The ideal situation is that the team is self-led, but some scrum teams do have project managers.

To start a project, the team meets with the product owner and picks items from the backlog list and places those items on the sprint backlog list. The team only works from the sprint backlog list. The sprint can range from two to five weeks or longer but should be kept short, with one day at the beginning of the sprint for planning and one day at the end for review. The goal of each sprint is to develop finished functionality that can be reviewed by the product owner and outside stakeholders. During the sprint, no changes or modification can be made to the sprint backlog.

Figure 9.1. Imagining an Actual Scrum.

Image reprinted with permission of the artist, Kristin Bittner.

Often upon reviewing the results of the sprint, outside stakeholders or the product owner provide feedback and typically additional emergent requirements, which are then placed on the product backlog and reprioritized. This is the part of the process that allows for changes and modifications; in the next sprint the modifications can be made if they are of a high enough priority. The process allows for software to be developed quickly and changes to be easily incorporated into the process, which improves the quality of the final product, reducing risk and increasing return on investment. One tenet of scrum is to prioritize the product backlog and subsequent sprint backlog according to likely return on investment.

To keep the team focused during the sprints, daily meetings called scrums are planned. Daily scrums bring the entire team together and address three questions from each team member to keep the scrum short and focused. The questions are

- What have I done since the last meeting?

- What do I still need to do?

- What obstacles have I encountered?

To make sure the daily meetings run smoothly, to ensure that the scrum team is not pulled in different directions by others in the organization, and to oversee the entire project, scrum employs a scrum master.

The scrum master is not the team leader; he or she acts as a gatekeeper to make sure the scrum team works without impediment and provides guidance and mentoring throughout the process. The scrum master also helps team members think through problems that might be causing delay or issues. Progress of the entire project is tracked with a tool called a burn down chart, which visually shows how much work is left to do versus how much time remains and usually is posted in a visible place so all team members can view it. Typically, there is a burn down chart for each sprint and a burn down chart for the entire project.

Hybrid

Most gamification efforts in organizations do not involve the amount of work and person power required for large scale MMOs or even for a project like Angry Birds, so the scrum model can sometimes be too much for a smaller scale project. But the ADDIE model doesn't easily allow for the inevitable changes that occur during the design and development of a game. So the size of the gamification project you are undertaking will have direct influence on the complexity, time, and effort spent on design, development, and implementation.

The development effort and process to create a stand-alone downloadable fifteen-minute game to teach a few vocabulary words is one thing, while the effort to create a web-based multi-player role-play game to teach leadership skills across fourteen different countries is something altogether different.

The process described below is a hybrid of the two models and will, most likely, require modification according to project size, scope, and level of complexity. The goal here was to present a gamification creation process that has been used successfully to create a game for learning. You will most likely need to make some changes based on your project, but the basic elements are described.

The first step in the development process is to determine what you want the outcome of the learning to be. Is it an affective change or a behavioral change? Will productivity improve? What will be different as the result of a successfully developed game-based intervention? These questions need to be answered so that impactful outcomes can be developed. This is akin to the analysis phase of the ADDIE model.

Once you have answered those questions, determine the type of content that will be taught. Often content will cover many different learning domains, from conceptual learning to problem solving. Identify the types of content and the domains. Also identify learning objectives related to each type of content. This will help you to identify what types of game structures and elements are required. At this step also determine whether the motivation of most of the learners is intrinsic or extrinsic, as that will have an impact on how you create the rewards and points system.

Then get a group together and brainstorm ideas with subject-matter experts, programming team members, artists, game designers, and instructional designers. The brainstorming process should result in the right amount of content and process knowledge being integrated into the game along with flow of the prototype, the "teachable" moments in the game, and an understanding of what is technically possible from a programming perspective. This step includes developing a rough storyline for the game and considering any point or reward systems. It also includes identifying in-game activities that most effectively teach the identified educational standards using a framework like the one in Table 9.1.

One result of the brainstorming process and alignment of concepts to be taught with game activities is the creation of a gamification design document outlining the design of the game, assumptions upon which the game is based, and the specific activities that will be used to convey the content. This is not a two-hundred-page specifications document; it is a high-level piece to give everyone a general understanding of the game that is to be developed. Think of this as the product backlog items from the scrum process.

Table 9.1. Linking In-Game Activities to Assessment of Learning.

Concept to Be Taught	In-Game Activity	Assessment of Learning
Negotiation skills related to obtaining the best price in the shortest time for a given product.	Bartering and purchasing supplies. (For example, in a space game, jetpacks might be rare but extremely helpful within the game but expensive and hard to obtain, while oxygen tanks might be abundant and easy to obtain.)	Learners will be required to purchase a jetpack and oxygen tank within "the right price range" based on the scarcity of the item. Learners will be assessed based on starting bid, subsequent bids, and amount of time to acquire object.

At this point, for your first sprint, it is a good idea to create a paper mockup of the game and play it. The mockup doesn't need to be elaborate; it just needs to convey the concepts of the game as accurately as possible. If the paper mockup is boring or not fun to play, any electronic version is not going to fun. With easy-to-use software for prototyping, this step is really tempting to skip. Don't skip it. There is nothing as telling as trying to play a paper-based version of an instructional game. The insights gained into the design and instructional assumptions will be invaluable and will provide great formative feedback.

In parallel, as another sprint, have an artist and an instructional game designer create storyboards and concept art. The storyboards, including the concept art, will demonstrate the flow and interactions of all the game play of the prototype. The goal is to place the entire sequence of activities in the game on paper. The storyboarding is so the team can easily explain the process to others who may not be able to visualize the game without artistic renderings.

Typically, the gamification design document is helpful for the development team to keep track of the game concepts and ideas, but people not directly involved with a gamification project cannot really understand what will happen or be able to provide appropriate feedback until they see the storyboards and the concept art. Then their feedback is more insightful and helpful to the team.

The completed storyboards and concept art should be tested by showing it to focus groups who can provide feedback on the storyboards and answer a series of questions the design team provides. If focused questions are not provided, the feedback may be scattered and not as helpful as it could be. The questions should be related to impression of the gamification project, how closely it matches instructional objectives, how trainers or teachers envision using the game, and the anticipated obstacles to using the game.

Once feedback is obtained, it should be incorporated into the necessary documents and storyboards to track the requirements. From this point, start a development sprint. Get the team together and create the first level of in-game functionality. Then have a meeting with stakeholders to see the results, and then conduct another sprint. Daily scrum meetings are important throughout the process of game development. After each sprint, have a play-test to see how the new features work out from both a playability perspective and an educational perspective.

When a gamification project if finally completed, release it through an implementation step and then gather summative feedback. Following these steps will lead to positive results for your gamification effort.

Team

The following team members typically are involved with a project for the gamification of learning and instruction. Not all of these individuals will be involved every time. It depends on the size and scope of the project. However, a project manager, instructional game designer, artist, at least one subject-matter expert, and a programmer or two are almost always involved. And it's a good idea to have a representative from the learner population on the team as well. Most instructional games only have this core team. If using a scrum approach, you will also have a product owner representing the key stakeholder, the scrum master who coaches the team along, and the project team itself.

Project Manager

The project manger is responsible for coordinating the activities of the other members of the group. This is a critical role. Again, on some teams a project manager is replaced by the scrum master and a product owner is involved in the process as well. Regardless of the configuration, someone needs to lead the project and all the interconnected and dependant activities. Someone on the team must ensure that the different individuals on the team are speaking the same language and working toward the same instructional goals.

Instructional Game Designer

Right now there are not too many of these people in existence. More likely, you'll need to hire an instructional designer, but look for one who plays games. An instructional designer is responsible for developing the instructional framework and the pedagogy to make the learning effective within the game. This is the person who is responsible for thinking through the entire learning experience and linking instructional objectives with game play. As mentioned previously, this person is often missing from instructional game development teams. Over time, as more instructional designers gain experience creating games, more instructional game designers will exist. For now, look for someone who likes to play games.

Subject-Matter Expert

This is the person who knows the subject matter to be learned within the game. This person has to supply the content knowledge and information necessary for the learning to occur. However, many subject-matter experts are not familiar with games and want to present in a linear method and add all kinds of conventional "checks" just in case. Try to find a subject-matter expert who really understands games.

Artist

This is the person responsible for creating the look and feel of the game. Artists create the characters, the setting, and the screen interfaces. This might be more than one person, depending on the complexity of the project. Sometimes there is a lead artist and then a shader who either works on the lighting in 3D renderings or who "colors" images and maintains style of art throughout project. Sometimes there is separate concept artist, who creates the drawings up-front but is not involved later. The point is that aesthetics are important in a gamification project and an artist must be part of the team.

Programmer

This person is responsible for writing code that makes the game function as desired. This can be one person or may involve an entire group. More typically, it is one or two people who are creating a way to keep the score and pass it to a learning management system, and performing other types of programming tasks.

Information Technology Representative

When implementing game-based instruction, a representative from the information technology department must be included to ensure it will run on the organization's computer infrastructure. This person knows the technical requirements necessary to run a robust and effective game.

Representative of Learner Population

One often overlooked team member is someone who represents the typical learner, someone from the target population who can help to inform the team of the mindset of the learners. This person can help make suggestions and contribute ideas that will shape the gamification experience and make it more comfortable for the learners.

Music/Sound Technician

This person is responsible for how the game sounds, from special sounds to any music or sound effects. Sounds and music play a key role in games. Sounds can provide feedback, set the tone of an environment, and even help the learner know what to do next.

Animator

If the game involves a great deal of character animation, an animator is needed to create character walks, animate jumping sequences, and any other type of animation you desire within the game.

Level Designer

This is the person who creates the challenges and sets parameters for the game play on each level. Smaller games do not involve level designers, and typically instructional games do not have the budget for multiple, complex levels.

Design Document

No two gamification design documents are exactly alike; there are many variations to the basic document. No universal guidelines exist for the perfect game document; in fact, some people don't even think a game document is necessary. However, some type of documentation within an organization is helpful to guide the design team to success.

As a starting point, a gamification design document can help establish the foundation for development. The document is a place to collect thoughts, ideas, and approaches to creating the game. It is not meant to be an exact step-by-step roadmap. No matter how much thought, and information goes into the game design document, there will always be changes. It is a living document and should be treated as such.

Here is the outline of a gamification design document that you might want to consider using.

Overview of Concept

In this section of the document provide information about your overall concept and what you are trying to accomplish. Describe the goal and intended audience, and provide a high-level overview of the game theme and what type of game you are designing.

Academic Concept Example

The concept is to create a multi-player online game for middle school students that provides engaging, relevant, and personalized learning while reinforcing educational standards in an interdisciplinary environment. Topics covered in the game are tied to the Pennsylvania academic standards in mathematics and English. The game is a time-traveling game where the learners will travel back in time and try to work out mathematical formula and craft great works of literature before they actually happen in a first-person thinker-type game. The more the player can solve before the NPCs, the more rewards will be provided.

Corporate Concept Example

The concept is to create a web-based single-player online game for pharmaceutical sales representatives that provides engaging, relevant, and personalized learning on the topic of opening and closing a conversation with a physician. Topics covered in the game are tied to our ABC engagement model. The game is set in a realistic setting, a physician's office. The game will happen from a third-person perspective and the learners will be evaluated on credibility, affability, and the ability to become an information source for the physician.

Outcome

What do you want to have happen as the result of the game. This is not specific, like an objective, but a general goal you have for the learners after they have played the game. Ask yourself: "If this instructional gamification project is successful, what will a learner who successfully completed it be able to do? What will be different because he or she has played the game."

Academic Outcome Example

Students will be able to correctly answer questions pertaining to English and mathematical standards and will perform well on standardized tests assessing those standards.

Corporate Outcome Example

Pharmaceutical sales representatives will properly use the ABC model to gain more time with the physician and become valuable resources to the physician.

Instructional Objectives

The instructional objective needs to be up-front because you are creating games for learning and instruction; be sure your objectives are front and center. Most good instructional design books tell you to place the objectives in a behavioral format to ensure measurement, but writing measurable objectives for higher-order thinking skills can be difficult for a game environment. However, it is a critical step to ensure that learners are actually learning within the context of the game. One way to address the issue is to have learners make a decision based on a higher-order skill like synthesizing information or making a prediction on the outcome of an event. Another is to include objectives for which the learner has to apply the knowledge.

If you are including any affective domain objectives within the game, this is the place to include them as well. For example, in the game for middle school students, the affective domain goal is aimed at helping kids to learn to positively respond to requests for help. The game designers will have to consider how that can be accomplished through the game story, mechanics, and reward structure.

This section should also contain information about how you plan to measure the outcomes of the objectives. The goal of an instructional game is to help the learners acquire new knowledge, so you need a method to assess whether or not new knowledge has been obtained.

Academic Instructional Objectives Example

At the end of the game, the learners will be able to:

Math

- Describe how a change in the value of one variable in a formula that utilizes linear variables affects the value of the measurement.
- Predict how a change in the value of one variable in a formula affects other variables.

(Continued)

English

- Analyze the ways in which a text's organizational structure supports or confounds its meaning or purpose.
- Apply knowledge of genre styles to correctly identify the genre from a one-page passage.

Affective

- Positively respond to requests for help.

Corporate Instructional Objectives Example

At the end of the game, the learners will be able to:

- Properly apply the three steps of an ABC opening.
- Properly apply the two steps of the ABC closing.
- Appropriately prepare for a call on a physician.

Affective

- Behave in a warm, friendly, professional manner toward the physician.

Description of Character or Characters

Not all games have an underlying story, so for some game designs you may not need to consider characters at all. However, in a game that does involve characters, you are going to want to give some thought to each character. You might want to consider questions such as: Are the characters customizable? Do the characters accurately reflect the diversity of our organization? What do the characters represent within the game? and How do the characters interact with the player or players?

Academic Character Description Example

The students will be able to choose a basic character type and then customize the eyes, skin, hair, and clothing in terms of color. The characters the students interact with represent diversity around the world. In the multi-player game students will interact with each other and NPCs who provide instructions and problems; students will need to partner on some tasks to achieve the desired goals.

Corporate Character Description Example

The learners will be able to customize an avatar in terms of eyes, skin, and hair and be able to select different styles of clothing. The learners will interact with six NPCs, three female and three male, each representing ethnic and personality diversity. The NPC physicians will each have different amounts of time they are able to spend with the sales representative.

Description of the Game Environment

This section describes the environment in which the game takes place. It provides an overview description and a listing of the key locations within the game. The artist can use this to create concept art. It also helps the team think through the type of environment that needs to be created to support the activities within the game.

Academic Game Environment Description Example

There will be four locations. The first will be the main headquarters, which will look a little like a situation room with large monitors and screens and people sitting in rows observing the monitors with smaller computer screens in front of them. There will be a transporter room to the right, which will be used for moving the students from one time period to the next. There will be three time periods in which they interact. One is the Old West in the United States in the 1800s, one is London in 1960s, and the third is in the future, 2055.

Old West—Typical Western town, two rows of buildings with a dirt road in between. Places to tie horses, dusty with a slight wind.

London 1960s . . .

Corporate Game Environment Description Example

Home office for the learner and then six different offices. Learner will walk their characters to a car that has a map on the passenger's seat. The map has images, each representing a different physician's office location. The learner will click on the map to arrive at the front door of that location. Six physician offices need to be created.

Office one: Rural small family practice. Older filing cabinets, small waiting room space with six chairs.

Office two:. . . .

Description of the Game Play

In this section, describe the play of the game. What happens in the game? This can be done in a series of vignettes describing first how a person enters the game, then what he or she does when in the game and what interactions he or she will have within the game. This can be a lengthy description if it is a large game. This is the description of the flow of the game outlining how the players are on-boarded into the game, how they perform actions in the game, and what the anticipated outcomes of the game are.

Academic Game Play Example

Upon typing in a pre-assigned username and password, students enter into headquarters and are met by an NPC who asks them to step over to the customizer space so they can customize the look of the avatar for time travel. The first activity will be for the students to customize their characters. Once that occurs, the students will be directed over to the mission director, who will provide the students with information about a randomly chosen mission occurring in the future, Old West, or London. The characters will be given folders, which go into their inventory, which can be viewed at any time. Next. . . .

Corporate Game Play Example

Upon entering into the learning management system and launching the game, the learner is placed into an office where customization can occur. After the learner customizes an avatar, he or she hears an audio of a phone ringing. The learner must click on the phone to answer it. At that time, the voice provides instructions on how to navigate through the game. At the end of the call, instructions are given as to the next step. When the call is over, the learner must click on the computer to view a list of physicians. Each image and name is clickable to receive more information. The learner must then prioritize the list to decide in what order to visit the physicians. Next. . . .

Reward Structure

Determining how to reward the player is a critical task. Do you want to create rewards (points, currency, badges) for completion of activities or for performance. Chapter Ten, written by game researcher Lucas Blair, describes the many considerations and best practices for creating reward structures within the game. Careful consideration needs to be given to ensure that the reward system does not undermine the learners' intrinsic motivation to participate within the game.

Academic Reward Structure Example

The reward structure will consist of both badges for achievements and currency that the students can spend on purchasing upgrades for their avatar characters. The idea is to use measurement achievements instead of completion achievements to increase intrinsic motivation through feedback.

Corporate Reward Structure Example

The points in this game will be based on three variables: credibility, affability, and the ability to become an information source for the physician. Each will be

(Continued)

scored separately and then an overall score will be provided (the "engagement score"). Within the game, a focus will be on mastery of the goal. This means each learner works to master the content in the game and his or her overall score is not related to any other learner's scores. Feedback will be provided immediately with an unobtrusive pop-up accompanied by a longer explanation available after play.

Look and Feel of the Game

This section of the game design document describes the aesthetics of the game. Does the game rely on high-fidelity, photo-realistic environmental settings and characters, or are they a little more comic or cartoon-like? What color palette will be used for the game? How "clean" is the interface? What does the heads-up display (HUD) look like? Is a map of the environment available? Is there a player inventory and how is it accessed? How many things do you want to display at once to the player? These elements influence the learners' experiences with the game.

Audio considerations should also be documented in this section. Is there any music that accompanies the game? What sound effects are needed? Do NPCs talk? Do players talk to one another? Careful use of audio can enhance the game play experience. Poor audio becomes highly distracting.

Academic Look and Feel Example

A stylized approach will be used for the characters, with minimal details. The environment will be bright primary colors and provide a somewhat crowded aspect within the game. No music will be used, but students will be able to communicate with each other through voice over IP protocol if that is enabled by the school; otherwise, they can use text chats. The interface will be divided into quadrants. In the first will be the map of the immediate area. The map will be a light brown with darker circles indicating positions of key elements. Next. . . .

Corporate Look and Feel Example

The goal is to provide a realistic-looking avatar in three dimensions. The player will be able to see both the front and back of the avatar through a spinning function. The environment will contain 3D objects that are typical colors: black phone, gray computer terminal, brown briefcase. The heads-up display will contain six elements. The first is. . . .

Technical Description

This section describes the technical aspects of the game. Will the game require the player to download software to play or will it be entirely web-based? Does the software reside on a server or is it distributed via portable technology like a jump drive? What types of software will be required to create the game: 3D modeling software, game development software, server-side software? Any potential compatibility issues? Does the game need to interface with an LMS? These are the types of considerations that should be documented in the technical description of the document.

Academic Technical Description Example

The game will be distributed via the web and housed on a server outside of the school. The students will access the game via Internet Explorer with a plug-in specific to the game software. The graphics programs required to create the textures for the game include. . . .

Corporate Technical Description Example

This game will be developed using Caspian's ThinkingWorlds software to provide the 3D environment required. The game will be accessed via the corporate

(Continued)

intranet and will not require any client downloads. The results need to flow into our learning management system when the player completes the game in a compatible format. Additionally, . . .

Project Timeline

This is the projected development schedule for the project, providing start dates, end dates, and dates for key milestones. It provides an estimate of how long each phase of the project will take. It is used for planning purposes and to allocate resources as necessary.

Tips for Managing the Gamification Process

Eric Milks

As the senior game designer for the creation of an educational game to teach middle school students engineering and math concepts, I recommend that you keep a number of design lessons in mind. Here are a few:

- It's best to choose your gaming development platform *after* you design. We did the opposite. We changed software more than four times. Sure, there are limitations to any development software, but that should not distract you from designing. Design first and foremost. After your ideas are formulated, then find software that will bring your ideas to life. Technology should not dictate pedagogy. You may need to alter some gaming activities to match particular software limitations, but if you have a solid concept/activity in mind, that alteration will be easier. It would be wise to understand basic gaming engine limitations before serious designing, but don't just choose a title and say you're going to design for that. There are many software engines/titles out there now. Place the education out front. As I said, this will make it easier later if you do need to alter something. All members will have a clear idea of how to alter it without having to start the concept or activity from scratch.

- You can never have too much communication in the design team. Whether your team is local or like us, in different states, communication is king. It could be to suggest an idea or find a flaw. The more everyone is up to speed the better.

- Create a decision model or standard to follow. Then stick to it. For example, tell your team they all have five business days to respond to a new concept. If they don't get back within five days with concerns or approval, the standard is to either move forward with the new concept or put it to bed. Make standards and then abide to them. Nothing hurts the team or deadline worse than everyone waiting on a particular person's response or approval.

- Sign off on items or milestones. Too much time between approvals and signoffs can lead to more changes.

- It is always difficult when balancing "fun" with pedagogy. There is time and manpower allotted for all things fun. You are tasked to find a happy middle ground, keep the players interested yet educate them. We were tasked to teach math and science concepts. It's best to know your limitations (money, time, and resources) but also know your players' expectations.

- When working with an array of age groups on a design team, expectations and basic gaming knowledge could greatly differ. Our team consisted of individuals ranging in age from twenty-one to sixty. Some were ritual Xbox 360 players; others may have watched their sons or daughters play World of Warcraft; still others thought avatars were blue aliens on the planet Pandora. It took some time away from design to get all member acclimated with gaming and game play. It would help if, in early sessions, team members collaboratively play games and discuss game play and concepts.

Eric Milks was a former instructional game designer for the Institute for Interactive Technologies at Bloomsburg University in Bloomsburg, Pennsylvania. Currently, he is the plant training manager for Kellogg Company in Muncy, Pennsylvania.

Paper Prototyping

Games are tricky. What might seem fun and engaging to one person might be boring and condescending to another. A great game concept may turn out to be horrible when it's executed. Games can only be truly assessed for playability, engagement, and learning when they are played. The game play may have unexpected instructional or motivation consequences; it may be too easy or it may confuse the learner.

Unfortunately, building a game and then finding out that it's not engaging or instructional is too expensive of an endeavor. The cost/benefit ratio is too high. The game needs to be effective once it's deployed. The answer is to create a paper-based version of the game first and use that to test the rules, reward structure, and playability.

The process is not difficult. First, design the game and then get an artist to draw any of the key images that are required. Write down the rules so everyone knows how to play. Then create a paper-based game board; if you want to get fancy take it to an office supply store and have the board laminated. If the game takes place in several different environments like the academic game described above, have each environment laminated. If the game requires it, gather up some game pieces and get started. The game pieces can be anything that you want; even action figures can work.

Next, play the game and keep track of the players' impressions of the game, difficulties or problems with scoring, and how rules of the game are working. Often inconsistencies in scoring will arise, difficulties with what to do in certain situations will occur, and complications with piece movement will be encountered. The paper-based prototype is the place to find those problems and work them out before programming the game. The little bit of time it takes to create the paper-based prototype will pay dividends in terms of shortening the development cycle and improving the quality. In some case, the paper-based prototype proved so effective and engaging that the programmed version wasn't even created.

■ ■ ■

Key Takeaways

The key takeaways from this chapter are

- Creating an effective and engaging gamification project takes time, careful planning, and a great deal of thought.

- A hybrid method between following the ADDIE model and using a scrum model for game design is most effective for learning games.

- A game design document can provide a solid foundation to collect thoughts and keep the design and development team on track.

- The core game design team typically consists of a project manager, instructional game designer, artist, at least one subject-matter expert, and a programmer or two.

- Create a paper prototype before programming the gamification product. The process will help avoid inevitable problems moving the concept to actual game play.

10

Congratulations! Selecting the Right In-Game Achievements

Lucas Blair

CHAPTER QUESTIONS

At the end of this chapter, you should be able to answer these questions:

- What is an in-game achievement?
- What are the different types of in-game achievements?
- Which in-game achievement is appropriate in which situation?

Introduction

Achievements are a hot topic in the gaming industry. Player feelings toward them range from obsession to indifference and designers seem equally torn over their use. Controversial or not, achievements appear to be here to stay, so designers need to learn to utilize them to their fullest potential. Achievements, if they are intended to have a positive effect on players, must be a forethought and not an afterthought during the game design process. In most cases they are carelessly tacked on to a game after it is already close to completion. Unfortunately, the benefits of a carefully crafted game can be undermined when a poorly designed achievement is attached to it. Alternatively, if achievements are designed in the same manner as other aspects of games, they can be used to improve the player's experience and the quality of a game.

There is an established body of scientific study covering a wide range of topics which should guide the design of achievements. However, before we can apply the lessons learned from scientific studies, we must deconstruct how achievements are currently used in games and create a taxonomy of design features. The goal of this exercise is to distill mechanisms of action out of achievement designs, which have been shown by research to affect performance, motivation, and attitudes.

Measurement vs. Completion Achievements

The first branch in the taxonomy contrasts measurement and completion achievements, which describe two distinct conditions under which we reward players for their actions. Measurement achievements are given to players for completing a task to a certain degree. Their performance can be measured against other players' performance, their own performance, or some standard set by game designers. An example of this would be the star rating used in Angry Birds, which gives the player a number of stars based on how well they beat the level. A measurement achievement can be likened to feedback because it is evaluative in nature. The literature regarding the use of feedback in training and education indicates that feedback is beneficial to players because it allows them to reflect on their performance in relation to goals they have set for themselves.[1] This reflection increases the players' perception of competence, which in turn increases their intrinsic motivation; a term used to describe a task one finds inherently rewarding.[2] That increase in perceived competence could also mediate the negative effects of other design decisions, like overusing rewards, which decrease intrinsic motivation.

On the other hand, completion achievements do not tell the players how well they've performed the task; instead they are offered as an award once a task is completed. Completion achievements can be split into two subcategories: performance contingent achievements and non-performance contingent achievements. Performance contingent achievements require skill to complete, while non-performance contingent achievements are awarded for simply being present.

Performance contingent completion achievements, like those received for finishing a dungeon for the first time in World of Warcraft, can be better understood by reviewing what we know about the use of rewards as an extrinsic motivator. Some incentive programs have been shown to have a significant positive effect on task performance. However, these types of rewards can decrease a player's sense of autonomy, especially when given in excess.[3] This decreased sense of autonomy leads to lower intrinsic motivation. Rewards also create an artificial ceiling for performance at the reward threshold.[4] Once players have earned the reward, they are unlikely to continue on with the task that they were persuaded to do. For game developers this translates into the replay value of their game. Using rewards makes players less likely to take risks, as they do not want to hurt their chances of being rewarded.[5] This is especially relevant to rewards used in video games, where designers wish to encourage creative and experimental play.

Non-performance contingent achievements, like earning an article of clothing or a pet for attending an in-game event, have no negative effect on intrinsic motivation. However these types of rewards do not have a performance measure, so players are unlikely to be interested in earning them unless they are paired with some sort of social reinforcement.

Best Practice

Use measurement achievements instead of completion achievements to increase intrinsic motivation through feedback.

Boring vs. Interesting Tasks

Achievements are earned for the completion of a task or series of tasks. These required actions will fall on a spectrum ranging from boring to exciting from the player's perspective. If a task is boring, the reward structure associated with it has to be different from tasks that are inherently interesting to the player.

Boring tasks (such as trade skills in MMOs) can be paired with extrinsic motivators, like achievements, in order for players to engage in them. Because players are not inclined to do these tasks on their own, intrinsic motivation is unaffected by the use of rewards as an incentive. Two common strategies are used to motivate people to engage in dull tasks. The first strategy is to make the player aware of the inherent value of the task through the wording of the achievement. An example of this would be the "Lifesaver" achievement in Deadliest Catch: Sea of Chaos, which is given for rescuing a crewmember. The use of the term "Lifesaver" implies that the task is important because you are helping others. The second strategy is to add additional rules or fantasy to the task itself, which is what all achievements do at their most basic level.[6]

Interesting tasks, which the player would engage in without any form of additional motivation, do not need to be reinforced with rewards. Players will engage in these tasks without any coaxing, so achievements (especially those that are completion achievements) should be used sparingly. Instead of trying to create artificial interest in a task, the achievements should be attentional, in that they focus the player's attention on important lessons or strategies for the task. This could improve player performance by scaffolding "hints" about what the most effective strategy is. A good example of this would be the achievement "The Flying Heal Bus" in StarCraft 2, which leads players to utilize a specific unit more effectively.

Best Practice

Reward players for boring tasks and give them feedback for interesting ones. Make achievements for interesting tasks attentional.

Achievement Difficulty

The difficulty of achievements is addressed twice by designers. First, the actual difficulty of achievements needs to be on a level that is attainable but challenging to the players. Second, players' self-efficacy for the task(s) associated with the achievement must be high enough that they feel confident in attempting it.

Achievements should provide challenging goals for players to fulfill as moderate difficulty leads to superior gains in performance and a greater sense of accomplishment upon completion.[7] However, achievements that are too difficult will not even be attempted by players, and those that are too easy will be completed quickly and won't provide an adequate challenge. A common strategy to keep in-game tasks interesting is to provide alternative objectives for those players who have reached a mastery level of performance.

Player self-efficacy (which refers to an individual's perception about his or her own ability to produce a desired result for a specific task) is another important factor that game designers must consider. Increasing player self-efficacy is important because it has been linked to increased goal commitment, increased strategy creation and use, and a more positive response to negative feedback. There are four factors that designers can address in order to affect a player's self-efficacy.[8] The first is *level of expertise* on the subject matter. This is another important reason to make sure there are achievements available for players at all skill levels. Seeing people around you succeed, or *vicarious experience*, is the second factor that influences self-efficacy. This affect is likely to be particularly powerful if the person being observed appears to be at the same ability level of the observer. Examples of utilizing this in games are leaderboards for online games or the "brags" in systems like Onlive. *Social persuasion* (giving someone a verbal boost) is the third method of influencing self-efficacy. This can be as simple as telling someone "good job" after a performance or the "50 NOTE STREAK!" messages that appear in Guitar Hero. *How a person feels* is the fourth factor, which includes stress level, emotional condition, and perceived physical state.

Best Practice

Make achievements challenging for the greatest returns in player performance and enjoyment. Phrase achievements and design interactions to increase player self-efficacy.

Goal Orientation

Players' goal orientation must be considered when designing achievements, as it will influence how they experience a game through goals they set for themselves. There are two types of goal orientation, commonly referred to as performance orientation and mastery orientation. Players who favor a performance orientation are concerned with other people's assessment of their competence. Players who have a mastery orientation are concerned more with improving their own proficiency.

Games tend to push players toward a performance orientation, as they are constantly emphasizing direct goals like time and points earned. Unfortunately, players who gravitate toward this type of orientation take fewer in-game risks and spend less time exploring, because they are afraid that doing so might affect their scores.[9] This occurs frequently in first-person shooters, where players use the same weapons and tactics over and over again because they think it is the best way to optimize their kill-to-death ratio. However, research has shown that when individuals are given performance-oriented goals, they typically perform better only with simple, non-complex tasks.[10]

To balance out player predisposition toward performance orientation, designers must actively try to instill mastery orientation in the goals and feedback they create. There are several benefits associated with having a mastery orientation. Players who have this mindset will accept errors and seek challenging tasks that provide them the opportunity to develop their competencies. When given mastery goals, players will have higher self-efficacy and utilize more effective strategies. Research has also shown that people given mastery-oriented goals perform better on complex tasks.[11] To help foster this type of orientation designers should create achievements that acknowledge the effort players are putting forth and support them during challenges. Games should treat errors and mistakes the players make as an opportunity to provide diagnostic feedback and encouragement.

The names and wording of achievements are very important when trying to effectively communicate this. For example, Heavy Rain's "So Close . . ." trophy, which is given to players for reaching, yet failing, the completion of a difficult task, could be seen as encouragement and recognition of effort. In contrast, a similar achievement in Guitar Hero III, named "Blowing It," is worded in such a way that it could be perceived as discouraging.

Best Practice

For complex tasks requiring creativity or complicated strategies, try to instill a mastery orientation. For simple or repetitive tasks, instill a performance orientation. Try to keep new players who are still learning how to play in a mastery orientation.

Expected vs. Unexpected Achievements

When players earn an achievement, the notification they receive can come as a total surprise or as the finish line they were striving for. The expectation that players have when starting a game stems from the design decision to let them know what they can achieve. Players either know what achievements can be earned before they play a game or they come upon them unexpectedly during play. Expected and unexpected achievements have different effects on players and can both be utilized to improve player experience.

Expected achievements allow players to set goals for themselves before they begin. There are four well-established benefits to having players set goals for themselves.[12] First, goals will allow the players to have objectives and allocate their resources to complete them. This could mean brushing up on certain skills, setting aside extra time, or asking a friend for help. Second, having a goal increases the amount of effort someone is willing to put into something. For game makers this will directly translate into more play time. Third, players who have goals are much more likely to not give up when facing a difficult task in a game, as compared to players without such goals, who quit playing once the going gets too tough. Fourth, players who establish goals for themselves will acquire new knowledge and skills in order to meet those goals. This is also important to game makers because those players who obtain new skills will in turn want to play their game more.

In addition to the benefits of goal setting, expected achievements also allow players to create a schema, or a mental model, of game play before they begin. Players then refer to this schema to make sense of how the game is structured and what actions they need to take to succeed. If players purchase a new game and look over all the achievements they can earn, they will develop a better understanding of the game itself. In fact, schema creation is often similarly used in training programs to help increase user performance.

On the other end of the spectrum are unexpected achievements. Unexpected achievements are relatively uncommon in video games but can also have potential benefits to players. One such perk would be encouraging experimental play. An extreme example of this strategy can be seen in the game Achievement Unlocked, in which players can earn quirky achievements for almost everything they do. Although the developers intended it to be a jab at the overuse of game achievements, Achievement Unlocked effectively illustrates the meta game that can be created through convincing players to run and jump around the screen randomly in hopes of earning all the mystery achievements.

Best Practice

Primarily use expected achievements so players can establish goals for themselves and create a schema of the game. Make sure achievement descriptions accurately reflect what needs to be done by the player and why it is important. Unexpected achievements can be used sparingly to encourage creative play.

When Achievement Notification Occurs

After an achievement is earned players must be made aware of their accomplishment. Players can be notified immediately while play is still going on or after some amount of time has passed at a natural break in the action. The decision between using immediate and delayed notifications should be influenced by game type as well as the players' level of experience.

Achievement notifications that occur during play, like those in World of Warcraft, are a form of immediate feedback. Studies have shown that immediate feedback can improve learning and efficiency, This is especially important when using measurement achievements that directly relate to player performance. It should be noted, however, that newer players benefit more from this type of feedback than more experienced players would. As players become more experienced, giving them increasingly delayed feedback will be more effective, as it gives them an opportunity to evaluate their own performance.

Another important consideration when giving players achievement notification during play is the potential obtrusiveness of the alert itself. A disruptive alert could break the flow state, or what players often call "the zone," with unfavorable results. When in a state like this, the outside world melts away, time becomes irrelevant, and focus is increased, probably a common experience when you play your favorite game. Players who are in a flow state have increased motivation[13] to continue playing and experience more enjoyment,[14] so disrupting this sensation with an in-your-face achievement may not be ideal.

In order to avoid distracting the player, games that require a lot of mental muscle (such as those in the real time strategy genre) will delay when they notify the player about earned achievements. Games like StarCraft, which have clearly defined play sessions, tend to give players achievement notification after a natural break in play. These types of notifications also have the benefit of acting like delayed feedback, which has been shown to produce increased retention when learning something new.[15] So a player who performs an action for the first time in a new game and is recognized for it a little while after the fact is more likely to remember how to perform it in future game sessions.

Best Practice

For games with no clear break in play, give immediate feedback with an unobtrusive popup accompanied by a longer explanation available after play. For games with clearly defined play sessions and those that require a greater deal of concentration, it is better to use delayed notification. Try to give new players immediate feedback and give more experienced players delayed feedback.

Achievement Permanence

Long after a player earns an achievement, he or she may want to reflect on the experience. Permanent achievements allow players to relive their former glory, while impermanent ones exist only when the player is first notified.

Permanent achievements come in two varieties: digitally tangible and stored lists. These terms basically reflect the difference between the reward you receive for earning an achievement and a catalogued description of the achievement. The tangibility of a digital item is an abstract concept because the item only exists in a virtual world. However, an item that is "digitally tangible," like a pet or a tabard given as a reward, can be manipulated by the player and admired by others, just like a physical reward. If all of the same rules that apply to rewards in the real world apply to rewards in a digital one, then there should be some concern about the overuse of digitally tangible rewards. Rewards have been shown to decrease intrinsic motivation[16] (one's natural desire to do something), lower the player's sense of self-determination, and decrease the likelihood that a player will return to a task.[17,18] Stored lists of earned achievements, on the other hand, like those featured on Xbox Live, allow players to reflect on their accomplishments long after they have earned them. The act of reflecting on past events will give players a greater understanding of the experience through recall.

Temporary achievements, like the phrases "Unstoppable" or "God-like" in first-person shooters, amount to verbal reinforcements. Unlike tangible achievements, these verbal boosts increase intrinsic motivation[19] and do not infringe on the player's sense of self-determination.[20] After the notification is gone, any record of the achievement disappears.

Best Practice

Give players the opportunity to go over their earned achievements using some kind of stored list. Digitally tangible rewards are a great incentive but won't keep the player around after the reward is earned.

Who Can See Earned Achievements?

Achievements that a player has earned are often visible to others in single player and multiplayer games. What information is shared varies by game. Some games take the decision out of the player's hands. These mandatory systems make an individual's achievements an open book. Player-defined public achievements, like those in Farmville and StarCraft 2; give the players the ability to decide what they want to share.

Social approval is a big part of why people play video games. Making earned achievements visible to others will encourage players to earn them for recognition. Social recognition has been shown to have a positive effect on performance when used as an incentive.[21] Making earned achievements visible also gives the player's peers the opportunity to see the reward and decide whether they want it for themselves. Striving for and eventually earning those rewards will improve their self-efficacy, their belief that they can accomplish other in-game tasks.[22] Having visible achievements can also act like a gaming résumé. Another player's earned achievements might reveal that he or she would make a good teammate or someone to ask for help.

Earned achievements that are visible to the community have potential downsides, however. Earned achievements that act as a résumé, as discussed above, can have the unintended consequence of excluding players. This phenomenon often takes place in MMOs, where players ask potential teammates to link a completed achievement before allowing them to participate in game events. This creates a Catch-22 situation wherein players must have experience to gain experience. Another problem with relying on social recognition as a motivator is that it is not a good predictor of future performance once the recognition has been doled out or is no longer available.[23]

Best Practice

Making earned achievements viewable to other players is a powerful incentive. To prevent players from being excluded because of their lack of experience, create achievements for players who take other players under their wing. Let players display a few achievements they are proud of to increase motivation and highlight their play style.

Negative Achievements

Most achievements are given to players after they have done something noteworthy and positive. However, some achievements are given to players for a notable performance at the other end of the spectrum. When a player fails, he or she may earn a negative achievement. Examples of negative achievements include the Command & Conquer 3 achievement "awarded" to a player who loses a ranked game to someone twenty places below in the official rankings, and the "Getting my ass kicked" trophy for repeatedly dying in PS3's God of War.

Negative achievements are the digital equivalent of pouring salt on a wound. Earning this type of achievement can cause players to lose their sense of competence and independence, which will make the game they are playing feel less fulfilling. If players know that there are negative achievements in the game, they will try to avoid them. Avoidance goals that are constantly in the back of the player's mind can be tiring and will make the overall experience less enjoyable.[24] Negative achievements can also make design flaws in the game a double whammy. Someone who dies repeatedly due to poor level design or a broken mechanic is not going to take a "You suck" achievement in stride. The player's response will be to blame the game and not him- or herself.

Best Practice

Don't use negative achievements as a punishment for failure. Provide feedback within the system that can assist struggling players.

Achievements as Currency

Earned achievements could be used as virtual currency in games. Players may receive such currency in the form of points, coins, or stars and later use them to purchase in-game items or real-world objects. Games like League of Legends, that use micro transactions, sometimes also have an alternative currency that is earned through game play. Achievements are an obvious choice for a metric when giving out virtual currency. They are memorable moments, with defined requirements, that are already important to players. Using achievements as currency, however, may have a pretty wide range of effects on players.

There is a great deal of research on giving money as an incentive for performance. Monetary rewards have greater returns on task performance than tangible rewards.[25] This is probably due to the fact that acquiring currency allows players to decide what they want to purchase with it. This takes the responsibility of choosing an appropriate reward out of the hands of designers. School systems have recently used monetary rewards with some success. In some cases class attendance, test scores, and even the likelihood of attending college all improved when monetary rewards were offered.[26] Other studies reported similar increased accomplishment, but only when rewards were tied to inputs rather than outputs.[27] This means that students were rewarded for things like the amount of time they spent studying but not directly for earning a particular grade. The idea is that if students are paid for good behaviors the grades will take care of themselves.

The other side of the argument concerning currency is the same one that is often made against tangible rewards. Currency rewards have been shown to decrease intrinsic motivation for the recipients of the reward. Players will end up caring about the reward system more than the game itself. More than one game company has exploited this kind of reward system in order to keep players strung out on boring tasks. Currency systems, like other reward programs, may also lower player creativity by inadvertently encouraging a hyper focus on the reward path.

Best Practice

Offer players currency for completing tasks instead of rewards to give them a greater sense of control. Use a currency system to enhance a game, but don't attempt to make currency acquisition the main reason players engage in an activity.

Incremental and Meta Achievements

Most of the time achievements are earned for completing a single task. Incremental and meta achievements, however, are given for completing more than one task. Incremental achievements are awarded in a chain for performing the same task through scaling levels of difficulty. Examples of incremental achievements are killing 250, 500, and 1,000 enemies in a first-person shooter and earning different colored ribbons in Farmville. Meta achievements are earned for completing a series of achievements that are for different tasks, for instance, earning the title of "chef" by completing all cooking related achievements in World of Warcraft.

Both incremental and meta achievements can be used as a type of scaffolding, a "training wheels" approach used in teaching. Here, players are given a seemingly complex task to do, only it's broken up into smaller pieces and sequenced like a training program. Breaking the task up into pieces also has the side benefit of helping players create a schema about how the more complex task is structured.

Incremental and meta achievements usually take extended periods of time to complete. This is similar to long-term incentive programs. These types of programs have been shown to elicit greater performance gains than short-term programs, which give rewards for single actions. Another benefit of these types of long-term goals is that players will spend more time in the game trying to complete them.

These types of achievements, however, can have a potential downside. If players feel like they are only following a trail of breadcrumbs with little self-direction, they may lose their sense of autonomy. The number of achievements, the spacing between them, and the amount of challenge each one provides are important things to keep in mind.

Best Practice

Use these types of achievements to hold the players' interest for longer periods of time and guide them to related activities. Make the spacing between incremental achievements, both in time and physical location, separated enough so that players don't feel too controlled.

Competitive Achievements

Competitive achievements require players to face off with one another in either direct confrontations or indirectly through their scores on solo tasks. This type of achievement can be completed individually or in teams where members work together to defeat other groups of players.

Some research indicates that competition can increase overall enjoyment and attitude toward a given task.[28] Being successful in a competition has been shown to increase intrinsic motivation by influencing a person's perception of his or her own competence,[29] and such competitive environments have also demonstrated increased performance on simple repetitive tasks.[30] Computer science classes in particular have noted success in their implementation of competition to make classes more interesting.

Although some studies have seen positive results from the implementation of competitive environments, other studies indicate that under certain circumstances competition should be avoided.

More often than not, competitive environments have a tendency to impede the learning process.[31] This is in part due to the egocentric behavior that competitive environments often induce, which in turn make people less likely to help one another.[32] Competition has also been shown to have a negative effect on the self-efficacy of learners.[33] This makes players rate themselves and their teammates more harshly, especially when they lose.

Players who have a higher level of skill are more likely to enjoy competitive achievements and be less affected by the negative aspects. They will be at a place where the game is familiar to them and will not be as stressed out with the addition of competition. Another consideration is the motivation of the individual players. Players who are high in achievement motivation enjoy competitive tasks to a greater extent and have more intrinsic interest than their counterparts who are low in achievement motivation. Gamers in general may have a higher overall achievement motivation, which can also vary depending on the game type. It is important to understand your target demographic and give players what they are most comfortable with.

Best Practice

If competitive achievements are used in a game, make them available only after players are comfortable with game play and no longer learning the ropes.

Non-Competitive Cooperative Achievements

Cooperative achievements are earned by players working toward a goal together in a game. These types of achievements are most common in multi-player games where players can interact with peers. The achievements can be rewards for group tasks like killing a monster, or built into multi-player games to encourage teamwork, like earning 1,000 assisted kills in a first-person shooter.

Most research supports the use of cooperative environments to improve performance. Cooperative settings have been associated with academic achievement,[34] increased self-esteem,[35] and higher positivity when evaluating peers. Incentive programs that require teamwork have a greater effect on performance than those that can be accomplished by an individual. Another great benefit of working cooperatively is that it gives players a wider range of goals that they may not be able to complete on their own. To facilitate this, achievements should encourage veteran players to engage with those less experienced. The sidekick system in City of Heroes is a great example of this. Research shows that people who are protégés in businesses have a greater promotion rate and more job satisfaction than individuals who were not mentored. The mentors also benefit from these types of systems by seeing their own performance and social status increased.

Although cooperation has many benefits, there are some risks associated with this type of environment. One risk is attitude polarization in groups, which often leads to more cautious or risky decision making as a whole. In these instances, team members will collectively make poor decisions they otherwise would not make if given the opportunity to decide by themselves.[36] Another problem that can affect groups is process loss, which can take place if the additional workload from coordinating communication and assisting others hinders group performance.[37] The communication difficulties that can cause process loss could be accentuated in games because of the limitation of the available technology. A good example of this takes place during raids in MMOs when some group members do not have access to voice chat. Another problem caused by group size is social loafing.[38] This is a problem in larger groups when individuals' performance is hidden and so they will put forth less effort.

Best Practice

To foster a cooperative environment, offering achievements for more advanced players to assist less experienced players is an option. The groups for cooperative achievements should be kept relatively small to decrease social loafing and process loss. The metrics used for earning achievements should assess individual performances within the group setting.

■ ■ ■

Key Takeaways

The key takeaways from this chapter are:

- Use measurement achievements instead of completion achievements to increase intrinsic motivation through feedback.

- Reward players for boring tasks and give them feedback for interesting ones. Make achievements for interesting tasks attentional.

- Make achievements challenging for the greatest returns in player performance and enjoyment. Phrase achievements and design interactions to increase player self-efficacy.

- For complex tasks requiring creativity or complicated strategies, try to instill a mastery orientation. For simple or repetitive tasks, instill a performance orientation. Try to keep new players who are still learning how to play in a mastery orientation.

- For games with no clear break in play, give immediate feedback with an unobtrusive popup accompanied by a longer explanation available after play. For games with clearly defined play sessions and those that require a greater deal of concentration, it is better to use delayed notification. Try to give new players immediate feedback and give more experienced players delayed feedback.

- Give players the opportunity to go over their earned achievements using some kind of stored list. Digitally tangible rewards are a great incentive but won't keep the player around after the reward is earned.

- Don't use negative achievements as a punishment for failure. Provide feedback within the system that can assist struggling players.

- Offer players currency for completing tasks instead of rewards to give them a greater sense of control. Use a currency system to enhance a game, but don't attempt to make currency acquisition the main reason players engage in an activity.

- Make the spacing between incremental achievements, both in time and physical location, separate enough so that players don't feel too controlled.

- If competitive achievements are used in a game, make them available only after players are comfortable with game play and no longer learning the ropes.

- To foster a cooperative environment, offering achievements for more advanced players to assist less experienced players is an option. The groups for cooperative achievements should be kept relatively small to decrease social loafing and process loss. The metrics used for earning achievements should assess individual performance within the group setting.

11

Perspective of a Gamer

Nathan Kapp

CHAPTER QUESTIONS

At the end of this chapter, you should be able to answer the following questions:

- What makes games more fun than school?
- Why do kids pay more attention to video games than they do to school?
- Can video games be effective learning tools?
- Why can a game be a better teaching method than a traditional teaching method?

Introduction

Often textbooks, pundits, and experts speak about the gamer generation and how the kids today have different learning expectations and have learned from video games, but rarely do we hear from that generation itself. In this chapter a seventeen-year-old male who has grown up playing video games sheds some insights into video games he has played and the learning outcomes that have been achieved. A careful read of the chapter indicates that many of the research- backed conclusions can be seen in this anecdotal review of the games played.

Gamer Generation

Growing up in the gamer generation, I have been exposed to games my entire life. Throughout my lifetime I have seen video games evolve from the original Game Boy to the Game Boy Color, from the PlayStation to the PlayStation 3, from the Nintendo to the Wii. I have played all types of games, from racing games to first-person shooters. By playing all these games I have learned that there is true value in playing games. In fact, playing video games has taught me a lot.

Mario Kart: Thinking Outside the Box

The first game I remember playing was Mario Kart 64 for the Nintendo 64. Mario Kart 64 is a racing game where the player can choose from eight different characters and race against friends head to head or against the computer in the Grand Prix mode. To make the game more interesting, you can collect different power ups, such as mushrooms, which give your character a speed boost, or shells that slow down your opponents. The game has three levels, 50cc, 100cc, and 150cc. These levels are essentially easy, medium, and hard, respectively. There were many courses to choose from, so the game was always changing.

Mario Kart 64 was fun because it was fast-paced. You were always trying to do something, whether it was trying to pass the person next to you or trying to avoid a green shell coming toward you. Mario Kart 64 was both fun and challenging. Even though Mario Kart 64 was very fun, it was not a mindless video game.

This game actually forced me to use my brain. I had to figure out which character was the fastest and what strategy to use to win the race. Each course was different and required a unique strategy. Whenever I thought the game was getting too easy I would move up to the next difficulty level. This game taught me problem-solving skills and how to think outside the box.

For example, one day when I was playing on the hardest difficulty, I could not win the race. I had memorized the entire course and knew exactly where the turns were and where I could get power ups, but I was repeatedly getting fourth or fifth place against the computer. This was not good enough for me. I had tried all the normal ways on the course, and I still could not win. Thinking back, I remembered that many of the previous courses at the lower difficulty levels had obvious shortcuts, but this course didn't seem to have one. I had looked everywhere for a noticeable shortcut, but could not find one.

Finally, I forced myself to think outside the box. I thought, "If I could somehow create my own shortcut, then I could win the race." I ran through the course a few more times and figured out I could jump over one of the walls of the racetrack and essentially cut the course in half. I tried this, and it worked! I got first by a mile. If I had kept racing the course without trying to jump over the wall, I never would have won the race. Thinking outside the box is a valuable skill, not only in video games but in the real world as well. Thinking outside the box is what leads to innovation and is a good skill to learn as a young video game player.

Madden Football: Analyzing Problems

After Mario Kart 64 the next game I really got into was the Madden Football series for the PlayStation, a football game where you can control all aspects of your favorite NFL team from the offense to the defense to the special teams. You can play against your friend or against the computer. You could play single games, or you could play in franchise mode, where you control your team season after season.

Madden, just like Mario Kart 64, is a very fast-paced game. You have to choose your play and then execute it on the field. When playing offense you have to choose your formation, the personnel you want on the field, and what play to run. Then you must execute the play. Whether you choose to run or pass, you must make split-second decisions on where to run or throw the ball. These decisions either result in yards gained or yards lost. To be a successful offensive Madden player, you must learn which plays are the best for your style and which teams fit well with how you play. If you like to run the ball, then you should play with the Steelers rather than the Patriots. The Patriots throw the ball more than they run because they have Tom Brady as their quarterback. You also must learn what formation the defense is in and how you can beat the defense. However, controlling your offense in Madden is the easy part. The real challenge is when it comes to controlling your defense.

On defense you must try to guess what the offense is going to call, then choose a play you think can stop the other team. You must counter the other player or computer. Once the play is called and the other team lines up on the line of scrimmage, you must analyze their offensive formation and what plays they can run from that formation, then make any changes to your defense to stop their potential plays. You have about thirty seconds to do this.

Success on defense means you have the ability to analyze the offensive formation and learn what defensive play can stop the other team's offense. There are literally hundreds of plays for the offense and defense to choose from, which make the game very challenging. Although Madden is a fun game, it has also taught me how to analyze things. In Madden I am able to analyze the formations and figure out what play my opponent is going to run before he runs it.

This ability to analyze data has been extremely helpful in school, especially on my chemistry final. In chemistry class, I was given ten labeled solutions to identify and memorize. Eventually, I was going to be given those same ten solutions unlabeled as a final. I had to collect and analyze data so that I would be able to properly identify each solution. The analytical skills I learned by playing Madden helped me to correctly identify all of the unknown solutions because I was able to memorize and determine from a dataset which solutions were which.

RuneScape: The Art of the Deal

RuneScape is a massively multiplayer online role play game (MMORPG) set in a medieval world where you control your own character, who interacts with the hundreds of thousands of other players. You can create your character's destiny, whether you want him to be a fierce warrior, a wizard, or even just a good cook. You can train your character in any of twenty-five different skills. Upgrading your character takes a lot of time and gold coins, the currency used in RuneScape. When you first create your character, you have no gold coins, just a set of weak armor. It is up to you to figure out a way make money.

You can make money by completing quests, killing monsters, or trading with other characters. Completing quests takes a long time, and you receive less than five gold coins when you kill a monster, which means killing monsters is a slow way to accumulate wealth. This leaves making trades with other players as the best way to make money. This takes good negotiation skills. There are hundreds of thousands of other players, and you must convince other players to buy your products. There is a place called the Grand Exchange on RuneScape where lots of players gather to try and sell their products. The Grand Exchange could be equated to a stock exchange. Everyone is buying and selling goods. I had just chopped down one thousand maple trees and went to the Grand Exchange to sell them for a profit. To my dismay, there were five other players selling maple trees. I had to think fast if I wanted to sell the trees. Luckily, this was not the first time I ran into a problem like this on RuneScape.

In fact, this actually occurs quite often in RuneScape. I was able to use the negotiating and communication skills I had acquired from being a long-time player to sell my maple trees. Being able to sell yourself is an extremely important talent. You must sell yourself whenever you are trying to get a job. In fact, I used the skills I learned in RuneScape to land a job in real life. I applied for a job and about a week later I was called in for an interview. When I arrived at the job site I noticed there were two other people already waiting for their interviews. I knew I really had to sell myself in order to be offered the job. When I was finally called in for my interview, I used the negotiating and communication skills I learned in RuneScape to convince the employer that I was the best man for job. In the end I received the job, in part, because of what RuneScape taught me.

Civilization Revolution: Balancing Resources

Civilization Revolution is another installment of the popular Sid Meier's Revolution games. In the game you take control of a civilization at the beginning of time and lead your civilization into the space age. You can win the game in four ways: economic victory, which is where you get the most money; technological victory, which is where you discover and develop the most advanced technology; cultural victory, which is where you build the most world wonders; or domination victory, which is where you capture all the enemy's capitals. You must decide which victory you want to achieve.

Within the game, you create cities and each city produces money or science. The money can be used to build up an army or build world wonders. The science is used to upgrade technology. Cities can produce only money or money and science or just science. It is up to the player to decide how he or she wants to use resources. Balancing the game's resources is important to victory. By playing Civilization Revolution for so long, I have found that specializing in one area makes winning a lot easier, but you can't ignore the other areas.

For example, if you make all your cities produce gold, then you will make money much more quickly and earn an economic victory much sooner than if you had all your cities produce both gold and science. However, once you start producing gold, other civilizations will want to attack your cities to take your gold. So you need to build armies and you also need to have some cities producing science because you must create the technology to build modern weapons to keep the other civilizations from destroying your cities. Balancing resources is a very important skill to have.

Throughout life you are going have to make decisions and balance variables. I have found that, by applying the lesson I learned in Civilization Revolution, I can achieve my goals much more easily. I must balance my schoolwork, cross country, and hanging out with friends. I dedicate a couple hours of my day to schoolwork, an hour for running, and an hour for hanging out with friends, just as I balance the different elements in the game. I have also found that I must keep them separate. It is very difficult to study for an economics test while shooting hoops with my friends. The lessons in the game translate to lessons in my life. I work to balance everything in my life and achieve my personal goals. I achieve good grades, while excelling in cross country and maintaining a healthy social life.

Games vs. School

Games can be extremely helpful in teaching important skills. School and video games differ in the following ways. Video games have the ability to keep kids' attention, which is extremely important when it comes to learning. If you don't pay attention, you will not learn anything. In addition to keeping kids' attention, video games also offer instant gratification. When playing a video game you are always challenging yourself.

The main thing people complain about when it comes to school is that it is boring. However, video games are fun. Video games are fast-paced, as compared with school, which has a slow pace aimed at keeping all learners at the same level. Because games are fast-paced, they keep the players' attention. Players must always be alert if they want to excel in the game. Decisions must be made instantly, gold or other valuable items are at stake during negotiations, and balancing resources correctly leads to a tangible victory. In school, the payoffs are not as obvious or as exciting. There is a delay between achievement and reward. If the concepts of learning and feedback could be combined, school would become much more exciting.

Video games give you instant gratification. Whenever you beat a level, you always unlock something new. For example, if you win a race in Mario Kart 64, the next course automatically becomes unlocked. In school, you do not receive instant gratification. You must wait at least a day or until you receive your grade on a test to receive any gratification. Rewards motivate students. Unfortunately, school doesn't provide the type of instant feedback that can be achieved in games. If students received more immediate recognition and perks for working hard, then they would work harder.

Third, video games allow you to challenge yourself. Once you think the game has become too easy, you can move onto the next level or increase the difficulty. This is different from school because in the classroom everyone must work at the same pace. Students who really grasp the concept cannot move on until everyone in the class has grasped the concept. This creates a disincentive to get ahead because you really can't go anywhere until the rest of the class is ready. Using games in learning would allow students to all work at their own pace. This would also help students who are having trouble understanding the concepts. They would not have to feel pressured by the other students in the class.

In conclusion, videogames have taught me helpful skills that I have already applied directly in the classroom and outside of the classroom. Games have many benefits that conventional teaching does not, but these could be incorporated into the learning process. Games keep students' attention, they allow the students to receive instant gratification, and they allow students to be challenged no matter the level of other students.

■ ■ ■

Key Takeaways

The key takeaways from this chapter are

- Video games are fun because of the challenge, fast pace, and meaningfulness of the tasks.

- Video games can teach valuable life skills

- The lessons learned in video games are not lost on the players.

12

Casual Games Site: DAU Case Study

Alicia Sanchez

CHAPTER QUESTIONS

At the end of this chapter, you should be able to answer these questions:

- How can casual games be used in an organization?
- Is it possible to teach concepts rather than specific tasks with games?
- What are the advantages of having a "games common"?

Introduction

Defense Acquisition University services the acquisition, technology, and logistics (AT&L) workforce for the Department of Defense. All goods that cannot be created by the U.S. government must be acquired, and DAU's primary responsibility is to provide training and education related to the procurement process. The AT&L workforce continues to expand, currently numbering approximately 143,000 employees, necessitating the DAU infrastructure to support voluminous courses and content for its students. DAU offers more than one hundred resident and blended courses, as well as hundreds of continuous learning modules that are required curriculum for many AT&L employees.

Games and Simulations in the Curriculum

In 2007, DAU began to explore the use of games and simulations within their curriculum to provide enhanced learning experiences for their students. The resulting games initiative evolved into a three-fold approach that the university has continued to expand. The targets and intentions of each of the three approaches are as follows:

Games in Curriculum

It was determined early in the exploration of the appropriate use of games within DAU's extensive curriculum that games that might be implemented into the formal DAU curriculum would need to be based on the very specific learning objectives that each course addressed. Essentially, games that are introduced into DAU courses would need to be highly customized to the acquisition process. As courses are updated and revised, each course receives a games evaluation to determine whether a game could enhance the learning experience and the learning outcomes by providing experiential learning opportunities, opportunities to practice the skills introduced in the course, and increase retention of the course content. DAU games are designed specifically to enhance and therefore supplement the curriculum and do not introduce concepts or skills.

CLM Games

DAU's continuous learning modules (CLMs) are often shorter formal courses, ranging in length for two to six hours and offered exclusively online. CLMs are often targeted toward specialty areas of acquisition expertise and heavily driven by policy and doctrine surrounding the acquisition process. In order to enhance learning outcomes, the games that are implemented into CLMs provide learners with opportunities to apply the concepts and policy introduced within the modules, including the appropriate application of the concepts, practice opportunities to demonstrate when and where the concepts might be used, and experiential games allowing students to have varied practice opportunities with the content.

Casual Games

Most recently, DAU introduced the first-ever DOD casual games initiative. This initiative was devised to provide learning opportunities for the AT&L workforce in an informal setting. Specifically, through analysis of the two preceding initiatives, DAU determined that because of the highly specialized nature of the acquisition process, games were being used to enhance acquisition specific practice solely. Further analysis clearly indicated that, despite the highly specialized nature of the acquisition process, there were core competencies that AT&L employees would universally be expected to have, such as a basic understanding of their overarching career field. The casual games initiative was designed to provide practice opportunities to increase proficiency and engagement with the basic concepts of the acquisition career field. Several examples of games and the characteristics of the games site itself will be discussed here.

DAU Casual Games Initiative

In December 2010, DAU successfully launched the DAU Casual Games portal with thirteen games that were created in order to or determined to support the core competencies of the acquisition process. The site currently hosts more than twenty games, with plans to continue expanding the offerings. The casual games available through the portal are primarily

2D Flash-based games. Several of the games on the site are used in other games initiatives in courses throughout the university, but many of the games were designed and produced specifically for use on the site. The main intent of the site was to provide students with informal learning opportunities to interact with the core DAU principles.

The core competencies DAU hoped to reinforce initially were a cross-section of basic principles that are addressed in a foundational course that all students must successfully complete prior to proceeding on to any other DAU course. By identifying these core competencies, DAU was able to inform the design of games for the site that would be challenging, but that would be able to be successfully completed by all AT&L employees. The nature of the competencies also allowed DAU to explore several facets of game design in low-risk environments. Many of the games range in length from ten to twenty minutes of total play time, allowing students to have short interactions with meaningful content.

Continuous Process Improvement Game

One of the first games developed for the DAU casual games site was targeted to present the tools used for continuous process improvement (CPI), a process used throughout the acquisition curriculum. While the application of each of the tools requires data sets and calculations that students might not be expected to be able to demonstrate until later in the curriculum, a basic understanding of the concepts of continuous process improvement is expected of all DAU students.

The initial requirement for the game outlined the learning objectives: the ability to understand in which circumstances it would be appropriate to utilize each of the seven concepts of the continuous process improvement process. As continuous process improvement is often used within a production environment, the requirement for this game did not mandate that the game be limited to realistic factory settings, allowing for creative license.

Instead, the game as it was developed and delivered by the Retro Lab at the University of Central Florida puts the learners into a simulated factory assembly line that is tasked with creating enough missiles to prevent the earth from being smited by an impending alien attack. (See Figure 12.1.)

Figure 12.1. Building Missiles to Save the Earth from Aliens and to Learn Continuous Process Improvement.

This approach allowed players of this game to use a real existing process within a fantasy based setting, therefore creating an element of cognitive and not physical fidelity of the situations in which the seven tools might be utilized. By creating a novel and fantasy based meta story for this game, it was hoped that students would be motivated (by saving the earth), engaged (as the impending attack requires that missiles be produced efficiently) and challenged (to appropriately leverage the 7 tools to create enough missiles).

The challenges within the game require that players determine which of the seven tools would best alleviate several problems that arise in the missile production. Feedback is immediate, and students proceed with either creating missiles, turkeys or toasters.

Logistics Lifecycle—Select A Cell

Also created by UCF's Retro Lab, the Select A Cell game was designed to provide students an opportunity to use a macro-level approach to the logistics of procurement. The ability to consider sustainability, availability, and

Figure 12.2. Gathering Requirements for the Right Cell Phone.

requirements are core competencies for all DAU students. The objective of the game was to allow students to check out the lifecycle of a product from cradle to grave, providing a big picture overview. Select A Cell, a game in which students receive requests for cell phones with specific abilities from troops in the field, gives players the opportunity to meet with contractors, select phones that are viable for inclusion, test each phone's limitations, and make a recommendation of which phone would have the highest likelihood of success. (See Figure 12.2.)

Select A Cell simulates the context a student would be most likely to experience and expects students to apply the concepts of lifecycle logistics. By using a situational fidelity approach to this game, students gain a better understanding of the process in a realistic situation.

Contracting Principles—Charge!

Created by the ADL Co-Lab, Charge! was designed to target the core principle of contracting, procuring the lowest cost solution that meets the minimum requirements for any need. In order to provide students with an engaging experience that allows them to apply the core competency in a

Figure 12.3. Saving the World and Learning About Pricing.

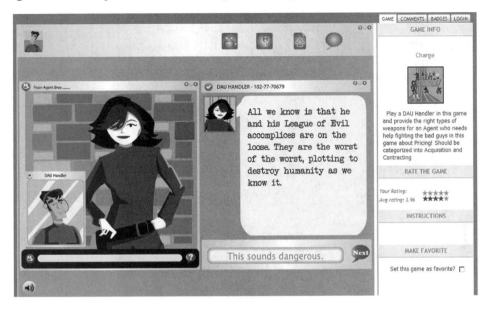

variety of situations, Charge! puts students in the role of a James Bond–type character. (See Figure 12.3.)

Specifically, players are cast as a Q–type character responsible for providing the weapons necessary to defeat villains. Players are asked to review three proposals and determine which of these represents the best value for the government. If a player selects the right contract, he or she is thanked for his or her efforts. If a player chooses the wrong contract, he or she is presented with an agent who is bruised and angry and provides feedback specific to the decision.

Acquisition Lifecycle—Acquisition Proposition

Created by the ADL Co-Lab, Acquisition Proposition was designed to reinforce an understanding of the acquisition lifecycle in general. The cycle consists of many phases, each requiring many components and reviews to proceed. The game focuses on the ability of students to identify and categorize what was required during each phase and the ability for a student to move through the entire acquisition cycle in a short amount of time. The resulting game was a stylized game that is commonly used in entertainment-based games. (See Figure 12.4.)

Figure 12.4. Learning About the Acquisition Lifecycle.

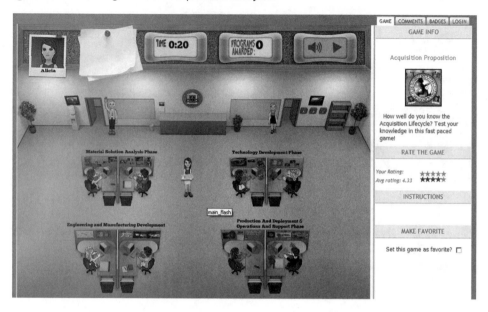

Acquisition Proposition requires students to collect the appropriate documents required for the multiple phases of the acquisition lifecycle and walk these documents through the process. The game is set in an office and requires students to quickly identify the next steps in the process. The game consists of several levels with increased time sensitivity and required documentation to challenge students' skills.

Games Portal

While most of DAU's efforts focused on the development of the game, the development of the portal itself was also an important component. The focus on creating a high-quality experience that was like the types of interactions students were having in their entertainment-based casual gaming experiences was a critical factor in developing the infrastructure that would house the games. Created by APPTIS, Inc., the site was designed to allow students to come to the site and play games within their web browsers at any time. Students could also create logins and user profiles on the site that would allow them access to additional components. (See Figure 12.5.)

Figure 12.5. Opening Screen of the DAU Games Portal.

Visitors to the DAU Casual Games Portal may select games that are categorized in a variety of ways. Players may select games from a sliding album cover, from thumbnails of favorites or recently played games, or by content area. Players who choose to create a login can a store their favorite games, leave comments about a game, and collect badges and achievements for their successful completion of games. Several of the games housed on the portal include high-score tables as well, allowing players to save their scores and compare their performance to the performance of others. By creating a high-quality experience, it is hoped that students will keep visiting the site and interacting with the content.

■ ■ ■

Key Takeaways

The key takeaways from this chapter are

- Casual games can be an effective tool to produce organizational learning.
- Games can be used to promote learning information.
- A games portal can provide reinforcement of key organizational concepts through short but targeted games.

13

Alternate Reality Games for Corporate Learning

Koreen Olbrish

CHAPTER QUESTIONS

At the end of this chapter, you should be able to answer these questions:

- What is an alternate reality game?
- What is an augmented reality game?
- Why are they useful?
- How should they be designed?

Introduction

Each year learning technologists and innovative instructional designers attend a conference hosted by the eLearning Guild called DevLearn. It is a forum where learning and development professionals gather to discuss learning innovations, technologies, theory, and instructional design methods. Imagine their surprise when they heard that they would be fighting off zombies in order to make it to the conference.

The story behind the zombies is that the program executive for DevLearn was looking for a way to give conference attendees hands-on experience using social media. At the same time, he wanted to arm attendees with data and case studies for how to overcome objections to the use of social media tools within their own organizations. Tandem Learning created a solution to meet both needs—an alternative reality game (ARG).

The goal of the game was to provide attendees with an opportunity to utilize a broad variety of social media tools and to help participants identify the benefits and usefulness of the tools for organizational learning. Throughout the conference, attendees collected data, case studies, and game clues from industry experts through various social media channels that presented evidence of the benefit of using social media to support learning initiatives.

Zombie Apocalypse

The premise for the ARG was simple and was only revealed to DevLearn attendees through the use of social media channels. A few weeks before the event, a "news video" surfaced and informed participants that the conference was "under attack" by zombies and conventional communication systems of telephone and e-mail had been eliminated. Participants were challenged to use social media channels to collaborate and defend the conference from the zombie hordes.

Slowly, more clues became evident and a game portal was presented to allow participants to work as teams and compete for top honors in the challenge. Significant buzz was generated about the experience, and soon conference attendees had joined forces to create a social learning community skilled in the use of technology for communication and collaboration.

The ARG at DevLearn achieved the identified goals better than anyone expected. The last session of the conference was a debriefing session, allowing participants to share their experiences and lessons learned. Not only did participants walk away having had a richer conference experience, but they also had success stories and evidence of the effectiveness of social media for collaboration and learning. The experience created by Tandem Learning for DevLearn was considered by everyone involved to be a great success.

What Is an ARG?

Alternate reality games (ARGs), also called pervasive games or transmedia storytelling, are designed to combine real life and digital game play elements. Typically, ARGs are "tracked" online, but the actual game play consists of real-life activities. There are many entertainment-based examples such as the games, I love bees, The Lost Experience, Numb3rs Chain Factor, and examples of ARGs for social issues such as Urgent Evoke and World Without Oil. A new area of focus is how ARGs can be leveraged for training and learning.

There continues to be a lot of confusion about the term ARG—some people use "*alternate* reality games" and "*augmented* reality games" interchangeably. For a point of clarification, *alternate* reality games refer to game play that integrates real life and online game play through a storyline that seeks to engage learners in an experience that seems real.

On the other hand, augmented reality games refer to games where there is a technology overlay on reality that contributes to play. An example is the yellow first down line superimposed on the football field. Often smart phones are used with augmented reality games.

The really confusing part comes in when augmented reality is used as part of an alternate reality game. To keep them straight, think about the meaning of the words: "alternate reality" seeks to create a different reality for game play purposes. "Augmented reality" adds additional information or a layer to real-life environments and objects.

ARG Terminology

Some key terms related to alternate reality games differentiate them from other types of serious games. These definitions help better define what differentiates ARGs from other types of serious games.

Puppetmaster. The puppetmaster in an ARG is the master controller of the game experience. Usually, the puppetmaster was also the game designer, and as part of the responsibility of managing the game play, the puppetmaster watches how players are engaging and interacting with the storyline and makes adjustments to the story, scoring, or game mechanisms as necessary to keep players focused and addressing the goals of the game. Because ARGs are played with the real world as the game environment, the puppetmaster's role is absolutely critical to keeping the game and players on track.

The Curtain. Much like the curtain behind which "the Wizard" hid in *The Wizard of Oz*, the puppetmaster operates behind a theoretical curtain that separates the game management activities from the game play environment. The curtain is the veil that provides the illusion that the game is playing out naturally, and when it is managed well, the curtain masks the existence of the puppetmaster.

Trailhead. The trailhead is a clue that leads players into the game. For marketing and media brand ARGs, lots of such clues are typically provided to attract as many players as possible. For learning ARGs, the same theory could be applied, especially for event-based ARGs. Another name for this is "rabbit hole." Rabbit hole is more commonly used when there is one specific entry point for an ARG.

TINAG or "This Is Not a Game." TINAG is the abbreviation commonly used to describe the tone of an ARG. The goal in the design is to create an experience in which the players don't necessarily feel like they are playing a game. The actions they take, the decisions they make, and the puzzles they solve shouldn't be extraneous to the storyline. That said, many ARG themes have a more fantastical feel, so the designer's responsibility is to create a game experience that mirrors realistic activities as part of the game play, even when the storyline makes it clear that the game is not "real."

Design Principles for ARGs

It's difficult to make generalizations of what an ARG is or looks like for learning. Just as there are an unlimited number of games and rules for game play, the same is true for ARGs. Designs could range from something very simple (a scavenger hunt) to something very complex (large-scale, problem-based learning or leadership development). There are, however, some basic design principles and "lessons learned" that have become apparent as we have designed more and more ARGs for corporate learning events and initiatives.

Design Is the Key. Just as with any game or game-mechanics described in this book, ARGs are most successful when they are both designed for the type of play and outcomes that make them fun and engaging and focused on the achievement of the desired learning goals. This is not instructional design; this is game design with learning goals. A huge misconception is that, because you've played games, you know how to design them. Don't underestimate the amount of time, energy, thought, and expertise that it takes to design a fun game, let alone a fun game that accomplishes your organizational learning goals.

What's Your Story? As mentioned earlier in the book, stories and narrative are important for games focused on helping people to learn. Everyone loves a good story. The most successful ARGs embrace storytelling as a key element of the game play. For corporate training initiatives, the storytelling elements can either mirror real-life scenarios or be more of a fantastical overlay. Strategy for the storyline should align with the design and objectives, but should not be overlooked as a critical aspect of the experience. The storyline is carefully crafted to elicit the targeted interactions and behaviors while at the same time presenting a theme that will draw learners into the experience and keep them engaged.

Stick to the Point. It might be fun to plan an ARG with a "Mission Impossible" theme, but it might not be appropriate for a game focused on team building. Make sure that your design is led by and focused on your learning objectives. Recognize that anything that doesn't support your goals might distract from them and be strategic about what you focus on to reduce cognitive overhead.

Although a compelling theme and storyline are critical to an effective ARG, the context and setting should remain authentic to allow learners to apply knowledge and practice new skills in realistic situations.

Follow the Rules. People play games to win, and rules dictate what you need to do to win. Part of the complexity of game design is setting rules of play to balance game play at the sweet spot between "too hard" and "too easy." If your game is too difficult, players will become frustrated and engagement will drop off. If games are too easy, they won't be fun. As mentioned in Chapter Three, this is the concept of flow. When designing an ARG, think about what makes a task difficult and then create rules and scoring mechanisms to support the behaviors that will challenge players but allow them to be successful in realistic ways.

Play to Learn Not Learn to Play. Beware of designing game play rules that are so complex that there's a significant learning curve to figure out how to play the game. Unless, of course, the goal of the game is to promote critical thinking skills. Then it might be appropriate. But in general, ARGs should be designed with clear rules of play to help players focus on the content and accomplishing the learning goals instead of figuring out how to play or win the game. If the game design is too complicated, players will be focused on figuring out the game, not practicing and learning.

Should You Keep It on the Down-Low? In the past, part of the intrigue and appeal of ARGs is that they have been secret or subversive, which created an atmosphere of being "in the know." For learning, you don't want your training experiences to be secret; the goal is for everyone to participate. It might not be a bad idea to think about how you can still create that feeling of subversiveness, however. Secret clues, bonuses, and secret codes are all examples of ways that you can create a "secret" feel to game play.

Technology Drives the Experience. You shouldn't underestimate the importance of the game design, but neither should you underestimate the importance of having a solid technology plan for driving and tracking the game play. Much of the basis of a good game is the mechanics—you can't play Yahtzee without dice or poker without cards. Technology enables game play, should support the design and the context that players are playing in, and is an essential element of what makes an ARG successful.

Will They Play? Just because they're gamers doesn't mean they'll play your game! And just because they aren't doesn't mean they won't! Think about it . . . gamers don't want to waste their time on a game unless it's fun and engaging—just like anyone else. It's absolutely essential that you design your game for engagement, understanding your audience and providing ample information to involve people in the game early. Subversive game play, even for gamers, seems like work when you're in the middle of a conference. Keeping game elements obvious and instructions simple goes a long way when people are busy managing their normal workloads in addition to a learning experience.

Get Some Celebrity Endorsements. A key to ARG success that Tandem Learning has seen over and over is that, if key players are involved, other people will be more engaged too. Identify who the people are within your organization who are the key influencers. Sometimes, this is as simple as getting your management or executive team to play along. In other examples, senior leadership within the organization has acted as characters in the game experience. Designing for recognition and visibility of players within an organization is a great storyline device to communicate the value of the ARG experience.

Design as You Go. The importance of the puppetmaster in an ARG can't be emphasized enough. As you see how people are engaging in your game, it's critical that you are thinking of how to make dynamic adjustments to tweak and improve the game play experience. ARGs are not a static experience, and their execution should be as fluid and intentional as the nature of playing them.

Potential of ARGs

Corporate training initiatives and live events and conferences are great opportunities to leverage the strengths of ARGs at a comparatively low cost and with the ability to spread out the game play over a period of time with short intervals of play time. Because of the flexibility of player time commitment, use of technology, and cost, ARG use has enormous potential to change the way learners think about training. As a designer, ARGs allow you to create realistic practice environments as part of a training experience. Ask yourself: What kind of shared experiences could an ARG provide as a basis for learning and relationship building? The possibilities and opportunities are endless.

■ ■ ■

Key Takeaways

The key takeaways from this chapter are

- Creating an effective and engaging ARG takes careful design and special considerations.

- Augmented reality and alternative reality games are not the same, although they can share common elements.

- Augmented reality games add a game layer on top of reality.

- Alternative reality games integrate real life and online activities through a storyline that seeks to engage learners in an experience that seems real.

- Use specific design principles to ensure successful alternative reality game such as keeping rules and instructions simple, add an element of intrigue or "in the know," and obtain visible endorsements of the game.

14

If You Want to Learn More, Play Games

CHAPTER QUESTIONS

At the end of this chapter, you should be able to answer the following questions:

- What is an example of a non-technical approach to gamification?
- What are some examples of gamification?
- How can we make research-informed decisions about instructional game design?

Introduction

Quick, name three countries that begin with the letter U. It's much easier this time—isn't it? You probably had no problem rattling off the country names. You learned from the game-like interaction at the beginning of this book. The process of using game-based mechanics, aesthetics, and game thinking to engage people, motivate action, promote learning, and solve problems works. The gamification of learning and instruction is not a fad; it is here to stay. The reality is that engaging, meaningful learning occurs when game-based thinking and mechanics are integrated into the instructional design process.

The theory indicates and research strongly supports the assertion that games can be both motivational and instructional. The combination of the two is powerful, effective, and the wave of the future. It is fitting to end a book that describes research in gamification, motivation, game elements, and player types with two examples of gamification for learning. One is a simple example that requires no computer and is designed to encourage adult learning professionals to think about mobile learning solutions. It is included because, with the push toward technology, it's easy to forget that card and board games can be a great alternative to online games. They're easier to prototype and don't require a massive team to build.

The other is an example of a videogame created to teach middle school students math, science, and engineering concepts. It was funded through the National Science Foundation and has been successfully prototyped in a number of school districts.

Pick a Card, Any Card—A Game of Phones*

By Alicia Sanchez and Kris Rockwell

The appropriate use of games includes the determination of the appropriate use of technology. While people often think of video games when they consider serious games, developers of games often focus on how to best provide the learning outcomes to their users, regardless of the technological implementation.

---

*Vignette courtesy of Hybrid Learning Systems and Czarina Games, all rights reserved.

A Game of Phones is a card game designed by Hybrid Learning Systems and Czarina Games (see Figure 14.1). The primary intention of A Game of Phones was to get players thinking through the types of mobile learning solutions that could be possible for a variety of organizational and learning challenges.

In creating a game to provide that outcome, several types of games were initially included in design concepts, including an obvious mobile game, a card game, a board game, and a web-based game. The game designers quickly realized that a large amount of the learning accomplished within the game would be through exposing players to a variety of ideas, including the successes and failures that other players might have experienced in their

Figure 14.1. Sample Card from the Game of Phones Card Deck.

mobile learning efforts. To give players these opportunities, using a digital format was ruled out during the design phase. The decision to move forward with a card game allowed for easy distribution of the game and provided a metaphor that most people are familiar with. Ensuring the instructions were clear and that game play was simple allowed players to focus on creating their own strategies for mobile learning possibilities. The game, initially distributed at the MLearnCon Conference consists of a typical fifty-two card deck. Each deck was comprised of an instruction card and four types of cards:

- *Twenty-One Challenge Cards*—These cards describe a real-world problem that provides a mobile learning challenge. (See Figure 14.2.)

- *Twelve Technology Cards*—These cards feature possible solution technologies such as Native App, Web App, Email or SMS. (See Figure 14.3.)

- *Nine Hardware Cards*—These cards feature various hardwares such as smart phones or tablets. (See Figure 14.4.)

Figure 14.2. Sample Challenge Card.

CHALLENGE

You've been tasked with creating a mobile asset targeted at ensuring that your organization's employees are able to respond accurately to an impending site survey and safety inspection from your governing agency.

CODE: CHAL-C7

Figure 14.3. Sample Technology Card.

Web App

TECHNOLOGY

A computer software application that is hosted in a browser-controlled environment or coded in a browser-supported language (such as JavaScript, combined with a browser-rendered markup language like HTML) and reliant on a common web browser to render the application executable.

CODE: TECH-T1

Figure 14.4. Sample Hardware Card.

Smart Phones

HARDWARE

A smartphone is a mobile phone that offers more advanced computing ability and connectivity than a contemporary feature phone. A smartphone allows the user to run and multitask applications that are native to the underlying hardware. Examples: iPhone, Droid

CODE: HARDW-H1

- *Nine Speaker Cards*—These cards featured a use case from a variety of MLearnCon Speakers (examples include games, job aids, augmented reality, qr codes). (See Figure 14.5.)

In order to play A Game of Phones, each player must have his or her own deck of cards. A single player challenges another player or players with a Challenge card. All players then play one or two Technology cards, one or two Hardware cards, and one (or no) Speaker cards from their decks to form their argument. Once all of the players have made their card selections, which are often placed face down on the table in front of them, they all reveal their cards and verbally present their strategies. At this point, it is up to the players to determine which strategy is "best" if they choose to keep score; but the learning value actually comes in the discussion of the strategies proposed by all the players.

Each of the cards was structured to provide multiple approaches that, when individually considered, could be architected by each player to support his or her ideas and parameters for designing mobile solutions.

Figure 14.5. Sample Speaker Card.

Kris Rockwell
Augmented Reality

CODE: SPKR-S3

In play-testing, players rarely were confronted with a draw situation, but when a draw did occur the players often still verbally presented very differing strategies. Players were able to discuss their strategies from their individual and organizational approaches, and frequently chose cards that were representative of the technologies and hardware that were available to them, indicating they were overlaying their own constraints onto their play strategies.

At the conference, a tournament was hosted, allowing for formal game play, with winners assigned as judged by a panel of experts, but the game was designed to additionally serve as an idea generator that its players could take back to their home organizations and leverage in their workplace challenges.

Survival Master

The Survival Master game is a joint project of Hofstra University, Bloomsburg University, and the CUNY Graduate Center, sponsored by the National Science Foundation. The project seeks to teach students engineering and technology skills through the use of a video game that is designed to be used in the classroom by teachers covering topics related to engineering and math.

The game involves teaching the students concepts of volume, heat flow, R-value, and other information in the context of a video game. The learners need to solve a series of obstacles or problems as they work to become "survival masters." The game teaches a variety of science, technology, engineering, and math concepts while being fun and engaging for middle school students.

The pedagogy behind the educational elements of this video game is the "informed design process," providing students with a series of knowledge and skill builder activities that build on one another to provide students with knowledge and skills necessary to perform a design task.

In the first part of the game, the students play independently. In each activity, they are required to solve problems based on a knowledge and skill builder activity. There are four levels in this part of the game, all designed to teach students basic skills related to engineering. The students learn about topics related to volume, material conductivity, heat flow, and structural integrity. Figure 14.6 shows a player within the "cave of volume," where the student needs to calculate volume of solid objects and cylinders and match the volumes to receive a reward.

Each subject or skill is done in the context of the students training to become "survival masters" so they can teach others how to survive in a hostile environment. Students earn points for their accomplishments and unlock items like power bars to boost their energy levels throughout the game. The activities at each level contain common elements of commercially available video games, such as unlocking chests with hidden surprises, shooting snowballs at targets, and jumping from one platform to another. Figure 14.7 shows a player hiding in an alcove deciding which direction to go to avoid snowball cannons.

Unbeknown to the players, each of the levels in the individual part of the games is preparing them for a group challenge in which they must apply the knowledge and skills learned individually into a group project.

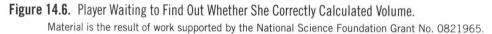

Figure 14.6. Player Waiting to Find Out Whether She Correctly Calculated Volume.
Material is the result of work supported by the National Science Foundation Grant No. 0821965.

Figure 14.7. Deciding Which Direction to Go to Complete the Mission.
Material is the result of work supported by the National Science Foundation Grant No. 0821965.

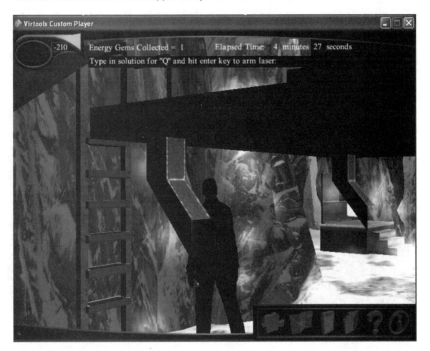

The second part of video game is multiplayer. Here, students must work in a group of four to build a shelter that will withstand extreme temperatures, a wind storm, and snow load. The concept is that the skills learned by the students in the first part of the game will be applied to the multiplayer, game with the students working together to weigh tradeoffs and to develop reasonable compromises involved with the building of the shelter.

The goal is to teach basic concepts related to engineering a structure while helping students to think like engineers by considering tradeoffs in terms of material usage, shape of the structure, structural integrity, and cost in terms of energy used by players. The individual portion of the game ensures that all students have the basic skills needed to understand the larger engineering problem of building a shelter. The group portion of the game forces students to work together and to think through developing a shelter to withstand cold temperatures and wind and snow load. The game has high-quality graphics,

Figure 14.8. Creating a Group Shelter.

Material is the result of work supported by the National Science Foundation Grant No. 0821965.

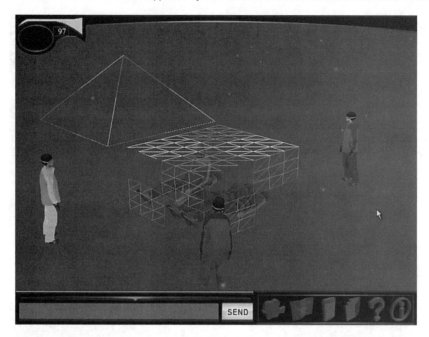

an interesting story line, and activities similar to commercially available video games. The game can be seen at http://gaming2learn.org/

The Virtue of Gamification

As Jane McGonigal, author of *Reality is Broken*, states, "Gamers are ultimately super-powered, hopeful individuals" because they have become virtuosos of four key concepts through their interactions with games:[1]

- *Urgent Optimism*—the desire to act immediately to tackle an obstacle combined with the belief that we have a reasonable hope of success.

- *Social Fabric*—gamers form a bond with other gamers quickly; research shows that we like people better after we play a game with them because it takes trust to engage in a game activity. Playing a game together builds trust, bonds, and cooperation.

- *Blissful Productivity*—People playing games are happier working hard in the game than just "hanging out." Humans are optimized to do challenging and meaningful work.

- *Epic Meaning*—Gamers love to be attached to awe-inspiring missions.

These skills are just some of the "epic wins" we can accomplish if we appropriately gamify instruction and learning. But she is not alone in her optimism; Sebastian Deterding discusses the elements that make a gamification experience matter by describing the need for meaning, mastery, and autonomy.[2]

Wouldn't it be great if all learning experiences contained blissful productivity, feelings of mastery, and epic meaning? Why can't they? If we focus on properly applying gamification concepts to learning and instruction, we can revolutionize learning, energize stale training classrooms, and engage students like never before.

Next Steps

Grokking the research and ideas in this book is helpful in understanding gamification, perhaps even critical to the process, but it is not enough. To truly grok the gamification process, play games. Play them as a learner and as an instructional game designer. Notice the reward structures, understand when the game let's you switch between first- and third-person perspectives, notice the aesthetics, participate in the story of the game, experience failure by getting your player killed on purpose to see what happens. Find the greater meaning in games like FoldIt and Darfur Is Dying.

Gamification elements cannot be fully described in text. They must be experienced in game play. Find instructional and non-instructional games, play them, and witness the impact. Use the research in this book to carefully design gamification experiences that motivate and educate learners. The research provides a path toward effective gamification of learning and instruction. Follow it and your gamification efforts will be successful—epic learning will result.

■ ■ ■

Key Takeaways

The key takeaways from this chapter are

- Gamification doesn't always have to involve online video games; simple elements like timing or a card game can add game-based thinking to learning.

- The research provides a clear path for gamification that links game elements to learning outcomes.

- Epic learning can occur with the proper application of gamification.

- Gamers are virtuosos of four key concepts: Urgent Optimism, Social Fabric, Blissful Productivity, and Epic Meaning.

- Gamification that matters includes meaning, mastery, and autonomy for the players.

- You have to play games to understand gamification. Go to http://tinyurl.com/gamificationLI and continue the discussion about the gamification of learning and instruction.

Glossary

Achiever—Player type who wants achievement within the content of the game. He or she wants to be at the top of the leaderboard. One of Bartle's player types.

ADDIE—A model for developing instruction with five phases, each represented by the first letter in the acronym: Analysis, Design, Development, Implementation, and Evaluation.

Affective Domain—Deals with attitudes, interest, values, beliefs, and emotions.

Agôn—The pattern of play that relates to competition.

Alea—The pattern of play related to chance.

Alternate Reality Game (ARG)—A game where the game play integrates real life and online activities through a storyline that seeks to engage learners in an experience that seems real.

America's Army—A massively multi-player online role play game (MMORPG) where a player assumes a role of a soldier in the U.S. Army and then goes through missions as that soldier. Missions include acting as a medic or an infantry solider. The game is one of the recruitment tools of the Army.

Anthropomorphic—Having human-like characteristics or form. Something that is not human but has taken on human-like characteristics and/or form. The personification of an object, in this case, the characteristics of a computer animated character that interacts with the learner in a human-like interface.

ARCS Motivation Model—Motivational model originally created to develop instruction that represents the concepts of attention, relevance, confidence, and satisfaction.

Augmented Reality Game—A game where a game level is superimposed on top of reality. An augmented reality game adds additional information to real-life environments and objects usually through a smart phone or specially made glasses.

Avatar—Virtual character a person assumes as he or she moves about within a game.

Behavior Rules—Rules that govern the social contract between two or more players, in other words the rules related to being a good sport about the game. These rules are game etiquette. Also see Implicit Rules.

Conceptual Knowledge—Knowledge about ideas, events, or objects that have a common attribute or a set of common attributes.

Constituative Rules—The underlying formal structures dictating game functionality. Also see Foundational Rules.

Curtain—In alternative reality games, a theoretical curtain that separates the game management activities from the game play environment. The curtain provides the illusion that the game is playing out naturally,

Curve of Interest—The idea that you need to hook a player with interesting content or activities in the game. If you plotted the interest of the player in the game, it would look like a series of peaks and valleys on a line graph.

Declarative Knowledge—Knowledge that can only be learned through memorization. Also known as verbal knowledge or factual knowledge.

Distributed Practice—A method whereby the learner distributes time dedicated to learning content or information over a series of small time periods rather than doing it all at once, which is known as mass practice or cramming.

Easter Egg—A message, graphic, sound effect, or an unusual change in program behavior that occurs in response to some undocumented set of commands, mouse clicks, keystrokes, button presses, or other stimuli intended as a joke, an amusing entertainment piece, or to display program credits.

Episodic Memory—Memory of information, details, and surroundings about a specific event or episode that involved the self and occurred at a particular time and place.

Explorer—Player type who try to find out as much as they can about a game environment. They want to understand the breadth of the game and learn all the nooks and crannies. One of Bartle's player types.

Extrinsic Motivation—Behavior undertaken in order to obtain some reward or avoid punishment.

First-Person Shooter—A game that involves moving around an environment encountering obstacles from a first-person perspective and using weapons to dispatch enemies.

First-Person Thinker—A game that involves moving around an environment encountering obstacles from a first-person perspective but not using violence to overcome the obstacles or solve problems.

Fixed Interval—Reinforcement for a behavior provided after a fixed amount of time has elapsed.

Fixed Ratio—Reinforcement after a pre-selected number of times a behavior is exhibited.

Flow State—A state of mind whereby a person playing a game player forgets his or her normal cares and the passage of time. The gamer derives intense satisfaction from the sheer pleasure of performing the activity required by the game and becomes engrossed within the game itself. The game becomes a sort of reality and the gamer reacts just as he or she would in an actual situation. The concept was developed by Mihaly Csikszentmihalyi.

Foundational Rules—The underlying formal structures dictating game functionality. Also see Constituative Rules.

Game—A system in which players engage in an abstract challenge, defined by rules, interactivity, and feedback, that results in a quantifiable outcome often eliciting an emotional reaction.

Gamification Design Document—Document to provide an outline and guidance to a team involved with a gamification project.

Gamification—Game-based mechanics, aesthetics, and game thinking to engage people, motivate action, promote learning, and solve problems.

Halo—A video game in the first-person shooter genre available for the Xbox series of game consoles. Subsequent versions include Halo 2. The game revolves around a character named Master Chief, a human super-soldier equipped with battle armor who battles aliens.

Hero's Journey—Common story structure used in games where the hero is forced out of a comfortable, albeit boring, lifestyle and undergoes a transformation through mental and physical trials and tribulations.

Ilinx—The pattern of play related to a state of dizziness or disorder, which could be physical or mental.

Implicit Rules—Rules that govern the social contract between two or more players, in other words, the rules related to being a good sport about the game or game etiquette. Also see Behavior Rules.

Intrinsic Motivation—When a person undertakes an activity for its own sake, for the enjoyment it provides, the learning it permits, or the feeling of accomplishment it evokes.

Jack Principles—A series of ideas and thoughts developed by Jellyvision, Inc., to create an Interactive Conversation Interface (iCi) (rhymes with "sticky"). The idea is that the Jack Principles—based on their popular game You Don't Know Jack—describes how to create an interface where it feels like the "host" of the learning is speaking right to you.

Killer—Player type who is interested in defeating others by killing them or defeating them in any way possible. One of Bartle's player types.

Leaderboard—List of the players who have the high score in a game or a game-like activity.

Massively Multiplayer Online Role Play Game (MMORPG)—Games in which the player assumes a role and identity not typically related to his or her real-world self and attempts to earn points to move to a higher level within the game. Players interact within a persistent online world. Once a role is assumed, the player embarks on adventures or quests with a team, guild, or clan. They seek treasure, battle monsters, or accomplish other specific goals and objectives that are an inherent part of the world.

Massive Multiplayer Online War Game Leveraging the Internet (MMOWGLI)—The Military's attempt at crowdsourcing the problem of the Somali pirates. The premise is to have players work as pirates and work against pirates and then to determine what works from solutions developed by the players.

Meta-Analysis—A study of studies where researchers take the results from many separate studies and compare them to find commonalities.

Mimicary—The pattern of play related to simulation or role play.

Multi-User Dungeon (MUD)—A real-time virtual world described entirely in text. MUDs were one of the first virtual environments in which people could interact online. The term "dungeon" was used because these text-based games were an extension of the board games in the genre of Dungeons and Dragons. The characters, rooms where chats took place, topics, and environment where similar to the Dungeons and Dragons games. Also referred to as multi-user dialogue or multi-user dimension.

Non-Player Character (NPC)—A computer-controlled character that can interact with the human player in the game. Non-player characters typically provide instruction, give hints, or otherwise communicated pre-scripted dialogue.

Operant Conditioning—The use of consequences or rewards to modify the occurrence and form of behavior.

Operational Rules—Rules that describe how a game is played.

Persistent World—A virtual world that continues to exist even after a learner exits. Changes made by a participant remain after the participant logs out.

Procedural Knowledge—Knowledge of step-by-step instructions for performing a particular task.

Progressive Disclosure—This is a technique in which a computer program, in this case a game, displays information in small "chunks" a little bit at a time. The technique is used so that a player is not overwhelmed by the amount of information displayed on the screen.

Pro-Social Behavior—Behavior that is not aggressive and contributes positively to a social situation.

Psychomotor Domain—The intersection of physical skills and cognitive skills.

Puppetmaster—The person in an alternative reality game who is responsible for overseeing the game experience.

Rule-Based Knowledge—Knowledge that expresses the relationships between concepts, indicating cause-and-effect and if/then relationships.

Scaffolding—The design of instruction that encourages a learner to move from one level of knowledge to the next with increasing difficultly and the need to apply more skill to master the new level.

Self-Determination Theory—A macro theory that explains human motivation to perform a task or an activity as being internally driven as opposed to the externally driven theory of operant conditioning. The three main components are autonomy, competence, and relatedness. The theory has been used to describe motivation in a broad range of human activities, including sports, healthcare, religion, work, and education.

Scrum—A development process based on the agile software development model whereby multiple small teams work intensively and interdependently for small quick bursts and then reconvene to reassess progress and create new priorities. Led by a scrum master who facilitates the process.

Serious Game—A game designed for a primary purpose other than pure entertainment.

Simulation—A self-contained immersive environment in which the learner interacts within the environment in an attempt to learn or practice skills or knowledge. Typically, only one person can navigate the on-screen avatar, and interactions are only between the computer and the learner. One of the most common types of simulations, is a branching story, which asks the learner a series of questions and the learner chooses the branch that most mimics what he or she would say or do in that situation.

Socializers—Player type who is interested in relationships with other players and in organizing players, that is, connecting with others through the game environment. The game is merely a backdrop in which socializers can enjoy the company of others. One of Bartle's player types.

This Is Not a Game (TINAG)—Commonly used to describe the tone of an ARG. The goal is to create an experience in which the players don't necessarily feel like they are playing a game. The actions they take, the decisions they make, and the puzzles they solve should not be extraneous to the storyline.

Trailhead—In an alternative reality game, the trailhead is a clue that leads players into the game. Also sometimes called a rabbit hole.

Variable Interval—Reinforcement for a behavior provided after a variable amount of time has elapsed.

Variable Ratio—Reinforcement for a behavior provided in unpredictable intervals.

Virtual Social World (VSW)—The concept of creating a virtual world in which socialization is the primary focus. Can be expansive virtual spaces in which different types of interactions between avatars can occur in different areas, commonly the commercial virtual worlds such as Second Life.

Virtual World—A generic term for discussing a wide variety of online spaces in which participants, as avatars, interact with one another.

Uncanny Valley—A design principle that states that if an avatar or character is made more humanlike in its appearance and motion, the emotional response from a human being will become increasingly positive until a point is reached at which the response suddenly becomes strongly repulsive.

UI—An acronym for User Interface. The user interface is the elements on the computer screen with which the player must interact to gain information, navigate, and work the game being played.

World of Warcraft (WoW)—One of the most popular massively multiplayer online role play games. Players assume one of many roles and do battle against each other or travel on quests.

Zone of Proximal Development—A concept introduced by Soviet psychologist and constructivist Lev Vygotsky. The zone of proximal development is the distance between the actual developmental level as determined by independent problem solving and the level of potential development as determined through problem solving under adult guidance, or in collaboration with more capable peers.

Notes

Chapter 1

1. Here is a list of counties that begin with the letter "U." Uganda, Ukraine, United Arab Emirates, United Kingdom, United States of America, Uruguay, and Uzbekistan. How did you do?
2. Saatchi & Saatchi. (2011, June). Engagement unleashed: Gamification for business, brands, and loyalty. www.slideshare.net/Saatchi_S/gamification-study.
3. You can watch a great video showing this concept in action at www.thefuntheory.com.
4. Check out Zombies Run at www.zombiesrungame.com/
5. This vignette is based on several news stories, including www.alcoa.com/global/en/news/news_detail .asp?newsYear=2007&pageID=20070305005759en and http://etceteraedutainment.com/index.php.
6. Vignette contributed by World of Warcraft player Judy Unrein. Thanks, Judy!
7. Salen, K., & Zimmerman, E. (2004). *Rules of play: Game design fundamentals.* Cambridge, MA: MIT Press, p. 80.
8. Koster, R. (2005). *A theory of fun for game design.* Scottsdale, AZ: Paraglyph Press, p. 34.
9. Zichermann, G. (2010, October 26). Fun is the future: Mastering gamification. *Google Tech Talk.* http://youtu.be/6O1gNVeaE4g.
10. Kim, A.J. (2011, March 23). Gamification 101: Designing the player journey. *Google Tech Talk.* http://youtu.be/B0H3ASbnZmc.
11. Gartner Group. ((2011, April 12). Gartner says by 2015, more than 50 percent of organizations that manage innovation processes will gamify those processes. www.gartner.com/it/page.jsp?id=1629214
12. Gamification. (2011, June 16). http://en.wikipedia.org/wiki/Gamification.

13. Kim, A.J. (2011, March 23). Gamification 101: Designing the player journey. *Google Tech Talk.* http://youtu.be/B0H3ASbnZmc.
14. Bepi Entertainment. A brief history of wargaming. www.faculty.virginia.edu/setear/students/wargames/page1a.htm.
15. Entertainment Software Association. Game player data. www.theesa.com/facts/gameplayer.asp.
16. eMarketer:Digital Intelligence. (2011, January 12). Social gaming market to surpass $1 billion. www.emarketer.com/Article.aspx?R=1008166.
17. Caoili, E. (2010, March 9). Study: U.S. gamers spent $3.8 billion on MMOs in 2009. *Gamasutra.* www.gamasutra.com/view/news/27581/Study_US_Gamers_Spent_38_Billion_On_MMOs_in_2009.php.
18. Goldman, T. (2010, August 26). Videogame industry worth over $100 billion worldwide. *The Escapist.* www.escapistmagazine.com/news/view/103064-Videogame-Industry-Worth-Over-100-Billion-Worldwide.
19. Gartner Group. (2011, April 12).
20. eMarketer: Digital Intelligence. (2011, January 12).
21. Gartner Group. (2011, April 12).
22. Whitney, K. (2007, March 14). Cisco illustrates how gaming could work for corporate learning. *Chief Learning Officer.* http://clomedia.com/articles/view/cisco_illustrates_how_gaming_could_work_for_corporate_learning.
23. IBM Innov8. www-01.ibm.com/software/solutions/soa/innov8/index.html.
24. Ungerleider, N. (2011, May 10). Wannabe SEALs help U.S. Navy hunt pirates in massively multiplayer game. *Fast Company.* www.fastcompany.com/1752574/the-us-navys-massively-multiplayer-pirate-hunting-game.
25. Gartner Group. (2011, April 12).
26. King, R. (2011, April 4). The games companies play: Siemens, Hilton, and Target are using games to train workers and improve how they design and market products. *Bloomberg Businessweek.* www.businessweek.com/technology/content/apr2011/tc2011044_943586_page_2.htm.

Chapter 2

1. Klein, J.H. (1985, August). The abstraction of reality for games and simulations. *The Journal of the Operational Research Society*, 36(8), 671–678.
2. Salen, K., & Zimmerman, E. (2004). *Rules of play: Game design fundamentals.* Cambridge, MA: MIT Press, p. 80.
3. Salen, K., & Zimmerman, E. (2004). p. 259.
4. Salen, K., & Zimmerman, E. (2004).
5. Goldman, N. (2003, September 15). A textbook case: MIT students break the bank in Las Vegas. *ABC News Online.* http://semyon.com/abc%20primetime.htm.
6. Salen, K., & Zimmerman, E. (2004). p. 255.
7. Crawford, C. (2003). *Chris Crawford on game design.* Indianapolis, IN: New Riders Publishing, p. 8.
8. Hunicke, R. (2009). Wildflowers: The UX of game/play. *UX Week.* http://vimeo.com/6984481.
9. Schell, J. (2008). *The art of game design: A book of lenses.* Waltham, MA: Morgan Kaufmann. p. 233.
10. Schell, J. (2008). *The art of game design: A book of lenses.* Waltham, MA: Morgan Kaufmann, p. 273, and Monomyth (2011, June 16). http://en.wikipedia.org/wiki/Monomyth.

11. Schell, J. (2008). p. 247.
12. Juul, J. (2009). Fear of failing? The many meanings of difficulty in video games. In B. Perron & M.J.P. Wolf (Eds.), *The video game theory reader 2.* New York: Routledge, pp. 237–252. www.jesperjuul.net/text/fearoffailing/

Chapter 3

1. Lepper, M.R. (1988). Motivational considerations in the study of instruction. *Cognition and Instruction, 5*(4), 289–309.
2. Beswick, D. (2007, February 15). Management implications of the interaction between intrinsic motivation and extrinsic rewards. www.beswick.info/psychres/management.htm.
3. Lepper, M.R. (1988).
4. Keller, J. (1987). Development and use of the ARCS model of instructional design. *Journal of Instructional Development, 10*(3), 2–10.
5. Malone, T. (1981). Toward a theory of intrinsically motivating instruction. *Cognitive Science, 4.* 333–369.
6. Lepper, M.R. (1988).
7. Malone, T.W., & Lepper, M.R. (1988). Making learning fun: A taxonomy of intrinsic motivations for learning. In R.E. Snow & M.J. Farr (Eds.), *Aptitude, learning, and instruction: Vol. III. Cognitive and affective process analyses* (pp. 229–253). Mahwah, NJ: Lawrence Erlbaum Associates. Thanks to Brett Bixler for pointing out this reference.
8. Gredler, M.E. (1997). *Learning and instruction: Theory into practice* (3rd ed.). Upper Saddle River, NJ: Prentice Hall.
9. Biehler, R.F., & Snowman, J. (1986). *Psychology applied to teaching* (5th ed.). Boston: Houghton Mifflin.
10. Biehler, R.F., & Snowman, J. (1986).
11. Biehler, R.F., & Snowman, J. (1986).
12. Floyd, D. (2010, November 25). The Skinner box: Extra credits. *The Escapist.* www.escapist magazine.com/videos/view/extra-credits/2487-The-Skinner-Box.
13. Biehler, R.F., & Snowman, J. (1986).
14. Hopson, J. (2001, April 27). Behavioral game design. *Gamasutra.* www.gamasutra.com/view/feature/3085/behavioral_game_design.php.
15. Hopson, J. (2001, April 27).
16. Hopson, J. (2001, April 27).
17. Biehler, R.F., & Snowman, J. (1986). *Psychology applied to teaching* (5th ed.). Boston: Houghton Mifflin, and Hopson, J. (2001, April 27). Behavioral game design. *Gamasutra.* www.gamasutra.com/view/feature/3085/behavioral_game_design.php.
18. Ryan, R.M., & Deci, E.L. (2000). Intrinsic and extrinisic motivations: Classic definitions and new directions. *Contemporary Educational Psychology, 25,* 54–67, and Ryan, R.M., & Deci, E.L. (2000). Self-determination theory and the facilitation of intrinsic motivation, social development, and well-being. *American Psychologist, 55,* 68–78.
19. Ryan, R.M., Rigby, C.S., & Przybylski, A. (2006). The motivational pull of video games: A self-determination theory approach. *Motivation and Emotion, 30,* 347–364.
20. Ryan, R.M., Rigby, C.S., & Przybylski, A. (2006).

21. Ryan, R.M., Rigby, C.S., & Przybylski, A. (2006).

22. Ausubel, D.P., & Youssef, M. (1965). The effect of spaced repetition on meaningful retention. *Journal of General Psychology, 73,* 147–150, and Caple, C. (1996). *The effects of spaced practice and spaced review on recall and retention using computer assisted instruction.* Ann Arbor, MI: University of Michigan Press.

23. Clark, C.C., & Mayer, R.E. (2002). *e-Learning and the science of instruction: Proven guidelines for consumers and designers of multimedia learning.* San Francisco: Pfeiffer, and National Research Council. (1991). In D. Druckman & R.A. Bjork (Eds.), *In the mind's eye: Enhancing human performance.* Washington DC: National Academy Press.

24. Fleming, M., & Levie, H. (1978). *Instructional message design: Principles from the behavioral sciences.* Englewood Cliffs, NJ: Educational Technology Publications.

25. Vygotsky, L.S. (1978). *Mind and society: The development of higher psychological processes.* Cambridge, MA: Harvard University Press, and Zone of proximal development (2011). http://en.wikipedia.org/wiki/Zone_of_proximal_development#cite_note-0

26. Gredler, M.E. (1997). pp. 263–264.

27. Gredler, M.E. (1997). pp. 147, 153.

28. Gredler, M.E. (1997). pp. 147, 153.

29. Kapp, K.M., & O'Driscoll, T. (2010). *Learning in 3D: Adding a new dimension to enterprise learning and collaboration.* San Francisco: Pfeiffer.

30. Brown, J.S., Collins, A., & Duguid, P. (1989, January/February). Situated cognition and the culture of learning. *Educational Researcher, 18*(1), 32–42.

31. Gredler, M.E. (1997).

32. Brown, J.S., Collins, A., & Duguid, P. (1989, January/February).

33. Brown, J.S., Collins, A., & Duguid, P. (1989, January/February).

34. Gredler, M.E. (1997).

35. Buckley, K.E., & Anderson, C.A. (2006). A theoretical model of the effects and consequences of playing video games. In P. Vorderer & J. Bryant (Eds.), *Playing video games: Motives, responses, and consequences* (pp. 363–378). Mahwah, NJ: Lawrence Erlbaum Associates.

36. Csikszentmihalyi, M. (1975). Play and intrinsic rewards. *Journal of Humanistic Psychology, 15*(3), 41–63.

37. Csikszentmihalyi, M. (1975).

Chapter 4

1. An often cited meta-analysis is Dempsey, J.V., Rasmussen, K., & Lucassen, B. (1996). Instructional gaming: Implications for instructional technology. *Proceedings of the Annual Meeting of the Association for Educational Communications and Technology*, Nashville, Tennessee, was purposefully left out of this list because that meta-analysis focused on classifying game types and learning outcomes but did not offer any indication of the effectiveness of games for learning.

2. Randel, J.M., Morris, B.A., Wetzel, C.D., & Whitehill, B.V. (1992). The effectiveness of games for educational purposes: A review of recent research. *Simulation and Gaming, 23*(3), 261–276.

3. A number of studies were used to draw the conclusion. The number of actual studies reported in total in the research report is actually higher.

4. Randel, J.M., Morris, B.A., Wetzel, C.D., & Whitehill, B.V. (1992).

5. Wolfe, J. (1997) The effectiveness of business games in strategic management course work. *Simulation & Gaming, 28*(4), 360–376.

6. Wolfe, J. (1997).

7. Hays, R.T. (2005). *The effectiveness of instructional games: A literature review and discussion.* Naval Air Warfare Center Training Systems Division (No 2005–004).

8. Hays, R.T. (2005).

9. Hays, R.T. (2005).

10. Hays, R.T. (2005).

11. Vogel, J.J., Vogel, D.S., Cannon-Bowers, J., Bowers, C.A., Muse, K., & Wright, M. (2006). Computer gaming and interactive simulations for learning: A meta-analysis. *Journal of Educational Computing Research, 34*(3), 229–243.

12. Vogel, J.J., Vogel, D.S., Cannon-Bowers, J., Bowers, C.A., Muse, K., & Wright, M. (2006).

13. Ke, F. (2009). A qualitative meta-analysis of computer games as learning tools. In R.E. Ferdig (Ed.), *Effective electronic gaming in education* (Vol. 1, pp. 1–32). Hershey, PA: Information Science Reference.

14. Ke, F. (2009).

15. Sitzmann, T. (2011). A meta-analytic examination of the instructional effectiveness of computer-based simulation games. *Personnel Psychology, 64*(2), 489–528) and Sitzmann, T., & Ely, K. (2010). *A meta-analytic examination of the effectiveness of computer-based simulation games.* Binghamton, NY: ADL Research Lab.

16. Sitzmann, T. (2011).

17. Sitzmann, T. (2011).

18. Howard-Jones, P.A., & Demetriou, S. (2008, September 11). Uncertainty and engagement with learning games. *Instructional Science, 37,* 519–536.

19. Howard-Jones, P.A., & Demetriou, S. (2008, September 11).

20. Howard-Jones, P. A., & Demetriou, S. (2008, September 11).

21. Atkinson, J.W. (1957). Motivational determinants of risk taking behavior. *Psychological Review, 64,* 359–372.

22. Howard-Jones, P. A., & Demetriou, S. (2008, September 11).

23. Howard-Jones, P. A., & Demetriou, S. (2008, September 11).

24. Howard-Jones, P. A., & Demetriou, S. (2008, September 11).

25. Howard-Jones, P. A., & Demetriou, S. (2008, September 11).

26. Lepper, M.R. (1988). Motivational considerations in the study of instruction. *Cognition and Instruction, 5*(4), 289–309.

27. Lepper, M.R. (1988).

28. Malone, T. (1981). Toward a theory of intrinsically motivating instruction. *Cognitive Science, 4,* 333–369.

29. Deci, E.L., Ryan, R.M., & Koestner, R. (1999). A meta-analytic review of experiments examining the effects of extrinsic rewards on intrinsic motivation. *Psychological Bulletin, 125,* 627–668.

30. Lepper, M.R. (1988).

31. Harackiewicz, J.M., & Manderlink, G. (1984). A process analysis of the effectives of performance-contingent rewards on intrinsic motivation. *Journal of Experimental Social Psychology, 20,* 531–551.

32. Eisenberger, R., Rhoades, L., & Cameron, J. (1999). Does pay for performance increase or decrease perceived self-determination and intrinsic motivation? *Journal of Personality and Social Psychology, 77*(5), 1026–1040.

33. Eisenberger, R., Rhoades, L. & Cameron, J. (1999).

34. Eisenberger , R., & Armeli, S. (1997). Can salient reward increase creative performance without reducing intrinsic creative interest? *Journal of Personality and Social Psychology, 72*, 652–663, and Eisenberger, R., Armeli, S., & Pertz, J. (1998). Can the promise of reward increase creativity? *Journal of Personality and Social Psychology, 74*, 704–714.

35. Lepper, M.R. (1988).

36. Beswick, D. (2007, February 15). Management implications of the interaction between intrinsic motivation and extrinsic rewards. www.beswick.info/psychres/management.htm.

37. Harter, S. (1981). A new self-report scale of intrinsic versus extrinsic orientation in the classroom: Motivational and informational components. *Developmental Psychology, 17,* 300–312.

38. Lepper, M.R., Iyengar, S.S., & Corpus, J.H. (2005). Intrinsic and extrinsic motivational orientations in the classroom: Age differences and academic correlates. *Journal of Educational Psychology, 97*(2), 184–196.

39. Lepper, M.R., Iyengar, S.S., & Corpus, J.H. (2005).

40. Lepper, M.R., Iyengar, S.S., & Corpus, J.H. (2005).

41. Deci, E.L., & Ryan, R.M. (1985). *Intrinsic motivation and self-determination in human behavior.* New York: Plenum Press, and Lepper, M.R., & Henderlong, J. (2000). Turning "play" into "work" and "work" into "play": 25 years of research on intrinsic versus extrinsic motivation. In C. Sansone & J.M. Harackiewicz (Eds.), *Intrinsic and extrinsic motivation: The search for optimal motivation and performance* (pp. 257–307). San Diego: Academic Press.

42. Lepper, M.R., Iyengar, S.S., & Corpus, J.H. (2005).

43. Lepper, M.R., Iyengar, S.S., & Corpus, J.H. (2005).

44. Chandler, C.L., & Connell, J.P. (1987). Children's intrinsic, extrinsic, and internalized motivation: A developmental study of children's reasons for liked and disliked behaviours. *British Journal of Developmental Psychology, 5,* 357–365, and Deci, E.L., Eghrari, H., Patrick, B.C., & Leone, D.R. (1994). Facilitating internalization: The self-determination theory perspective. *Journal of Personality, 62,* 119–141.

45. Yee, N., & Bailenson, J.N. (2006). Walk a mile in digital shoes: The impact of embodied perspective-taking on the reduction of negative stereotyping in immersive virtual environments. *Proceedings of PRESENCE 2006: The 9th Annual International Workshop on Presence.* August 24–26, Cleveland, Ohio.

46. Fox, J., & Bailenson, J.N. (2009). Virtual self-modeling: The effects of vicarious reinforcement and identification on exercise behaviors. *Media Psychology*, 12, 1–25.

47. Yee, N., Bailenson, J.N., & Duchenaut, N. (2009). The Proteus effect: Implications of transformed digital self-representation on online and offline behavior. *Communication Research, 36*(2), 285–312.

48. Ersner-Hershfield, H., Bailenson, J., & Carstensen, L.L. (2008). *A vivid future self: Immersive virtual reality enhances retirement saving.* Chicago: Association for Psychological Science.

49. Yee, N., & Bailenson, J.N. (2007). The Proteus effect: The effect of transformed self-representation on behavior. *Human Communication Research, 33,* 271–290.

50. Yee, N., Bailenson, J.N., & Duchenaut, N. (2009). The Proteus effect implications of transformed digital self-representation on online and offline behavior. *Communication Research, 36,* 285–312.

51. Baylor, A.L., & Kim, Y. (2005). Simulating instructional roles through pedagogical agents. *International Journal of Artificial Intelligence in Education, 15*(1), 95–115.

52. Baylor, A.L., & Kim, Y. (2005).

53. Libby, L.K., Shaeffer, E.M., Eibach, R.P., & Slemmer, J.A. (2007). Picture yourself at the polls: Visual perspective in mental imagery affects self-perception and behavior. *Psychological Science, 18,* 199–203.

54. Libby, L.K., Eibach, R.P., & Gilovich, T. (2005). Here's looking at me: The effect of memory perspective on assessments of personal change. *Journal of Personality and Social Psychology, 88,* 50–62, and McIsaac, H.K., & Eich, E. (2002). Vantage point in episodic memory. *Psychonomic Bulletin & Review, 9,* 146–150, and Robinson, J.A., & Swanson, K.L. (1993). Field and observer modes of remembering. *Memory, 1,* 169–184.

55. Lisa, L. Personnel correspondence, May 23, 2011.

Chapter 5

1. Barlett, C.P., Anderson, C.A., & Swing, E.L. (2008, December 22). Video game effects— Confirmed, suspected, and speculative: A review of evidence. *Simulation Gaming, 40,* 377. http://sag.sagepub.com/content/40/3/377, and Green, C.S., & Bavelier, D. (2003). Action video game modified visual selective attention. *Nature, 423,* 534–537.

2. Barlett, C.P., Anderson, C.A., & Swing, E.L. (2008, December 22).

3. Barlett, C.P., Anderson, C.A., & Swing, E.L. (2008, December 22).

4. These items were first found in an online presentation titled Are Video Game Players Better at Laparoscopic Surgical Tasks? presented by J.C. Rosser, P.J. Lynch, A.L. Haskamp, A. Yalif, D.A. Gentile, & L. Giammaria. www.psychology.iastate.edu/~dgentile/MMVRC_Jan_20_MediaVersion.pdf.

5. Yuji, H. (1996). Computer games and information-processing skills. *Perceptual and Motor Skills, 83,* 643–647, and Brandil, B. (2007). The effect of video game laying and video game experience on anticipation. Missouri Western State University. http://clearinghouse.missouriwestern.edu/manuscripts/847.php.

6. Griffith, J.L., Voloschin, P., Gibb, G.D., & Bailey, J.R. (1983). Differences in eye-hand motor coordination of video-game users and non-users. *Perceptual and Motor Skills, 57*(1), 155–158.

7. Barlett, C.P., Anderson, C.A., & Swing, E.L. (2008, December 22).

8. Barlett, C.P., Anderson, C.A., & Swing, E.L. (2008, December 22).

9. Phend, C. (2007, February 19). Video games hone laparoscopic surgery skills. www.medpagetoday.com/Surgery/GeneralSurgery/5089, and Rosser, J.C, Lynch, Cuddihy, L.A.L., Gentile, D.A., Klonsky, J., & Merrell, M. (2007). The impact of video games on training surgeons in the 21st Century. *Archives of Surgery, 142*(2), 181–186.

10. Inskeep, S. (2008, January 21). Surgery trainees warm up using video games. *National Public Radio Broadcast.* www.npr.org/templates/story/story.php?storyId=18279048.

11. Check out the game for yourself at http://fold.it/portal/

12. Play the Phylo game at http://phylo.cs.mcgill.ca/eng/index.html.

13. Conquer the world yourself in Civilization V at www.civilization5.com/

14. Federation of American Scientists. (2006). Harnessing the power of video games for learning. www.fas.org/gamesummit/Resources/Summit%20on%20Educational%20Games.pdf.

15. Reeves, B., Malone, T.W., & O'Driscoll, T. (2008). Leaderships online labs. *Harvard Business Review,* pp. 58–66.

16. 70s board game contains eerie BP oil spill scenarios. (2010, July 6). *CNN News Blog.* http://news.blogs.cnn.com/2010/07/06/70s-board-game-contains-eerie-bp-oil-spill-scenarios/

17. LSU players use video games to prepare. (2008, January 5). *NBC Sports Online.* http://nbcsports.msnbc.com/id/22517376/

18. Banks, D. (2010, October 20). U.S. Army turns to videogames for training. GeekDat at *Wired.com.* www.wired.com/geekdad/2010/10/jtcoic/all/1.

19. Banks, D. (2010, October, 20).

20. Shaffer, D.M., & Collura, M.J. (2009). Evaluating the effectiveness of a personal response system in the classroom. *Teaching of Psychology, 36*, 273–277.

21. Information on gamification with audience response system. http://turningtalk.turningtechnologies .com/home/

22. NikePlus information. http://nikerunning.nike.com/nikeos/p/nikeplus/en_US/

23. Video game fans dance off extra pounds. (2004, May 23). *USA Today Online.* www.usatoday.com/tech/news/2004–05–23-video-health_x.htm.

24. Schmidt, T.S. (2007, February 1). Is the Wii really good for your health? *Time Online.* www.time .com/time/business/article/0,8599,1584697,00.html#ixzz1Onoij21f.

25. Laino, C. (2010, February 25). Wii games speed stroke rehab: Video games help stroke survivors regain arm strength in study. *WebMD.* www.webmd.com/stroke/news/20100225/wii-games-speed-stroke-rehab

26. Greitemeyer, T., & Osswald, S. (2010, February). Effects of prosocial video games on prosocial behavior. *Journal of Personality and Social Psychology, 98*(2), 211–221.

27. Greitemeyer, T., & Osswald, S. (2010, February).

28. Greitemeyer, T., & Osswald, S. (2010, February).

29. Liau, A.K. Khoo, A., Bushman, B.J., Huesmann, R., Sakamoto, A., Gentile, D.A., Craig, C.A., Yukawa, S., Ihori, N., Saleem, M., Ming, L.M., & Shibuya, A. (2009, March 25). The effects of prosocial video games on prosocial behaviors: International evidence from correlational, longitudinal, and experimental studies. *Personality and Social Psychology Bulletin, 35*(6), 752.

30. Peng, W., Lee, M., & Heeter. (2010). The effects of a serious game on role-taking and willingness to help. *Journal of Communication. 60,* 723–742.

31. Retrieved from Thinking Worlds website. How was a complex certification exam transformed into a pioneering new 3D serious game? www.caspianlearning.co.uk/company-news/how-was-a-complex-certification-exam-transformed-into-a-pioneering-new-3d-serious-game.htm.

32. Chuang, T.-Y., & Chen, W.-F. (2009). Effect of computer-based video games on children: An experimental study. *Educational Technology & Society, 12*(2), 1–10.

33. Basak, C., Boot, W.R., Voss, M.W., & Kramer, A.F. (2008). Can training in a real-time strategy video game attenuate cognitive decline in older adults? *Psychology and Aging, 23*(4), 765–777.

Chapter 6

1. Kim, A.J. (2011, February 16). Smart gamification: Designing the player journey. *Google Tech Talks.* www.youtube.com/watch?v=B0H3ASbnZmc.

2. Kim, A.J. (2011, February 16).

3. Bartle, R. (1996). Hearts, clubs, diamonds, spaces: Players who suit MUDS. Colchester, Essex, UK: MUSE Ltd. www.mud.co.uk/richard/hcds.htm#1, and Schell, J. (2008). *The art of game design: A book of lenses.* Waltham, MA: Morgan Kaufmann, pp. 110–112.

4. Salen, K., & Zimmerman, E. (2006). *The game design reader: Rules of play anthology: Caillois: The definition of play, the classification of games.* Cambridge, MA: The MIT Press.

5. Salen, K., & Zimmerman, E. (2006).

6. Salen, K., & Zimmerman, E. (2006).

7. Salen, K., & Zimmerman, E. (2006).

8. Salen, K., & Zimmerman, E. (2006).

9. Salen, K., & Zimmerman, E. (2006).

10. Crawford, C. (2003). *Chris Crawford on game design.* Indianapolis, IN: New Riders Publishing.

Chapter 7

1. Koster, R. (2005). *A theory of fun for game design.* Scottsdale, AZ: Paraglyph Press, p. 34.
2. Gredler, M.E. (1997). *Learning and instruction: Theory into practice* (3rd ed.). Upper Saddle River, NJ: Prentice Hall.
3. Gredler, M.E. (1997).
4. Gredler, M.E. (1997).
5. Rice, J. (2007, January). Higher order thinking in video games. *Journal of Technology and Teacher Education, 15*(1), 87–100.
6. Rice, J. (2007, January).
7. Rice, J. (2007, January).
8. Rice, J. (2007, January).
9. Kapp, K.M. (2007). *Gadgets, games and gizmos for learning: Tools and techniques for transforming know-how form boomers to gamers.* San Francisco: Pfeiffer.
10. Rice, J. (2007, January).
11. Kapp, K.M., & O'Driscoll, T. (2010). *Learning in 3D: Adding a new dimension to enterprise learning and collaboration.* San Francisco: Pfeiffer.
12. Rice, J. (2007, January).
13. Rice, J. (2007, January).
14. Case study provided by Designing Digitally. www.designingdigitally.com/
15. Bohannon, J. (2009, April 20). Gamers unravel the secret life of protein. *Wired Magazine Online.* www.wired.com/medtech/genetics/magazine/17–05/ff_protein?currentPage=all.

Chapter 8

1. Carey, B. (2007, May 22). This is your life (and how you tell it). *New York Times Online.* www.nytimes.com/2007/05/22/health/psychology/22narr.html?em&ex=1180065600&en=4d426931b2330fae&ei=5087%0A
2. Smith, P.L. & Ragan, T.J. (1999). *Instructional design* (2nd ed.). Upper Saddle River, NJ: Merrill.

Chapter 9

1. Chen, B.X. (2011, January 20). How Angry Birds is becoming the next Super Mario. *Wired.* www.wired.com/gadgetlab/2011/01/app-stars-angry-birds/2/.
2. Chen, B.X. (2011, January 20).

Chapter 10

1. Locke, E.A., & Latham, G.P. (2002). Building a practically useful theory of goal setting and task motivation: A 35-year odyssey. *American Psychologist, 57*(9), 705–717.
2. Deci, E.L. (1975). *Intrinsic motivation.* New York: Plenum Press.
3. Deci, E.L., & Ryan, R.M. (1985). *Intrinsic motivation and self-determination in human behavior.* New York: Plenum Press.
4. Csikszentmihalyi, M. (1975). Play and intrinsic rewards. *Journal of Humanistic Psychology, 15*(3), 41–63.

5. Amabile, T.M., Hennessey, B.A., & Grossman, B.S. (1986). Social influences on creativity: The effects of contracted-for reward. *Journal of Personality and Social Psychology, 50*(1), 14–23.

6. Lepper, M.R., & Gilovich, T. (1982). Accentuating the positive: Eliciting generalized compliance from children through activity-oriented requests. *Journal of Personality and Social Psychology, 42*(2), 248–259.

7. Campbell, D.J. (1982). Determinates of choice of goal difficulty level: A review of situational and personality influences. *Journal of Occupational Psychology, 55*(2), 79–95.

8. Bandura, A. (1999). Self-efficacy: Toward a unifying theory of behavioral change. In R.F. Baumeister (Ed.), *The self in social psychology* (pp. 285–298). New York: Psychology Press.

9. Dormann, T., & Frese, M. (1994). Error training: Replication and the function of exploratory behavior. *International Journal of Human-Computer Interaction, 6*(4), 365–372.

10. Winters, D., & Latham, G.P. (1996). The effect of learning versus outcome goals on a simple versus a complex task. *Group & Organization Management, 21*(2), 236–250.

11. Bangert-Drowns, R.L., Kulik, C.C., Kulik, J.A., & Morgan, M. (1991). The instructional effect of feedback in test-like events. *Review of Educational Research, 61*(2), 213–238.

12. Schooler, L.J., & Anderson, J.R. (1990). The disruptive potential of immediate feedback. *The Proceedings of the Twelfth Annual Conference of the Cognitive Science Society*, Cambridge, Massachusetts.

13. Bizzocchi, J., & Paras, B. (2005). Game, motivation, and effective learning: An integrated model for educational game design. *Proceedings of Digital Games Research Association Conference.*

14. Chen, H., Wigand, R.T., & Nilan, M.S. (1999). Optimal experience of web activities. *Computers in Human Behavior, 15*(5), 585–608.

15. Smith, T.A., & Kimball, D.R. (2010). Learning from feedback: Spacing and the delay–retention effect. *Journal of Experimental Psychology: Learning, Memory, and Cognition, 36*(1), 80–95.

16. Greene, D., & Lepper, M.R. (1974). Effects of extrinsic rewards on children's subsequent intrinsic interest. *Child Development, 45*, 1141–1145.

17. Bandura, A. (1986). *Social foundations of thought and action: A social cognitive theory.* Englewood Cliffs, NJ: Prentice Hall.

18. Dickinson, A.M. (1989). The detrimental effects of extrinsic reinforcement on "intrinsic motivation." *The Behavior Analyst, 12*(1), 1–15.

19. Deci, E.L., & Cascio, W.F. (1972, April). Changes in intrinsic motivation as a function of negative feedback and threats. Paper presented at the meeting of the Eastern Psychological Association, Boston.

20. Eisenberger, R., & Cameron, J. (1996). Detrimental effects of reward: Reality or myth? *American Psychologist, 51*(11), 1153–1166.

21. Stajkovic, A.D., & Luthans, F. (2001). Differential effects of incentive motivators on work performance. *Academy of Management Journal, 44*(3), 580–590.

22. King, D., & Delfabbro, P. (2009). Motivational differences in problem video game play. *Journal of Cybertherapy and Rehabilitation, 2*(2), 139–149.

23. Peterson, S.J., & Luthans, F. (2006). The impact of financial and nonfinancial incentives on business-unit outcomes over time. *Journal of Applied Psychology, 91*(1), 156–165.

24. Elliot, A.J. (2006). The hierarchical model of approach-avoidance motivation. *Motivation and Emotion, 30*(2), 111–116.

25. Condly, S., Clark, R.E., & Stolovitch, H.S. (2003). The effects of incentives on workplace performance: A meta-analytic review of research studies. *Performance Improvement Quarterly, 16*(3), 46–63.

26. Jackson, C.K. (2008). A little now for a lot later: A look at a Texas advanced placement incentive program. Retrieved from Cornell University, School of Industrial and Labor Relations site.

27. Fryer, R. (2010). Financial incentives and student achievement: Evidence from randomized trials. Working paper. Cambridge, MA: Harvard University.

28. Burguillo, J.C. (2010). Using game theory and competition-based learning to stimulate student motivation and performance. *Computers & Education, 55*(2), 566–575.

29. Reeve, J., & Deci, E.L. (1996). Elements of the competitive situation that affect intrinsic motivation. *Personality and Social Psychology Bulletin, 22*(1), 24–33.

30. Lam, S., Yim, P., Law, J.F., & Cheung, R.Y. (2004). The effects of competition on achievement motivation in Chinese classrooms. *British Journal of Educational Psychology, 74*(2), 281–296.

31. Goodman D.A., & Crouch, J. (1978). Effects of competition on learning. *Improving College and University Teaching, 26*(2), 130–133.

32. Bryant, B.K. (1977). The effects of the interpersonal context of evaluation on self- and other-enhancement behavior. *Child Development, 48*(3), 885–892.

33. Chan, J.Y., & Lam, S. (2008). Effects of competition on students' self-efficacy in vicarious learning. *British Journal of Educational Psychology, 78*(1), 95–108.

34. Slavin, R.E. (1980). Cooperative learning. *Review of Educational Research, 50*(2), 315–342.

35. Ames, C., & Felker, D.W. (1979). An examination of children's attributions and achievement-related evaluations in competitive, cooperative, and individualistic reward structures. *Journal of Educational Psychology, 71*(4), 413–420.

36. Myers, D.G., & Lamm, H. (1976). The group polarization phenomenon. *Psychological Bulletin, 83*(4), 602–627.

37. Steiner, I.D. (1972). *Group process and productivity*. New York: Academic Press.

38. Jackson, J.M., & Harkins, S.G. (1985). Equity in effort: An explanation of the social loafing effect. *Journal of Personality and Social Psychology, 49*(5), 1199–1206.

Chapter 14

1. McGonigal, J. (2007). Gaming can make a better world. TED Talk. www.ted.com/talks/jane_mcgonigal_gaming_can_make_a_better_world.html.

2. Deterding, S. (2011, January, 24) Meaningful play: Getting gamification right. www.youtube.com/watch?v=7ZGCPap7GkY.

Index

Page references followed by *fig* indicate an illustrated figure; followed by *t* indicate a table.